# The
# Industrial
# Design
# Reader

## Edited by Carma Gorman

**ALLWORTH PRESS**
NEW YORK

DESIGN MANAGEMENT INSTITUTE

07  06  05  04  03    5  4  3  2  1

Published by Allworth Press
An imprint of Allworth Communications, Inc.
10 East 23rd Street, New York, NY 10010

Cover design by Derek Bacchus
Cover photography by © Bilderberg/Photonica 2003
Interior design and layout by Sharp Des!gns, Inc.

ISBN: 1-58115-310-4

LIBRARY OF CONGRESS CATALOGING-IN-PUBLICATION DATA
The industrial design reader / edited by Carma R. Gorman.
p. cm.
ISBN 1-58115-310-4 (pbk.)
1. Design, Industrial—History. I. Gorman, Carma R.
TS171.4.I573 2004
745.2—dc22
2003017295

Printed in Canada

# Contents

## 1851-1875

## 1876-1900

## 1901-1925

# 1926-1950

# 1951-1975

# 1976-2000

# Foreword

Since its beginning in 1975, the Design Management Institute (DMI) has literally built the foundation of the design management profession. DMI is an independent, nonprofit organization with members and constituents; education; and research programs around the globe. From this independent position, DMI works with a variety of institutions and organizations to help design managers become leaders in their professions and business managers effectively utilize design for business success.

Our publishing partnership with Allworth Press is an important opportunity to further the Institute's commitment to continuously advancing the profession and the understanding of the crucial role of design in business. Because *The Industrial Design Reader* is the first anthology to focus exclusively on the history of industrial design, it is a perfect project for the Institute to help make available to the design management community. We are pleased indeed to be the copublishers of this invaluable resource.

Earl N. Powell, Doc. Letters (Hon.)
President, Design Management Institute
*www.dmi.org*

# Preface

I decided to edit this book for a simple reason: I could not find a text that contained the primary sources that I wanted my design history students to read. Anthologies of primary sources abound in the fine arts, architecture, and (thanks in large part to Allworth Press) graphic design. There are also good decorative arts anthologies available, namely Isabelle Frank's *The Theory of Decorative Art* and Paul Greenhalgh's *Quotations and Sources on Design and the Decorative Arts.* However, to my knowledge there are no other books available on the market today that (1) reprint full-length primary source essays—or substantial excerpts therefrom—that focus primarily on industrial design and related issues, and (2) cover both the second half of the nineteenth century and the entire twentieth century. This anthology does both. Its aim is to make some of the key texts of the history of industrial design more accessible to readers, and thereby to highlight ideas and issues that have significantly shaped the field over the last 150 years.

As those knowledgeable about design history will note, this is not an anthology that deals solely with aesthetics or theories of ornament. Nor does it address only mass production (as opposed to craft production), though that is certainly its focus. The authors of the articles, books, public addresses, and manifestos that are excerpted herein include designers, politicians, home economists, museum curators, architects, artists, social critics, manufacturers, advertisers, and educators. From widely varying perspectives, they discuss industrialization, mass production, machines, commodities, sales, labor, craft, aesthetics, technology, management, modernity, gender, race, class, and nationality.

I selected these texts using five criteria: canonicity (what one would *expect* to find in such an anthology, e.g., Walter Gropius's Bauhaus manifesto); the notoriety of the writer in the field of design or elsewhere; date (texts from every decade between 1850 and 2000); diversity of critical approach; and readability. However, practical considerations, such as my word count limit and the price and availability of copyright permissions, ultimately influenced my choices as well. As a result, this collection of texts is not, and does not pretend to be, comprehensive or exhaustive, though it does strive to be at least somewhat representative of the myriad ways in which design has been understood over the last century and a half.

# Acknowledgments

For permission to reprint texts and images, and for help in obtaining permissions, I am grateful to the following individuals (formal credit lines appear on the first page of each selection):

Donna Accorso
Faith Freeman Barbato
Michael Batterman
Charlotte Benton
Tim Benton
Gabrielle Bertemann
Karen Berube
Gui Bonsiepe
Bill Browne
Sandra Chin
Carol Christiansen
Jennifer Conrard
Catherine Crabtree
Marie Donatelli
Lindsay Doyle
John Dreyfuss
Taji Duncombe
Jenny Dunhill
Tela Durbin
Florence Eichin
Margaret Elliott
Sheila Emery
John Ferry

Agnes Fisher
Bette Gahres
Karen Gibson
Kristina Goodrich
Pamela Griffin
Sharon Hecker
Fawn Horvath
Susan Hult
Frances Hymas
Charles E. Inman
Marisa Inzaghi
Rekha Khimji
Sheilah Ledwidge
Marion Locke
Laurence Loewy
Jo Mattern
C. Thomas Mitchell
Bryn Mooth
Diana Mutersbaugh
Norah Piehl
Val Price
Lucie Prinz
Pamela Quick

Barbara Radice
David H. Rice
Ruth Rich
Kathleen Robbins
Lia Rojales
Mona Ross
Yehuda Safran
Gemma Sala
Stephen Schwartz
Diana Southern
Carolyn Sperry
Mark Strauss
Justine Tenney
M. K. Timme
Patrick Toensmeier
Rick Watson
Jo West
Susanna Wettin
Susan Wilson
Lydia Zelaya
Rebecca Zimmerman

For advice about the contents of this book, and/or for assistance in obtaining copies of hard-to-find items, my thanks to:

Steve Belletire
Isabel Breskin
Anna Brzyski
Christina Cogdell
Kathryn Feazel

Sharon Hecker
Patricia Hills
Margaretta Lovell
Victor Margolin
Jessica May

Kevin Muller
Serena Perrone
Eric Peterson
Natasha Zaretsky

For photographing, scanning, and printing the illustrations, I am grateful to:

Nathan Blank                    Eric Peterson                    Dave Hart

For various forms of institutional support for this project, my thanks to the following individuals and departments at Southern Illinois University, Carbondale:

Michael Batterman        Harris Deller            Morris Library
Anna Brzyski             LouAnn Elwell            Eric Peterson
Peter Chametzky          Rich Hausman            School of Art and
Connie Christy           Jabari Loving               Design

For their many efforts on behalf of this book, I am grateful to Allworth Press and the Design Management Institute, especially to:

Tad Crawford             Nicole Potter            Jessica Rozler
Michael Madole           Earl Powell
Birte Pampel             Cynthia Rivelli

For their support and patience, thanks to my parents and in-laws:

Paul and Janice Gorman    Gae and John Larson    Jim and Karen Peterson

And for his manifold contributions to this project, I am especially grateful to Eric Peterson, my colleague, husband, and friend.

# Editor's Note

In order to present a fairly broad sampling of the literature on industrial design, I excerpted many of these selections from longer works. The title and publication information for the original source always appears in the introduction to each chapter. Essays that have been reprinted in their entirety generally retain their original titles, but selections that have been excerpted from longer essays or from books (such as Karl Marx's *Capital*) are usually given titles that reflect the chapter or section from which they were taken (such as "The Capitalist Character of Manufacture"). In some cases, descriptive titles have been given to works that were not originally titled (as is the case with the selections from the first issue of the journal of the Hochschule für Gestaltung, Ulm). This is usually indicated by an absence of quotation marks around the title.

To retain the flavor (or flavour) of the original texts, I have retained British spellings, archaic spellings, and idiosyncratic punctuation, capitalization, etc., whenever possible. However, in those cases in which idiosyncrasies might be attributed to an error in transcription rather than to faithful reproduction of the original, I have indicated corrections or additions with square brackets. Bracketed ellipses ([ . . . ]), when placed within the body of a paragraph, indicate that a portion of that paragraph has been omitted. A freestanding bracketed ellipsis indicates that one or more full paragraphs have been omitted. If footnotes or endnotes that appeared in the original text have been omitted, that is noted in the introduction to the selection. Illustrations, when present in the original, have been reproduced here only when they are directly referenced in the original text, or are otherwise deemed integral to the author's argument.

# 1851-1875

# 1852

## Henry Cole, "On the International Results of the Exhibition of 1851"

Sir Henry Cole (1808–1882), an Englishman, was the chief organizer of the Great Exhibition of 1851, which was sponsored by Prince Albert and the Royal Society of Arts as a means of fostering international competition—and, thereby, improved design—in manufactures. The Great Exhibition took place in Hyde Park, London, in the famed Joseph Paxton-designed iron-and-glass "Crystal Palace." Cole, both before and after the exhibition, was a passionate advocate of design education. His collection of objects from the Great Exhibition formed the basis for the collections of the South Kensington (later the Victoria and Albert) Museum, an institution whose original purpose was to provide design students and manufacturers with examples of good design and decorative motifs. In these excerpts, taken from an 1852 lecture, Cole explains the rationale behind the exhibition, as well as some of its effects on manufacturing and international relations.

Excerpted from Henry Cole, *Lecture XII, Second Series,* December 1, 1852 (London: D. Bogue, 1852): 521–539.

[ ... ]

To come to causes nearer at hand which produced the International Exhibition, and placed in this country that first of the long series of Exhibitions, which I have no doubt will follow, I think must be named Free Trade, or, to substitute Latin for Saxon words, "unrestricted competition." It would have been a folly to have proposed an International Exhibition before that great statesman, Sir Robert Peel,[1] had loosened the fetters of our commercial tariff, so that it might be [in] the interest of foreigners to accept the invitation to show us the fruits of their Industry. Had an International Exhibition of Industry been proposed in the good old times, when our manufacturers of silk, and cotton, and metals, were protected from the competition of their foreign neighbours, we should have rejected the idea just as the French manufacturers did, whose developement [sic] is still cramped by protective tariffs. But it was decidedly [in] the interest of England to adopt the idea, and she did so on that account, and because she was ripe for it, which France was not, and is not, although she may be certainly advancing to that point of reason.

You are all well aware that the honour of the first idea of an International Exhibition does not belong to England. Like many other theories, it came from France, having been proposed by M. Buffet, the Minister of Commerce after the Revolution of 1848, and was submitted by him to the several Chambers of Commerce. He said to them: —"It has occurred to me, that it would be interesting to the country in general to be made acquainted with the degree of advancement towards perfection attained by our neighbours in those manufactures in which we so often come in competition in foreign markets. Should we bring together and compare the specimens of skill in agriculture and manufactures now claiming our notice, whether native or foreign, there would, doubtless, be much useful experience to be gained; and, above all, a spirit of emulation, which might be greatly advantageous to the country." He then requested that the Chambers would "give their opinion on the abstract principle of exhibiting the productions of other countries, and, if they should consider that the experiment ought to be made, to enumerate to him officially the articles they thought would most conduce to the French interest when displayed."

No doubt it would have been interesting to our neighbours to see the best we were doing; but the French manufacturers were not prepared to let the French ladies see the printed calicoes we were able to produce at fourpence and fivepence a-yard, or to allow the French gentlemen to examine the cutlery of Sheffield, the plated wares of Birmingham, or the pottery of Staffordshire in Paris. So the French Chambers of Commerce gave no encouragement to the abstract proposition of M. Buffet. They would not throw off their armour of protection, and will not do so until the French people themselves become more imperative in their desire to have a sight and taste of foreign manufactures. [ . . .]

In France an International Exhibition was a philosophical theory, and must remain a bauble to be talked about until she alters her commercial tariff. But in England the idea at once became a practical reality, receiving universal welcome as soon as our Royal President[2] directed that it should be submitted to our manufacturers for their consideration. As part of the history of the growth of the International Exhibition in this country, I would read to you a few opinions which I collected and submitted to Prince Albert in 1849:—

A committee of Manchester cotton-printers, consisting of Mr. H. Thomson, Mr. Hargreaves, and Mr. Herz, concurred in thinking that "It is very necessary that all parties should know what the French and all nations are doing, and should compare their manufactures with our own. The comparison would show what our manufacturers could do, and by generating increased knowledge and appreciation in our consumers would induce the production of a much higher class of work."

Mr. Nelson, of the firm of Nelson, Knowles, and Co., of Manchester, said,—

"One great argument for universality is that manufacturers ought to know all that is doing. Most manufacturers have much too high an opinion of their own excellence, and it is desirable they should measure it by that of others."

Messrs. Hoyle and Sons agreed unanimously that the Exhibition ought certainly to be international. "The Lancashire feeling eminently is," said Mr. Alderman Neild, "to have a clear stage and no favour."

Messrs. Kershaw and Co. of Manchester, said, "Open the Exhibition to receive productions of all nations, certainly."

[ . . . ]

And even in those manufactures where our own inferiority would probably be demonstrated in the Exhibition, manufacturers certainly welcomed the opportunity which would thus be afforded for comparison. Thus,—

Mr. J. Jobson Smith, of the firm of Messrs. Stuart and Smith of Sheffield, grate-manufacturers, thought "it most desirable to see the best metal work of all nations; but that England would be behind in ornamental metal work, particularly where the human figure is involved."

I do not think the Exhibition itself will have altered these opinions uttered two years before.

As England, beyond any other nation, was prepared, by the cosmopolitan character of its people and by its commercial policy, to be the first nation to carry out an International Exhibition of Industry—so the continuous labours of the Society of Arts in promoting National Exhibitions of Industry naturally led to its being the agent for carrying out such a work. I will not detain you with details of the Exhibitions which had been held in Manchester, Glasgow, Birmingham, and other provincial towns, or in Dublin; or of the eleven successive National Exhibitions which had been held in France, between 1798 and 1849. All of these, doubtless, had an important influence in directing public attention to the subject in this country.

But we must recollect that, even as early as 1756, nearly a century before, this Society had held Exhibitions of Manufactures; and for six years immediately preceding 1851 had, year by year, held Annual Exhibitions of some kind, each one growing in importance.

The idea of a National Exhibition became a common property. [ . . . ] Mr. S. Carter Hall, Mr. G. Wallis, Mr. F. Whishaw, Mr. Theophilus Richards, were all avowed public advocates of some kind of National Exhibition of Manufactures, and perhaps others whose names I do not know, before this Society pledged itself to hold a National Exhibition in 1851. Public conviction of its importance was of slow growth. So slow, that even after several Exhibitions had been proved to have been successful in these walls, the Government could not be induced to promise any assistance. But in 1848, the Council of the Society made some little way with the Government in obtaining the promise of a site for the building. In 1849 the Paris Exhibition was held, and M. Buffet's idea of internationality was brought to England. Our Royal President, always interested in the subject, spontaneously took the proposed Exhibition of 1851 under his own personal direction, and inscribed with his own hand the following passage on the Minutes of a Meeting held at Buckingham Palace, on the 30th June, 1849. It ran thus:—"It was a question whether this Exhibition should be exclusively limited to British industry. It was considered that, whilst it appears an error to fix any limitation to the productions of machinery, science, and taste, which are of no country, but belong, as a whole, to the civilised world, particular advantage to British industry might be derived from placing it in fair competition with that of other nations." Then followed the proofs of the concurrence of manufacturers in the expediency of internationality, and the issue of the Royal Commission confirming the idea. And thus that International feature was conferred on the Exhibition of 1851, the results of which I have now to attempt to examine.

Soon after the Royal Commission of the Exhibition was issued, communications were opened with all the Governments of the civilised world, except the Celestial Empire.[3] The Commissioners wrote to the Secretary of State for Foreign Affairs, and he wrote to our ministers and consuls abroad, directing them to bring the subject of the Exhibition before the Governments of the respective countries: each Government thereupon appointed the most eminent persons in Arts, Science, and Commerce, to be a committee representing the country, and to communicate direct with the Royal Commissioners. Subsequently, for the purpose of awarding the prizes, other eminent persons, distinguished for special knowledge, were named and placed in *direct* communication with the Commissioners, independently of their Governments. And thus the Foreign Commissioners and the Foreign Juries constituted Committees of the men most distinguished in the arts of peace in the civilised world. If you glance down the lists of these our foreign friends, you will find in the list of each country its aristocracy of Art, Science, and Commerce—men who have raised themselves into distinction, or, rather, been elected to their position by the unsolicited suffrages of their fellow-citizens. It would be superfluous to read to you these several hundred names, certainly a fair representation of the most eminent in the world. Thus, for the *first* time in the world's history, the men of Arts, Science, and Commerce, were permitted by their respective Governments to meet together to discuss and promote those objects for which civilised nations exist. The chief business of politicians, lawyers, and soldiers, is professedly to protect the results of men's industry; and up to this time, Governments, for the most part consisting of politicians, lawyers, and soldiers, have had the chief voice in regulating the interests of industry. The men of Art, Science, and Commerce, have hitherto had but a very subordinate voice in the regulation of their own interests, which had been too much left to the professional superintendence of their brethren of Politics, Law, and War. But a new principle was introduced by the Exhibition of 1851, and questions of Art, Science, and Commerce, were permitted to be discussed in a Parliament of Art, Science, and

Commerce. I believe the recognition of this principle is of the first importance for the progress of mankind, and is one which will be likely to stand each nation in good stead as occasion arises. [ . . . ] And I believe the Exhibition has opened the way to this kind of treatment,—more reasonable, more civilised, less costly and more consistent with religious convictions, than the most scientific arguments of parks of artillery and squares of infantry, which in the long [run] do not settle any questions, or we should not see dynasties restored which we have paid millions to depose. Success in war among civilised nations, after all, now resolves itself ultimately into the length of the purse; and the length of the national purse depends upon the strength of the national industry. We are the richest people in the world, and, I fear, the most pugnacious, partly in consequence of our superior wealth. I think I may say we have spent more for war than any other nation, and that we cannot boast of many practical results from our expenditure. I submit that we have spent much on behalf of Belgium, and Spain, and Portugal; and I apprehend it will be found that they, taking advantage of our friendship, have imposed as great, if not greater, impediments on our commercial relations with them than even France has done. I believe the Exhibition has had a tendency to prevent such mistakes in future, and to keep nations from going to blows as hastily and foolishly as they have been accustomed to do; and if this result follows, we shall owe it to the extended application of the great principle of international discussion of questions by parties most informed and most interested in them, which the Exhibition caused to be recognised by all the civilised nations in the world. Thus the old-fashioned, narrow suspicions and secrecy of diplomacy will be exchanged for public confidence and public discussion.

[ . . . ]

Foremost among the immediate and most practical of the international results of the Exhibition, I rank the consent—nay, eagerness, of all countries to discuss and revise their system of *Postal Communication*, which is now established as a great fact. The Postage Association was formed during the Exhibition, and arose out of the convictions that men of all countries entertained of the vital importance of a perfect and easy interchange of thought by means of writing, and of their sense of the indefensible impediments which now prevent it. Instead of the present postage treaties, the products of bureaucracy only, in which it appears to have been the aim of each nation to huckster and overreach one another, the object of the Postage Association is to have a uniform and intelligible system, based upon a due recognition of the importance of freedom of communication. To this principle France, America, Austria, Belgium,—in fact, almost all civilised countries, have already sent their adhesion, and upon this basis the discussion of a future international postage system, I cannot doubt, will proceed. [ . . . ] I have only to ask you to agree with me that freedom of international correspondence when it does arrive will have to be considered as one of the earliest results of the Exhibition.

The beginning of the *reform of our Patent Laws*, or laws for the recognition of the rights of intellectual labour, which I foresee may have great international results on industry, is due to the Exhibition. I say the beginning, for we have only just entered on the very threshold of the subject. Almost as soon as the Exhibition was announced, every one was sensible of the manifest absurdity of inviting exhibitors to display the fruits of their intellectual exertions, whilst at the same time they should be subjected thereby to pillage. So our Legislature promised inventors that they should not be liable to be robbed, at least, until the Exhibition was over, and a law was made to keep men from picking and stealing for a few months. Wonderful morality!—found to be so consistent with common sense, that the law was renewed for a few months longer. You will find an interesting account of the working of the Inventions Act during the Exhibition in the Report made by Mr. P. Le Neve Foster to the Commissioners of the Exhibition, and printed in their first Report (p. 109). Six hundred and twenty exhibitors obtained certificates or cautions against robbery. At last, after many struggles, our Legislature has passed a permanent law which forbids the robbery of inventions, provided that the inventor can muster some 5*l.* or 10*l.* to purchase the privilege. How great was the want of this reform may be seen in the fact, that since the 1st October last—a period of only nine weeks— upwards of 765 applications have been made for "protection" against robbery. Imperfect as this law is, it will have important results on industry, both abroad and in our colonies, and will affect inventive rights, more or less, over the whole world. I am happy to say, that we cannot now go to the Continent, pillage an invention in use, and introduce it here as a novelty; and that we cannot prevent a Belgian or French inventor from giving our own colonies the benefit of his skill. It must be obvious that in the proper administration of a wise Patent Law, and in order to prevent fraud and useless litigation, it will be necessary that ample means should exist for ascertaining in this country what inventions have been patented abroad. The American Government prints its own specifications, so I believe does the Belgian; and if the French Government does not, it, at least, gives every facility in the consultation of them. We ourselves are now bound to print the patents of the United Kingdom. With these facilities for doing so, it appears to me there ought to be an international exchange of printed Patents, and I think it would be a right work to be undertaken by our Government; but I am afraid there are little hopes of this being done so long as the administration of patent Law is treated in a legal rather than an industrial point of view. This Society, as the principal author of the new Patent Law, may very properly come in aid; and I would suggest to the Council at once to take measures for impressing on the Government the necessity of mutually exchanging copies of printed Patents with foreign countries, and of establishing, as early as possible, an International Library of Reference for manufacturers. We may take a lesson from the United States' Government, which yearly issues above 40,000 copies of the Annual Report on Patents, at a cheap rate; and also from France: one of the great features of the *Conservatoire des Arts et Metiers* in Paris being its *Salle du Portefeuille*, which contains about 12,000 drawings of machinery and 20,000 *brevets* of Inventions, all of which are accessible to the public at any time, and free of cost, to be copied or to be traced.[4]

[ . . . ]

If we look down the list of 164 Council Medals, and the objects to which they were awarded, I confess it seems to me that there is but ONE object with which the world became acquainted for the first time, and that as a direct result of the Exhibition. I am not speaking of the results which are deducible from the combination of the innumerable objects then displayed, but am looking only to the individual objects. I need not go through the list, but if I were to do so, I feel sure that as each object was mentioned, except a solitary instance, some one of this audience would be able to say, "I was acquainted with *that* object before the Exhibition." That solitary one, which no one was acquainted with, was the building itself which Paxton suggested.[5] The Exhibition has taught the world how to roof in great spaces: how to build with glass and iron in a way never done before. This is another instance of the logical mode in which supply follows demand: in which invention is shown to be the child of necessity. The one material thing absolutely necessary for an international exhibition was an adequate building, to be erected in six months. And after many galvanic struggles to get it one was obtained. Nothing very novel in iron columns resting on concrete foundations,—nothing novel in Paxton girders, which half-a-dozen persons claim to have invented, and possibly may have done so, but something very novel indeed in covering twenty acres with glass as an exhibiting room, a feat the world had not seen performed before. I look upon this building as one of great importance in its way, calculated to have vast beneficial influences on the occupations, health, and amusement of all northern nations. But how slow and progressive has been such a result in building?—evolved just at the time when it was wanted from little antecedents, as was printing, the steam-engine, and in fact all great results. Even in the material Glass house, as in the possibility of an International Exhibition, Sir Robert Peel appears as an agent. Had the excise duties on glass still remained, it is certain we could not have had the Crystal Palace.

[ . . . ]

It is said that the industrial progress of this country is not at the present time commensurate with that of other countries. To my view the Exhibition proved the contrary. If you admit the Exhibition as any evidence at all, I say it was proved by the reports of the Jurors, that certainly the *Industry*, and perhaps even the *Art* of the United Kingdom, took the first place in the race. [ . . . ]

Thus, out of a total of 164 Council Medals awarded among 13,937 Exhibitors, thirty foreign countries obtained 86 among 7076, whilst Great Britain, one country, obtained 78 among 6861 Exhibitors.

But the position I take seems to me corroborated by another fact, namely, the superior value of the British over the Foreign goods exhibited. The value of the articles on the Foreign side was estimated at 670,420*l.*, on the British side at 1,031,607*l.* The data in both cases were furnished by the Exhibitors.

[ . . . ]

I freely admit, that in the execution of art applied to industry, the French are, upon an average, better educated and better workmen than ourselves. But if we separate the almost mechanical execution of art from its general sentiment as displayed in the Exhibition, we cannot but remark the universal likeness which pervades the art of all Europe at the present time. You might have taken works of art from Russia, Saxony, England, France, Belgium, Austria, and Italy, and it would have been impossible to tell the country where they originated. But this feature is no novelty, for it has been the case for many centuries. [ . . . ] With certain modifications, we find a spirit of the age common to the most advanced nations of Europe at all periods, and the present is not an exception, as the Exhibition proved. [ . . . ]

[ . . . ] It was from the East that the most impressive lesson was to be learnt. Here was revealed a fresh well of art, the general principles of which were the same as those in the best periods of art of all nations—Egyptian, Grecian, Roman, Byzantine, Gothic. And turning from artistic to industrial objects, and speaking generally, I venture to submit whether our American cousins did not, in their reaping and other machines adapted to new wants and infant periods of society, teach us the next most valuable lessons.

[ . . . ]

And I will conclude this list of *Agenda,* the prospective fruits of the Exhibition, by mentioning the impulse which better *education,* and particularly *industrial education,* is likely to derive from it. Already the intention exists of making drawing a part of our national education, and thus we shall be learning a universal and international language, intelligible, as Mr. Redgrave recently pointed out, alike to the European as to the Chinese or South American. Already we have the School of Mines developing itself into a school of practical science. In a few years, on a site opposite that where the Exhibition stood, I hope we shall witness the foundation of an *Industrial University,* in the advantages of which all the nations of the world may equally share, which has been suggested by Prince Albert as the most legitimate application of the pecuniary success of the Exhibition. [ . . . ]

### N O T E S

1. Sir Robert Peel (1788–1850) was the prime minister of Britain from 1834–35 and 1841–46 and the founder of the Conservative Party. He was responsible for the 1846 repeal of the British "Corn Laws" that had restricted imports. "Peel, Sir Robert, 2nd Baronet," *Encyclopædia Britannica,* <*http://www.britannica.com/eb/article?eu=60419*>, (accessed 27 December 2002).
2. Prince Albert, the husband of Queen Victoria, was the president of the Royal Society of Arts.
3. The term "Celestial Empire" refers to China.

4. The *Conservatoire des Arts et Métiers* is the Academy of Arts and Crafts; the *Salle du Portefeuille* is the Portfolio Room; *brevets* are patents.
5. Sir Joseph Paxton was the architect of the iron-and-glass building that housed the Great Exhibition; it was popularly known as the Crystal Palace.

# 1852

# Horatio Greenough, "The Law of Adaptation"

Horatio Greenough (1805–1852) was a well-educated and well-traveled Boston neoclassical sculptor who is perhaps best known today for his over-life-size, half-nude, seated marble statue of George Washington (now in the National Museum of American Art, Washington, DC). However, under the pseudonym Horace Bender, he published his ideas on race, evolution, architecture, design, and the arts as *The Travels, Observations, and Experience of a Yankee Stonecutter*. In this book, which was published the year of his death, Greenough argued that beauty in architecture and design was a result of fitness to function. His is one of the earliest statements of the doctrine of functionalism that was so famously adopted in the late nineteenth and early twentieth centuries by architect-theorists such as Louis Sullivan and Ludwig Mies van der Rohe. Greenough's comparison of the "evolution" of design to biological evolution was also an early formulation of a pattern of thought that was later to characterize many modernist histories of design.

Excerpted from *The Travels, Observations, and Experience of a Yankee Stonecutter* (New York: G. P. Putnam, 1852): 136–141, 202–203.

I f, as the first step in our search after the great principles of construction, we but observe the skeletons and skins of animals, through all the varieties of beast and bird, of fish and insect, are we not as forcibly struck by their variety as by their beauty? There is no arbitrary law of proportion, no unbending model of form. There is scarce a part of the animal organization which we do not find elongated or shortened, increased, diminished or suppressed, as the wants of the genus or species dictate, as their exposure or their work may require. The neck of the swan and that of the eagle, however different in character and proportion, equally charm the eye and satisfy the reason. We approve the length of the same member in grazing animals, its shortness in beasts of prey. The horse's shanks are thin, and we admire them; the greyhound's chest is deep, and we cry, beautiful! It is neither the presence nor the absence of this or that part or shape or color that wins our eye in natural objects; it is the consistency and harmony of the parts juxtaposed, the subordination of details to masses, and of masses to the whole.

The law of adaptation is the fundamental law of nature in all structure. So unflinchingly does she modify a type in accordance with a new position, that some philosophers have declared a variety of appearance to be the object aimed at; so entirely does she limit the modification to the demands of necessity, that adherence to one original plan seems, to limited intelligence, to be carried to the very verge of caprice. The domination of arbitrary rules of taste has produced the very counterpart of the wisdom thus displayed in every object around us; we tie up the camel leopard to the rack; we shave the lion, and call him a dog; we strive to bind the unicorn with his band in the furrow, and to make him harrow the valleys after us!

When the savage of the South Sea islands shapes his war club, his first thought is of its use. His first efforts pare the long shaft, and mould the convenient handle; then the heavier end takes gradually the edge that cuts, while it retains the weight that stuns. His idler hour divides its surface by lines and curves, or embosses it with figures that have pleased his eye, or are linked with his superstition. We admire its effective shape, its Etruscan-like quaintness, its graceful form and subtle outline, yet we neglect the lesson it might teach. If we compare the form of a newly invented machine with the perfected type of the same instrument, we observe, as we trace it through the phases of improvement, how weight is shaken off where strength is less needed, how functions are made to approach without impeding each other, how the straight becomes curved, and the curve is straightened, till the straggling and cumbersome machine becomes the compact, effective, and beautiful engine.

[ . . . ]

Let us now turn to a structure of our own, one which from its nature and uses commands us to reject authority, and we shall find the result of the manly use of plain good sense so like that of taste and genius too, as scarce to require a distinctive title. Observe a ship at sea! Mark the majestic form of her hull as she rushes through the water, observe the graceful bend of her body, the gentle transition from round to flat, the grasp of her keel, the leap of her bows, the symmetry and rich tracery of her spars and rigging, and those grand wind muscles, her sails! Behold an organization second only to that of an animal, obedient as the horse, swift as the stag, and bearing the burthen of a thousand camels from pole to pole! What Academy of Design, what research of connoisseurship, what imitation of the Greeks produced this marvel of construction? Here is the result of the study of man upon the great deep, where Nature spake of the laws of building, not in the feather and in the flower, but in winds and waves, and he bent all his mind to hear and to obey. Could we carry into our civil architecture the responsibilities that weigh upon our ship-building, we should ere long have edifices as superior to the Parthenon for the purposes that we require, as the Constitution or the Pennsylvania is to the galley of the Argonauts.[1] Could our blunders on terra-firma be put to the same dread test that those of ship-builders are, little would be now left to say on this subject.

Instead of forcing the functions of every sort of building into one general form, adopting an outward shape for the sake of the eye or of association, without reference to the inner distribution, let us begin from the heart as a nucleus and work outward. The most convenient size and arrangement of the rooms that are to constitute the building being fixed, the access of the light that may, of the air that must, be wanted, being provided for, we have the skeleton of our building. Nay, we have all excepting the dress. The connexion and order of parts, juxtaposed for convenience, cannot fail to speak of their relation and uses. [ . . . ]

What a field of study would be opened by the adoption in civil architecture of those laws of apportionment, distribution and connexion, which we have thus hinted at? No longer could the mere tyro huddle together a crowd of ill arranged, ill lighted and stifled rooms, and masking the chaos with the sneaking copy of a Greek façade, usurp the name of architect. If this anatomic connexion and proportion has been attained in ships, in machines, and, in spite of false principles, in such buildings as make a departure from it fatal, as in bridges and in scaffolding, why should we fear its immediate use in all construction!
[ . . . ]

The normal development of beauty is through action to completeness. The invariable development of embellishment and decoration is more embellishment and more decoration. The *reductio ad absurdum* is palpable enough at last; but where was the first downward step?[2] I maintain that the first downward step was *the introduction of the first inorganic, non-functional element, whether of shape or color.* If I be told that such a system as mine would produce *nakedness,* I accept the omen. In nakedness I behold the majesty of the essential, instead of the trappings of pretension. [ . . . ]

Beauty is the promise of function. [ . . . ]
[ . . . ]

**N O T E S**

---

1. The *USS Constitution* ("Old Ironsides"), the oldest commissioned ship still serving in the U.S. Navy, is an American frigate that was first launched in 1797. The first *USS Pennsylvania*, a ship-of-the-line commissioned in 1812 (but not launched until 1837), was the largest sailing warship ever built for the U.S. Navy. See James L. Mooney, *Dictionary of American Naval Fighting Ships*, vol. II (Washington, D.C.: Navy Department, Naval History Division, 1963):

173–7, and Mooney, *Dictionary of American Naval Fighting Ships*, vol. IV (Washington: Navy Department, Naval History Division, 1969): 596–7. "The galley of the Argonauts" refers to the small oar- (rather than sail-) powered ship *Argo*, which in ancient Greek myth was the vessel of the hero Jason.

2. The Latin phrase *reductio ad absurdum* means "reduction to the absurd."

# 1853

## John Ruskin, "The Nature of Gothic"

John Ruskin (1819–1900) was the preeminent art critic in England for much of the third quarter of the nineteenth century; he was named the first Slade Professor of Fine Art at Oxford University in 1869. He was a prolific writer, acting not only as an historian and critic of the fine arts, but also of architecture and design. In his three-volume work, *The Stones of Venice*, Ruskin attempted to recuperate and vindicate the Venetian Gothic style, which had often been maligned in histories of art as degenerate or imperfect, particularly in comparison to Classical and Renaissance art. In these excerpts from chapter two of the second volume *The Stones of Venice*, Ruskin argued that imperfect execution of ornament—as was often visible in the gothic style—was an index of social conditions in which workers had freedom and dignity, whereas slick perfection in the execution of ornament—as in Victorian Britain—was a sign of social relations in which workers were enslaved and dehumanized. Ruskin's essay, which linked aesthetics to the conditions of labor, was one of the foundational texts of the Arts and Crafts movement.

Excerpted from *The Stones of Venice*, vol. 2 (1853; reprint, New York: E. P. Dutton & Co., 1907): 147–154, 156–157.

[ . . . ]

§ XI. [ . . . ] Now, in the make and nature of every man, however rude or simple, whom we employ in manual labour, there are some powers for better things: some tardy imagination, torpid capacity of emotion, tottering steps of thought, there are, even at the worst; and in most cases it is all our own fault that they *are* tardy or torpid. But they cannot be strengthened, unless we are content to take them in their feebleness, and unless we prize and honour them in their imperfection above the best and most perfect manual skill. And this is what we have to do with all our labourers; to look for the *thought-ful* part of them, and get that out of them, whatever we lose for it, whatever faults and errors we are obliged to take with it. For the best that is in them cannot manifest itself, but in company with much error. Understand this clearly: You can teach a man to draw a straight line, and to cut one; to strike a curved line, and to carve it; and to copy and carve any number of given lines or forms, with admirable speed and perfect precision; and you find his work perfect of its kind: but if you ask him to think about any of those forms, to consider if he cannot find any better in his own head, he stops; his execution becomes hesitating; he thinks, and ten to one he thinks wrong; ten to one he makes a mistake in the first touch he gives to his work as a thinking being. But you have made a man of him for all that. He was only a machine before, an animated tool.

§XII. And observe, you are put to stern choice in this matter. You must either make a tool of the creature, or a man of him. You cannot make both. Men were not intended to work with the accuracy of tools, to be precise and perfect in all their actions. If you will have that precision out of them, and make their fingers measure degrees like cog-wheels, and their arms strike curves like compasses, you must unhumanise them. All the energy of their spirits must be given to make cogs and compasses of themselves. All their attention and strength must go to the accomplishment of the mean act. The eye of the soul must be bent upon the finger-point, and the soul's force must fill all the invisible nerves that guide it, ten hours a day, that it may not err from its steely precision, and so soul and sight be worn away, and the whole human being be lost at last—a heap of sawdust, so far as its intellectual work in this world is concerned; saved only by its Heart, which cannot go into the form of cogs and compasses, but expands, after the ten hours are over, into fireside humanity. On the other hand, if you will make a man of the working creature, you cannot make a tool. Let him but begin to imagine, to think, to try to do anything worth doing; and the engine-turned precision is lost at once. Out come all his roughness, all his dulness, all his incapability; shame upon shame, failure upon failure, pause after pause: but out comes the whole majesty of him also; and we know the height of it only, when we see the clouds settling upon him. And, whether the clouds be bright or dark, there will be transfiguration behind and within them.

§XIII. And now, reader, look round this English room of yours, about which you have been proud so often, because the work of it was so good and strong, and the ornaments of it so finished. Examine again all those accurate mouldings, and perfect polishings, and unerring adjustments of the seasoned wood and tempered steel. Many a time you have exulted over them, and thought how great England was, because her slightest work was done so thoroughly. Alas!

if read rightly, these perfectnesses are signs of a slavery in our England a thousand times more bitter and more degrading than that of the scourged African, or helot Greek. Men may be beaten, chained, tormented, yoked like cattle, slaughtered like summer flies, and yet remain in one sense, and the best sense, free. But to smother their souls within them, to blight and hew into rotting pollards the suckling branches of their human intelligence, to make the flesh and skin which, after the worm's work on it, is to see God, into leathern thongs to yoke machinery with,—this it is to be slave-masters indeed; and there might be more freedom in England, though her feudal lords' lightest words were worth men's lives, and though the blood of the vexed husbandman dropped in the furrows of her fields, than there is while the animation of her multitudes is sent like fuel to feed the factory smoke, and the strength of them is given daily to be wasted into the fineness of a web, or racked into the exactness of a line.

§XIV. And, on the other hand, go forth again to gaze upon the old cathedral front, where you have smiled so often at the fantastic ignorance of the old sculptors: examine once more those ugly goblins, and formless monsters, and stern statues, anatomiless and rigid; but do not mock at them, for they are the signs of the life and liberty of every workman who struck the stone; a freedom of thought, and rank in scale of being, such as no laws, no charters, no charities can secure; but which it must be the first aim of all Europe at this day to regain for her children.

§XV. Let me not be thought to speak wildly or extravagantly. It is verily this degradation of the operative into a machine, which, more than any other evil of the times, is leading the mass of the nations everywhere into vain, incoherent, destructive struggling for a freedom of which they cannot explain the nature to themselves. Their universal outcry against wealth, and against nobility, is not forced from them either by the pressure of famine, or the sting of mortified pride. These do much, and have done much in all ages; but the foundations of society were never yet shaken as they are at this day. It is not that men are ill fed, but that they have no pleasure in the work by which they make their bread, and therefore look to wealth as the only means of pleasure. It is not that men are pained by the scorn of the upper classes, but they cannot endure their own; for they feel that the kind of labour to which they are condemned is verily a degrading one, and makes them less than men. [ . . . ]

§XVI. We have much studied and much perfected, of late, the great civilised invention of the division of labour; only we give it a false name. It is not, truly speaking, the labour that is divided; but the men:—Divided into mere segments of men—broken into small fragments and crumbs of life; so that all the little piece of intelligence that is left in a man is not enough to make a pin, or a nail, but exhausts itself in making the point of a pin, or the head of a nail. Now it is a good and desirable thing, truly, to make many pins in a day; but if we could only see with what crystal sand their points were polished,—sand of human soul, much to be magnified before it can be discerned for what it is,—we should think there might be some loss in it also. And the great cry that rises from all our manufacturing cities, louder than their furnace blast, is all in very deed for this,—that we manufacture everything there except men; we blanch cotton, and strengthen steel, and refine sugar, and shape pottery; but to brighten, to strengthen, to refine, or to form a single living spirit, never enters into our estimate of advantages. And all the evil to which that cry is urging our myriads can be met only in one way: not by teaching nor preaching, for to teach them is but to show them their misery, and to preach to them, if we do nothing more than preach, is to mock at it. It can be met only by a right understanding, on the part of all classes, of what kinds of labour are good for men, raising them, and making them happy; by a determined sacrifice of such convenience, or beauty, or cheapness as is to be got only by the degradation of the workman; and by equally determined demand for the products and results of healthy and ennobling labour.

§XVII. And how, it will be asked, are these products to be recognised, and this demand to be regulated? Easily: by the observance of three broad and simple rules:

1. Never encourage the manufacture of any article not absolutely necessary, in the production of which *Invention* has no share.
2. Never demand an exact finish for its own sake, but only for some practical or noble end.
3. Never encourage imitation or copying of any kind, except for the sake of preserving record[s] of great works.

The second of these principles is the only one which directly rises out of the consideration of our immediate subject; but I shall briefly explain the meaning and extent of the first also, reserving the enforcement of the third for another place.

1. Never encourage the manufacture of anything not necessary, in the production of which invention has no share.

For instance. Glass beads are utterly unnecessary, and there is no design or thought employed in their manufacture. They are formed by first drawing out the glass into rods; these rods are chopped up into fragments of the size of beads by the human hand, and the fragments are then rounded in the furnace. The men who chop up the rods sit at their work all day, their hands vibrating with a perpetual and exquisitely timed palsy, and the beads dropping beneath their vibration like hail. Neither they, nor the men who draw out the rods or fuse the fragments, have the smallest occasion for the use of any single human faculty; and every young lady, therefore, who buys glass beads is engaged in the slave-trade, and in a much more cruel one than that which we have so long been endeavouring to put down.

But glass cups and vessels may become the subjects of exquisite invention;

and if in buying these we pay for the invention, that is to say, for the beautiful form, or colour, or engraving, and not for mere finish of execution, we are doing good to humanity.

[ ... ]

§XX. [ ... ] Our modern glass is exquisitely clear in its substance, true in its form, accurate in its cutting. We are proud of this. We ought to be ashamed of it. The old Venice glass was muddy, inaccurate in all its forms, and clumsily cut, if at all. And the old Venetian was justly proud of it. For there is this difference between the English and Venetian workman, that the former thinks only of accurately matching his patterns, and getting his curves perfectly true and his edges perfectly sharp, and becomes a mere machine for rounding curves and sharpening edges, while the old Venetian cared not a whit whether his edges were sharp or not, but he invented a new design for every glass that he made, and never moulded a handle or a lip without a new fancy in it. And therefore, though some Venetian glass is ugly and clumsy enough, when made by clumsy and uninventive workmen, other Venetian glass is so lovely in its forms that no price is too great for it; and we never see the same form in it twice. Now you cannot have the finish and the varied form too. If the workman is thinking about his edges, he cannot be thinking of his design; if of his design, he cannot think of his edges. Choose whether you will pay for the lovely form or the perfect finish, and choose at the same moment whether you will make the worker a man or a grindstone.

[ ... ]

§XXIII. [ ... ] Hitherto I have used the words imperfect and perfect merely to distinguish between work grossly unskilful, and work executed with average precision and science; and I have been pleading that any degree of unskilfulness should be admitted, so only that the labourer's mind had room for expression. But, accurately speaking, no good work whatever can be perfect, and *the demand for perfection is always a sign of a misunderstanding of the ends of art.*

§XXIV. This for two reasons, both based on everlasting laws. The first, that no great man ever stops working till he has reached his point of failure; that is to say, his mind is always far in advance of his powers of execution [ ... ].

§XXV. The second reason is, that imperfection is in some sort essential to all that we know of life. It is the sign of life in a mortal body, that is to say, of a state of progress and change. Nothing that lives is, or can be, rigidly perfect; part of it is decaying, part nascent. The foxglove blossom,—a third part bud, a third part past, a third part in full bloom,—is a type of the life of this world. And in all things that live there are certain irregularities and deficiencies which are not only signs of life, but sources of beauty. No human face is exactly the same in its lines on each side, no leaf perfect in its lobes, no branch in its symmetry. All admit irregularity as they imply change; and to banish imperfection is to destroy expression, to check exertion, to paralyze vitality. All things are literally better, lovelier, and more beloved for the imperfections which have been divinely appointed, that the law of human life may be Effort, and the law of human judgment, Mercy.

Accept this then for a universal law, that neither architecture nor any other noble work of man can be good unless it be imperfect; and let us be prepared for the otherwise strange fact, which we shall discern clearly as we approach the period of the Renaissance, that the first cause of the fall of the arts of Europe was a relentless requirement of perfection, incapable alike either of being silenced by veneration for greatness, or softened into forgiveness of simplicity.

[ . . . ]

# 1856

## Owen Jones, *Grammar of Ornament*

The English architect and designer Owen Jones (1809–1874), a friend of Henry Cole, served as the superintendent of works for the Great Exhibition of 1851, and, in that capacity, designed the display spaces and color schemes inside Joseph Paxton's "Crystal Palace."[1] In his 1856 book, *Grammar of Ornament*, Jones argued that the ornament of "civilised" nations such as Britain was "enfeebled," but that the ornament of the "savage tribes" of New Guinea and New Zealand, and of the "Mohammedan" countries of India, Tunisia, Egypt, and Turkey, was vital and beautiful. In his lavishly illustrated book Jones provided examples of ornament from both ancient and modern civilizations, and promoted forms of ornament that were idealized or conventionalized, rather than closely copied from nature.

Excerpted from Owen Jones, *Grammar of Ornament* (1856; reprint, London: Bernard Quaritch, 1910): 16, 77–8, 154.

[ . . . ]

The ornament of a savage tribe, being the result of a natural instinct, is necessarily always true to its purpose; whilst in much of the ornament of civilised nations, the first impulse which generated received forms being enfeebled by constant repetition, the ornament is oftentimes misapplied, and instead of first seeking the most convenient form and adding beauty, all beauty is destroyed, because all fitness, by superadding ornament to ill-contrived form. If we would return to a more healthy condition, we must even be as little children or as savages; we must get rid of the acquired and artificial, and return to and develope [*sic*] natural instincts.

[ . . . ]

The Exhibition of the Works of Industry of all Nations in 1851 was barely opened to the public ere attention was directed to the gorgeous contributions of India.

Amid the general disorder everywhere apparent in the application of Art to manufactures, the presence of so much unity of design, so much skill and judgment in its application, with so much of elegance and refinement in the execution as was observable in all the works, not only of India, but of all the other Mohammedan contributing countries,—Tunis, Egypt, and Turkey,—excited a degree of attention from artists, manufacturers, and the public, which has not been without its fruits.

Whilst in the works contributed by the various nations of Europe there was everywhere to be observed an entire absence of any common principle in the application of Art to manufactures,—whilst from one end to the other of the vast structure there could be found but a fruitless struggle after novelty, irrespective of fitness, that all design was based upon a system of copying and misapplying the received forms of beauty of every bygone style of Art, without one single attempt to produce an Art in harmony with our present wants and means of production—the carver in stone, the worker in metal, the weaver and the painter, borrowing from each other, and alternately misapplying the forms peculiarly appropriate to each—there were to be found in isolated collections at the four corners of the transepts all the principles, all the unity, all the truth, for which we had looked elsewhere in vain, and this because we were amongst a people practising an art which had grown up with their civilisation, and strengthened with their growth. United by a common faith, their art had necessarily a common expression, this expression varying in each according to the influence to which each nation was subject. The Tunisian still retaining the art of the Moors who created the Alhambra; the Turk exhibiting the same art, but modified by the character of the mixed population over which they rule; the Indian uniting the severe forms of Arabian art with the graces of Persian refinement.

All the laws of the distribution of form which we have already observed in the Arabian and Moresque Ornament are equally to be found in the productions of India. From the highest work of embroidery, or most elaborate work of the loom, to the constructing and decorating of a child's toy or earthen vessel, we find everywhere at work the same guiding principles,—there is always the same care for the general form, the same absence of all excrescences or superfluous ornament; we find nothing that has been added without purpose, nor that could be removed without disadvantage. The same division and subdivision of their general lines, which forms the charms of Moresque ornament, is equally to be found here; the difference which creates the style is not one of principle, but of individual expression. In the Indian style ornaments are somewhat more flowing and less conventionalised, and have, doubtless, been more subjected to direct Persian influence.

[ . . . ]

We have endeavoured to show in the preceding chapters, that in the best periods of art all ornament was rather based upon an observation of the principles which regulate the arrangement of form in nature, than on an attempt to imitate the absolute forms of those works; and that whenever this limit was exceeded in any art, it was one of the strongest symptoms of decline: true art consisting in idealising, and not copying, the forms of nature.

We think it desirable to insist rather strongly on this point, as, in the present uncertain state in which we are, there seems a general disposition arising to reproduce, as faithfully as may be possible, natural form as works of ornament. The world has become weary of the eternal repetition of the same conventional forms which have been borrowed from styles which have passed away, and therefore can excite in us but little sympathy. There has risen, we say, a universal cry of "Go back to nature, as the ancients did;" we should be amongst the first to echo that cry, but it will depend much on what we go to seek, how far we may succeed. If we go to nature as the Egyptians and the Greeks went, we may hope; but if we go there like the Chinese, or even as the Gothic artists of the fourteenth and fifteenth centuries, we should gain but little. We have already, in the floral carpets, floral papers, and floral carvings of the present day, sufficient evidence to show that no art can be produced by such means; and that the more closely nature is copied, the farther we are removed from producing a work of art.

[ . . . ]

**N O T E S**

1. "Jones, Owen," *Encyclopaedia Britannica*, *<http://www.britannica.com/eb/article?=eu44953>*, (accessed 16 October 2002); and Michael Darby, "Jones, Owen," *The Grove Dictionary of Art Online*, *<http://www.groveart.com>*, ed. L. Macy (accessed 16 October 2002).

# 1867

# Karl Marx, "The Capitalist Character of Manufacture"

Karl Marx (1818–1883), a German-born resident of London from 1849 to his death, was the coauthor with Friedrich (or Frederick) Engels, of *The Communist Manifesto* (1848). Volume one of Marx's masterwork, *Capital*, was published in German as *Das Kapital* in 1867; however, Engels edited and completed volumes two and three of *Capital*, which Marx left unfinished at his death. In *Capital*, Marx not only lays out his theories about class struggle and the "inevitable" dictatorship of the proletariat, but also writes extensively about the "capitalist character of manufacture" and the effects of machine production and the factory system on workers. In these excerpts, Marx argues that capitalists do not make use of machines to ease or shorten labor, as one might expect. Rather, Marx claims, machines are used to make goods more cheaply, and to further subjugate the worker to the will of the "master."

Excerpted from Karl Marx, *Capital: A Critique of Political Economy*, vol. 1, edited by Frederick Engels; translated from the third German edition by Samuel Moore and Edward Aveling; revised and amplified according to the fourth German edition by Ernest Untermann (1867; reprint/translation, New York: Charles H. Kerr & Company, 1906): 395–6, 405, 431–2, 440, 462 (references omitted).

**M**anufacture proper[1] not only subjects the previously independent workman to the discipline and command of capital, but, in addition, creates a hierarchic gradation of the workmen themselves. While simple co-operation leaves the mode of working by the individual for the most part unchanged, manufacture thoroughly revolutionises it, and seizes labour-power by its very roots. It converts the labourer into a crippled monstrosity, by forcing his detail dexterity at the expense of a world of productive capabilities and instincts; just as in the States of La Plata[2] they butcher a whole beast for the sake of his hide or his tallow. Not only is the detail work distributed to the different individuals, but the individual himself is made the automatic motor of a fractional operation, and the absurd fable of Menenius Agrippa,[3] which makes man a mere fragment of his own body, becomes realised. If, at first, the workman sells his labour-power to capital, because the material means of producing a commodity fail him,[4] now his very labour-power refuses its services unless it has been sold to capital. Its functions can be exercised only in an environment that exists in the workshop of the capitalist after the sale. By nature unfitted to make anything independently, the manufacturing labourer developes [*sic*] productive activity as a mere appendage of the capitalist's workshop. [ . . . D]ivision of labour brands the manufacturing workman as the property of capital.

[ . . . ]

John Stuart Mill[5] says in his *Principles of Political Economy*: "It is questionable if all the mechanical inventions yet made have lightened the day's toil of any human being." That is, however, by no means the aim of the capitalistic application of machinery. Like every other increase in the productiveness of labour, machinery is intended to cheapen commodities, and, by shortening that portion of the working-day, in which the labourer works for himself, to lengthen the other portion that he gives, without an equivalent, to the capitalist. In short, it is a means for producing surplus-value.

[ . . . ]

In so far as machinery dispenses with muscular power, it becomes a means of employing labourers of slight muscular strength, and those whose bodily development is incomplete, but whose limbs are all the more supple. The labour of women and children was, therefore, the first thing sought for by capitalists who used machinery. That mighty substitute for [male] labour and labourers was forthwith changed into a means for increasing the number of wage-labourers by enrolling, under the direct sway of capital, every member of the workman's family, without distinction of age or sex. Compulsory work for the capitalist usurped the place, not only of the children's play, but also of free labour at home within moderate limits for the support of the family.

The value of labour-power was determined, not only by the labour-time necessary to maintain the individual adult labo[u]rer, but also by that necessary to maintain his family. Machinery, by throwing every member of that family on to the labour market, spreads the value of the man's labour-power over his whole family. It thus depreciates his labour-power. To purchase the labour-power of a family of four workers may, perhaps, cost more than it formerly did to purchase the labour-power of the head of the family, but, in return, four days' labour takes the place of one, and their price falls in proportion to the excess of the surplus-labour of four over the surplus-labour of one. In order that the family may live, four people must now, not only labour, but expend surplus-labo[u]r for the capitalist. Thus we see, that machinery, while augmenting the human material that forms the principal object of capital's exploiting power, at the same time raises the degree of exploitation.

[ . . . ]

If machinery be the most powerful means for increasing the productiveness of labour—*i.e.*, for shortening the working time required in the production of a commodity, it becomes in the hands of capital the most powerful means, in those industries first invaded by it, for lengthening the working day beyond all bounds set by human nature. It creates, on the one hand, new conditions by which capital is enabled to give free scope to this its constant tendency, and on the other hand, new motives with which to whet capital's appetite for the labour of others.

In the first place, in form of machinery, the implements of labour become automatic, things moving and working independent of the workman. They are thenceforth an industrial *perpetuum mobile*,[6] that would go on producing forever, did it not meet with certain natural obstructions in the weak bodies and the strong wills of its human attendants. The automaton, as capital, and because it is capital, is endowed, in the person of the capitalist, with intelligence and will; it is therefore animated by the longing to reduce to a minimum the resistance offered by that repellant yet elastic natural barrier, man. This resistance is moreover lessened by the apparent lightness of machine work, and by the more pliant and docile character of the women and children employed on it.

[ . . . ]

Every kind of capitalist production in so far as it is not only a labour-process, but also a process of creating surplus-value, has this in common, that it is not the workman that employs the instruments of labour, but the instruments of labour that employ the workman. But it is only in the factory system that this inversion for the first time acquires technical and palpable reality. By means of its conversion into an automaton, the instrument of labour confronts the labourer, during the labour-process, in the shape of capital, of dead labour, that dominates, and pumps dry, living labour-power. The separation of the intellectual powers of production from the manual labour, and the conversion of those powers into the might of capital over labour, is, as we have already shown, finally completed by modern industry erected on the foundation of machinery. The special skill of each individual insignificant factory operative vanishes as an infinitesimal quantity before the science, the gigantic physical forces, and the mass of labour that are embodied in the factory mechanism and, together with that mechanism, constitute the power of the "master."

### NOTES

1. Here, Marx means, literally, "hand-making" (as opposed to machinofacture or "machine-making").

2. Marx probably refers here to Argentina, Bolivia, Uruguay, and Paraguay, the former territories of the Viceroyalty of the Río de la Plata, which have long been known for their cattle production.

3. Menenius Agrippa was a Roman consul, circa 503 BCE, who represented the plebeian class. Agrippa was able to stop the plebeians from a planned revolt against the patrician class by telling them a parable about the belly and the limbs, in which the (productive and hard-

working) hands and legs of the body decided to starve the (seemingly inactive and parasiti-
cal) belly. However, as the limbs discovered, the belly did serve a purpose; without it, the
limbs weakened and could not function.

4. Marx means that the laborer does not own and cannot afford the tools or raw materials necessary to perform his craft or labor.

5. John Stuart Mill (1806–1873) was an English philosopher and economist who was a contemporary of Marx.

6. Perpetual motion machine.

# 1868

## Charles Eastlake, *Hints on Household Taste*

The Englishman Charles Eastlake (1836–1906) studied architecture as a youth
and served as the Keeper of the National Gallery in London during his mature
years. But Eastlake is best known as the writer of the immensely popular 1868
book, *Hints on Household Taste*, which was reprinted numerous times over the
following fifteen years in both England and the United States. In it, Eastlake
promoted a Gothic revival furniture style that featured incised decorative carving and turned legs and spindles, which seemed, at least in contrast to the
Renaissance revival and Neo-Rococo styles favored during the Victorian period,
simple and "honest" (see illustration on page 27). Eastlake, however, disliked
the heavily ornamented and often cheaply made American furniture that bore
his name, though it was inspired by his designs. He stated in the preface to the
fourth edition of his book that "I find American tradesmen continually advertising what they are pleased to call 'Eastlake' furniture, with the production of
which I have had nothing whatever to do, and for the taste of which I should
be very sorry to be considered responsible." In the following excerpts, Eastlake
laments what he considers to be the ugliness and shoddiness of most Victorian
design, and argues that simplicity, fitness to purpose, and truth to materials
should be the guiding principles of both designers and buyers.

Excerpted from Charles Eastlake, *Hints on Household Taste in Furniture, Upholstery
and Other Details,* 4th (revised) edition, (London: Longmans, Green and Company,
1878): 2–4, 91–92, 167, 172.

[ . . . ] **I**f we may believe those who have given their attention to the subject of technical design, [commonplace taste] pervaded and vitiated the judgment by which we were accustomed to select and approve the objects of everyday use in our houses. It crossed our path in the Brussels carpet of our drawing-rooms; it was about our beds in the shape of gaudy chintz; it compelled us to rest on chairs and to sit at tables which were designed in accordance with the worst principles of construction and invested with shapes confessedly unpicturesque. It sent us metal-work from Birmingham which was as vulgar in form as it was flimsy in execution. It decorated the finest modern porcelain with the most objectionable character of ornament. It lined our walls with silly representations of vegetable life, or with a mass of uninteresting diaper.[1] It bade us, in short, furnish our houses after the same fashion as we dress ourselves, and that is with no more sense of real beauty than if art were a dead letter.

It is hardly necessary to say that the general public did not recognise this fact. In the eyes of Mater-familias there was no upholstery which could possibly surpass that which the most fashionable upholsterer supplied. She believed in the elegance of window-curtains, of which so many dozen yards had been sent to the Duchess of ——, and concluded that the dinner-service must be perfect which was described as 'quite a novelty.' When did people first adopt the monstrous notion that the 'last pattern out' must be the best? Is good taste so rapidly progressive that every mug which leaves the potter's hands surpasses in shape the last which he moulded? Far from this, it is to be feared that, instead of progressing, we have, for some ages at least, gone hopelessly backward in the arts of manufacture. And this is true not only with respect to the character of design, but often in regard to the actual quality of material employed. It is generally admitted by every housewife who has attained a matronly age, that linen, silk, and other articles of textile fabric, though less expensive than formerly, are far inferior to what was made in the days of our grandfathers. Metal-workers tell us that it is almost impossible to procure, for the purpose of their trade, brass such as appears to have been in common use a century ago. Joinery is neither so sound nor so artistic as it was in the early Georgian era. A cheap and easy method of workmanship—an endeavour to produce a show of finish with the least possible labour, and, above all, an unhealthy spirit of competition in regard to price, such as was unknown to previous generations—have combined to deteriorate the value of our ordinary mechanics' work.

[ . . . ]

[ . . . ] The true principles of good design are universally applicable, and, if they are worth anything, can be brought to bear on all sorts and conditions of manufacture. There was a time when this was so; and, indeed, it is certain that they lingered in the cottage long after they had been forgotten in palaces.

Every article of manufacture which is capable of decorative treatment should indicate, by its general design, the purpose to which it will be applied, and

should never be allowed to convey a false notion of that purpose. Experience has shown that particular shapes and special modes of decoration are best suited to certain materials. Therefore the character, situation, and extent of ornament should depend on the nature of the material employed, as well as on the use of the article itself. On the acceptance of these two leading principles—now universally recognised in the field of decorative art—must always depend the chief merit of good design. To the partial, and often direct, violation of those principles, we may attribute the vulgarity and bad taste of most modern work.

[ . . . ]

In the sphere of what is called industrial art, use and beauty are, in theory at least, closely associated: for not only has the humblest article of manufacture, when honestly designed, a picturesque interest of its own, but no decorative feature can legitimately claim our admiration without revealing by its very nature the purpose of the object which it adorns. Yet, among half-educated minds, nothing is more common than to retain two distinct and utterly opposed ideals of beauty—one of a poetic and sentimental kind, which leads people to prefer certain conditions of form and colour in pictorial representations of 'still life'; and the other of a conventional and worldly kind, through which we not only tolerate, but approve, the dubious 'elegancies' of fashionable upholstery. [ . . . ]

[ . . . ]

[ . . . T]he modern English work-table, or any similar article of manufacture designed for fashionable households, is sure to belie its purpose in some way. It will probably have doors which look like drawers, or drawers which assume an appearance of doors. It will shroud up part of its wooden framing with silken plaits fringed with straight bands of gimp, and [be] decorated at each angle with lumpy little tassels. It will be made of deal[2] and veneered with walnut and mahogany. It will be 'enriched' with fictitious carving, and plastered over with delusive varnish.

Real art has no recourse to such tricks as these. It can accommodate itself to the simplest and most practical shapes which the carpenter or potter has invented, as well as to the most delicate and subtle forms of refined manufacture. There is no limit to the height of dignity which it can reach; there is no level of usefulness to which it will not stoop. [ . . . ]

[ . . . ]

## NOTES

1. A "diaper" is a regular geometric pattern, often of diamond shapes formed by intersecting diagonal lines.
2. Pine or fir; in the nineteenth century, both were considered cheap, inferior woods.

# 1873

## Christopher Dresser, *Principles of Decorative Design*

Christopher Dresser (1834–1904), a Scottish botanist and designer, was particularly interested in the economic value of beauty, as is evident in this excerpt from his 1873 book, *Principles of Decorative Design*. Like his contemporaries Henry Cole and Owen Jones (to whose *Grammar of Ornament* he contributed a design), Dresser advocated conventionalization of natural motifs, a belief probably strengthened by his 1877 travels in Japan, during which he purchased items for Tiffany & Co. and represented the British government.[1] Dresser has been declared by some historians to be the first "real" industrial designer, in that he worked for numerous firms in many media (including iron, silver, glass, ceramics, furniture, and wallpaper), and promoted machine production rather than handcraft. The austerity and functionalism of his designs, many of which straightforwardly revealed their means of fabrication by means of exposed joints and rivets, made his works popular even with twentieth-century historians and critics who otherwise had little interest in Victorian design.

Excerpted from Christopher Dresser, *Principles of Decorative Design* (London: Cassell Petter & Galpin, 1873): 1–2, 22–25 (references omitted).

There are many handicrafts in which a knowledge of the true principles of ornamentation is almost essential to success, and there are few in which a knowledge of decorative laws cannot be utilised. The man who can form a bowl or a vase well is an artist, and so is the man who can make a beautiful chair or table. These are truths; but the converse of these facts is also true; for if a man be not an artist he cannot form an elegant bowl, nor make a beautiful chair.

At the very outset we must recognise the fact that the beautiful has a commercial or money value. We may even say that art can lend to an object a value greater than that of the material of which it consists, even when the object be formed of precious matter, as of rare marbles, scarce woods, or silver or gold.

This being the case, it follows that the workman who can endow his productions with those qualities or beauties which give value to his works, must be more useful to his employer than the man who produces objects devoid of such beauty, and his time must be of higher value than that of his less skilful companion. If a man, who has been born and brought up as a "son of toil," has that laudable ambition which causes him to seek to rise above his fellows by fairly becoming their superior, I would say to him that I know of no means of his so readily doing so, as by his acquainting himself with the laws of beauty, and studying till he learns to perceive the difference between the beautiful and the ugly, the graceful and the deformed, the refined and the coarse. To perceive delicate beauties is not by any means an easy task to those who have not devoted themselves to the consideration of the beautiful for a long period of time, and of this be assured, that what now appears to you to be beautiful, you may shortly regard as less so, and what now fails to attract you, may ultimately become charming to your eye. In your study of the beautiful, do not be led away by the false judgment of ignorant persons who may suppose themselves possessed of good taste. It is common to assume that women have better taste than men, and some women seem to consider themselves the possessors of even authoritative taste from which there can be no appeal. They may be right, only we must be pardoned for not accepting such authority, for should there be any over-estimation of the accuracy of this good taste, serious loss of progress in art-judgment might result.

It may be taken as an invariable truth that knowledge, and knowledge alone, can enable us to form an accurate judgment respecting the beauty or want of beauty of an object, and he who has the greater knowledge of art can judge best of the ornamental qualities of an object. He who would judge rightly of art-works must have knowledge. Let him who would judge of beauty apply himself, then, to earnest study, for thereby he shall have wisdom, and by his wise reasonings he will be led to perceive beauty, and thus have opened to him a new source of pleasure.

Art-knowledge is of value to the individual and to the country at large. To the individual it is riches and wealth, and to the nation it saves impoverishment. Take, for example, clay as a natural material: in the hands of one man this material becomes flower-pots, worth eighteen-pence a "cast" (a number varying from sixty to twelve according to size); in the hands of another it becomes a tazza, or a vase, worth five pounds, or perhaps fifty. It is the art which gives the value, and not the material. To the nation it saves impoverishment.

A wise policy induces a country to draw to itself all the wealth that it can, without parting with more of its natural material than is absolutely necessary. If for every pound of clay that a nation parts with, it can draw to itself that amount of gold which we value at five pounds sterling, it is obviously better thus to part with but little material and yet secure wealth, than it is to part with the material at a low rate either in its native condition, or worked into coarse vessels, thereby rendering a great impoverishment of the native resources of the country necessary in order to [increase] its wealth.

Men of the lowest degree of intelligence can dig clay, iron, or copper, or quarry stone; but these materials, if bearing the impress of mind, are ennobled and rendered valuable, and the more strongly the material is marked with this ennobling impress the more valuable it becomes.

[ . . . ]

A principle of great importance in respect to design is, that *the material of which an object is formed should be used in a manner consistent with its own nature, and in that particular way in which it can be most easily "worked."*

Another principle of equal importance with that just set forth, is this: that *when an object is about to be formed, that material (or those materials) which is (or are) most appropriate to its formation should be sought and employed.* These two propositions are of very great importance, and the principles which they set forth should never be lost sight of by the designer. They involve the first principles of successful designing, for if ignored the work produced cannot be satisfactory.

*Curves will be found to be beautiful just as they are subtle in character; those which are most subtle in character being most beautiful.*

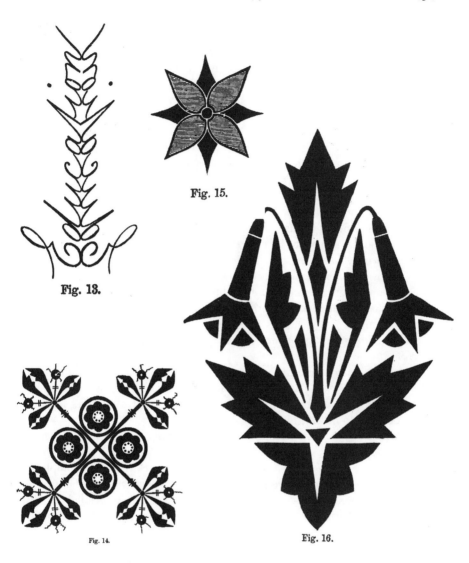

Fig. 15.

Fig. 13.

Fig. 14.

Fig. 16.

The arc is the least beautiful of curves (I do not here speak of a circle, but of the line, as a line, which bounds the circle); being struck from one centre its origin is instantly detected, while the mind requires that a line, the contemplation of which shall be pleasurable, must be in advance of its knowledge, and call into activity its powers of inquiry. The elliptic curve, or curve bounding the ellipse, is more beautiful than the arc, for its origin is not so strikingly apparent, being formed from two centres. The curve of the egg is more beautiful still, being formed from three centres. As the number of centres necessary to the formation of a curve increases, the difficulty of detecting its origin also becomes greater, and the variety which the curve presents is also proportionally great; the variety being obviously greater as the number of the centres from which it is struck is increased.

*Proportion, like the curve, must be of a subtle nature.*

A surface must never be divided for the purpose of decoration into halves. The proportion of 1 to 1 is bad. As proportion increases in subtlety it also increases in beauty. The proportion of 2 to 1 is little better; the proportion of 3 to 8, or of 5 to 8, or of 5 to 13, is, however, good, the last named being the best of those which I have adduced; for the pleasure derived from the contemplation of proportion increases with the difficulty of detecting it. This principle is true in relation to the division of a mass into primary segments, and of primary segments into secondary forms, as well as in relation to the grouping together of parts of various sizes; hence it is worthy of special note.

*A principle of order must prevail in every ornamental composition.*

Confusion is the result of accident, while order results from thought and care. The operation of mind cannot well be set forth in the absence of this principle; at least, the presence of a principle of order renders the operation of mind at once manifest.

*The orderly repetition of parts frequently aids in the production of ornamental effects.*

The kaleidoscope affords a wonderful example of what repetition will do. The mere fragments of glass which we view in this instrument would altogether fail to please were they not repeated with regularity. Of themselves repetition and order can do much. (Figs. 13 and 14.)

*Alternation is a principle of primary importance in certain ornamental compositions.*

In the case of the flower (as the buttercup, or chickweed, for example) the coloured leaves do not fall over the green leaves (the petals do not fall over the sepals), but between them—they alternate with them. This principle is not only manifested in plants, but also in many ornaments produced in the best periods of art (Fig. 15).

*If plants are employed as ornaments they must not be treated imitatively, but must be conventionally treated, or rendered into ornaments* (Fig. 16).

A monkey can imitate, man can create.

These are the chief principles which we shall have to notice, as involved in the production of ornamental designs.

[ . . . ]

**NOTES**

1. Rosamond Allwood, "Dresser, Christopher," *Grove Dictionary of Art Online*, ed. L. Macy, <*http://www.groveart.com*>, (accessed 16 October 2002).

# 1876-1900

# 1877

## William Morris, "The Lesser Arts"

William Morris (1834–1896), an English artist, poet, essayist, designer, and printer, was a prominent socialist and one of the foremost theorists of the Arts and Crafts movement. He was a member of the Pre-Raphaelite Brotherhood in the 1850s, and, in 1861, founded the firm of Morris, Marshall, Faulkner, & Co. (reorganized as Morris & Co. in 1875), the goal of which was to produce reasonably priced, well-designed furnishings, wallpapers, and textiles while employing skilled craftsmen at fair wages. Morris admired the writings of John Ruskin, particularly the chapter in *The Stones of Venice* called "The Nature of Gothic" (excerpts of which are reprinted earlier in this volume), and, like Ruskin, modeled his ideal society on medieval England (or, more accurately, on a heavily romanticized version thereof). Morris championed traditional craft production not only for the superior quality products that he believed resulted from this method of manufacture, but also for the well-paid and honorable employment that he felt craft production provided. The following excerpts are from Morris's first public lecture, in which he argued that aesthetics and quality of craftsmanship were linked to social conditions, and that only a "popular" art grounded in socialist principles could be noble, vital, and beautiful.

Excerpted from William Morris, "The Lesser Arts," a lecture delivered before the Trades' Guild of Learning, December 4, 1877; published in pamphlet form as *The Decorative Arts, Their Relation to Modern Life and Progress* (London: Ellis & White, 1878); reprinted in *The Collected Works of William Morris,* vol. XXII (London: Longmans, Green and Company, 1914): 5–6, 22–27.

[ . . . ]

To give people pleasure in the things they must perforce *use*, that is one great office of decoration; to give people pleasure in the things they must perforce *make*, that is the other use of it.

Does not our subject look important enough now? I say that without these arts, our rest would be vacant and uninteresting, our labour mere endurance, mere wearing away of body and mind.

[ . . . W]e all know what people have said about the curse of labour, and what heavy and grievous nonsense are the more part of their words thereupon;

whereas indeed the real curses of craftsmen have been the curse of stupidity, and the curse of injustice from within and without: no, I cannot suppose there is anybody here who would think it either a good life, or an amusing one, to sit with one's hands before one doing nothing—to live like a gentleman, as fools call it.

Nevertheless there *is* dull work to be done, and a weary business it is setting men about such work, and seeing them through it, and I would rather do the work twice over with my own hands than have such a job: but now only let the arts which we are talking of beautify our labour, and be widely spread, intelligent, well understood both by the maker and the user, let them grow in one word *popular*, and there will be pretty much an end of dull work and its wearing slavery; and no man will any longer have an excuse for talking about the curse of labour, no man will any longer have an excuse for evading the blessing of labour. I believe there is nothing that will aid the world's progress so much as the attainment of this; I protest there is nothing in the world that I desire so much as this, wrapped up, as I am sure it is, with changes political and social, that in one way or another we all desire.

[ . . . ]

There is a great deal of sham work in the world, hurtful to the buyer, more hurtful to the seller, if he only knew it, most hurtful to the maker: how good a foundation it would be towards getting good Decorative Art, that is[,] ornamental workmanship, if we craftsmen were to resolve to turn out nothing but excellent workmanship in all things, instead of having, as we too often have now, a very low average standard of work, which we often fall below.

I do not blame either one class or another in this matter, I blame all: to set aside our own class of handicraftsmen, of whose shortcomings you and I know so much that we need talk no more about it, I know that the public in general are set on having things cheap, being so ignorant that they do not know when they get them nasty also; so ignorant that they neither know nor care whether they give a man his due: I know that the manufacturers (so called)[1] are so set on carrying out competition to its utmost, competition of cheapness, not of excellence, that they meet the bargain-hunters half way, and cheerfully furnish them with nasty wares at the cheap rate they are asked for, by means of what can be called by no prettier name than fraud. England has of late been too much busied with the counting-house and not enough with the workshop: with the result that the counting-house at the present moment is rather barren of orders.

I say all classes are to blame in this matter, but also I say that the remedy lies with the handicraftsmen, who are not ignorant of these things like the public, and who have no call to be greedy and isolated like the manufacturers or middlemen; the duty and honour of educating the public lies with them, and they have in them the seeds of order and organization which make that duty the easier.

When will they see to this and help to make men of us all by insisting on this most weighty piece of manners: so that we may adorn life with the pleasure of cheerfully *buying* goods at their due price; with the pleasure of *selling* goods that we could be proud of both for fair price and fair workmanship; with the pleasure of working soundly and without haste at *making* goods that we could be proud of?—much the greatest pleasure of the three is that last, such a pleasure as, I think, the world has none like it.

You must not say that this piece of manners lies out of my subject: it is essentially a part of it and most important: for I am bidding you learn to be artists, if art is not to come to an end amongst us: and what is an artist but a workman who is determined that, whatever else happens, his work shall be excellent? or, to put it in another way: the decoration of workmanship, what is it but the expression of man's pleasure in successful labour? But what pleasure can there be in *bad* work, in *un*successful labour; why should we decorate *that?* and how can we bear to be always unsuccessful in our labour?

As greed of unfair gain, wanting to be paid for what we have not earned, cumbers our path with this tangle of bad work, of sham work, so the heaped-up money which this greed has brought us (for greed will have its way, like all other strong passions), this money, I say, gathered into heaps little and big, with all the false distinction which so unhappily it yet commands amongst us, has raised up against the arts a barrier of the love of luxury and show, which is of all obvious hindrances the worst to overpass: the highest and most cultivated classes are not free from the vulgarity of it, the lower are not free from its pretence. I beg you to remember both as a remedy against this, and as explaining exactly what I mean, that nothing can be a work of art which is not useful; that is to say, which does not minister to the body when well under command of the mind, or which does not amuse, soothe, or elevate the mind in a healthy state. What tons upon tons of unutterable rubbish pretending to be works of art in some degree would this maxim clear out of our London houses, if it were understood and acted upon! To my mind it is only here and there (out of the kitchen) that you can find in a well-to-do house things that are of any use at all: as a rule all the decoration (so called) that has got there is there for the sake of show, not because anybody likes it. I repeat, this stupidity goes through all classes of society: the silk curtains in my Lord's drawing-room are no more a matter of art to him than the powder in his footman's hair; the kitchen in a country farmhouse is most commonly a pleasant and homelike place, the parlour dreary and useless.

Simplicity of life, begetting simplicity of taste, that is, a love for sweet and lofty things, is of all matters most necessary for the birth of the new and better art we crave for; simplicity everywhere, in the palace as well as in the cottage.

Still more is this necessary, cleanliness and decency everywhere, in the cottage as well as in the palace: the lack of that is a serious piece of *manners* for us to correct: that lack and all the inequalities of life, and the heaped-up thoughtlessness and disorder of so many centuries that cause it: and as yet it is only a very few men who have begun to think about a remedy for it in its widest range: even in its narrower aspect, in the defacements of our big towns by all that commerce brings with it, who heeds it? who tries to control their squalor and hideousness? there is nothing but thoughtlessness and recklessness in the matter: the helplessness of people who don't live long enough to do a thing themselves, and have not manliness and foresight to begin the work, and pass it on to those that shall come after them.

Is money to be gathered? cut down the pleasant trees among the houses, pull down ancient and venerable buildings for the money that a few square yards of London dirt will fetch; blacken rivers, hide the sun and poison the air with smoke and worse, and it's nobody's business to see to it or mend it: that is all that modern commerce, the counting-house forgetful of the workshop, will do for us herein.

And Science—we have loved her well, and followed her diligently, what will she do? I fear she is so much in the pay of the counting-house—the counting-house and the drill-sergeant—that she is too busy, and will for the present do nothing. Yet there are matters which I should have thought easy for her; say for example teaching Manchester how to consume its own smoke, or Leeds how to get rid of its superfluous black dye without turning it into the river, which would be as much worth her attention as the production of the heaviest of heavy black silks, or the biggest of useless guns. Anyhow, however it be done, unless people care about carrying on their business without making the world hideous, how can they care about Art? I know it will cost much both of time and money to better these things even a little; but I do not see how these can be better spent than in making life cheerful and honourable for others and for ourselves; and the gain of good life to the country at large that would result from men seriously setting about the bettering of the decency of our big towns would be priceless, even if nothing specially good befell the arts in consequence: I do not know that it would; but I should begin to think matters hopeful if men turned their attention to such things, and I repeat that, unless they do so, we can scarcely even begin with any hope our endeavours for the bettering of the arts.

Unless something or other is done to give all men some pleasure for the eyes and rest for the mind in the aspect of their own and their neighbours' houses, until the contrast is less disgraceful between the fields where beasts live and the streets where men live, I suppose that the practice of the arts must be mainly kept in the hands of a few highly cultivated men, who can go often to beautiful places, whose education enables them, in the contemplation of the past glories of the world, to shut out from their view the everyday squalors that the most of men move in. Sirs, I believe that art has such sympathy with cheerful freedom, openheartedness and reality, so much she sickens under selfishness and luxury, that she will not live thus isolated and exclusive. I will go further than this and say that on such terms I do not wish her to live. I protest that it would be a shame to an honest artist to enjoy what he had huddled up to himself of such art, as it would be for a rich man to sit and eat dainty food amongst starving soldiers in a beleaguered fort.

I do not want art for a few, any more than education for a few, or freedom for a few.

No, rather than art should live this poor thin life among a few exceptional men, despising those beneath them for an ignorance for which they themselves are responsible, for a brutality that they will not struggle with,—rather than this, I would that the world should indeed sweep away all art for awhile, as I said before I thought it possible she might do; rather than the wheat should rot in the miser's granary, I would that the earth had it, that it might yet have a chance to quicken in the dark.

I have a sort of faith, though, that this clearing away of all art will not happen, that men will get wiser, as well as more learned; that many of the intricacies of life, on which we now pride ourselves more than enough, partly because they are new, partly because they have come with the gain of better things, will be cast aside as having played their part, and being useful no longer. I hope that we shall have leisure from war—war commercial, as well as war of the bullet and the bayonet; leisure from the knowledge that darkens counsel; leisure above all from the greed of money, and the craving for that overwhelming distinction that money now brings: I believe that as we have even now partly achieved LIBERTY, so we shall one day achieve EQUALITY, which, and which only, means FRATERNITY, and so have leisure from poverty and all its griping, sordid cares.[2]

Then having leisure from all these things, amidst renewed simplicity of life we shall have leisure to think about our work, that faithful daily companion, which no man any longer will venture to call the Curse of labour: for surely then we shall be happy in it, each in his place, no man grudging at another; no one bidden to be any man's *servant*, every one scorning to be any man's *master*: men will then assuredly be happy in their work, and that happiness will assuredly bring forth decorative, noble, *popular* art.

That art will make our streets as beautiful as the woods, as elevating as the mountain-sides: it will be a pleasure and a rest, and not a weight upon the spirits to come from the open country into a town; every man's house will be fair and decent, soothing to his mind and helpful to his work: all the works of man that we live amongst and handle will be in harmony with nature, will be reasonable and beautiful: yet all will be simple and inspiriting, not childish nor enervating; for as nothing of beauty and splendour that man's mind and hand may compass shall be wanting from our public buildings, so in no private dwelling will there be any signs of waste, pomp, or insolence, and every man will have his share of the *best*.

It is a dream, you may say, of what has never been and never will be; true, it has never been, and therefore, since the world is alive and moving yet, my hope is the greater that it one day will be: true, it is a dream; but dreams have before now come about of things so good and necessary to us, that we scarcely think of them more than of the daylight, though once people had to live without them, without even the hope of them.

Anyhow, dream as it is, I pray you to pardon my setting it before you, for it lies at the bottom of all my work in the Decorative Arts, nor will it ever be out of my thoughts: and I am here with you to-night to ask you to help me in realizing this dream, this *hope*.

### NOTES

1. Morris probably includes the phrase "manufacturers (so called)" to point out the irony of late nineteenth–century usage of the word *manufacture*. Although the word comes from the Latin roots meaning "hand" and "to make," to say that a product was manufactured usually meant—and still means—that it was made by machines rather than by hand.
2. "*Liberté, Egalité, Fraternité*" was the slogan of the French Revolution of 1789.

# 1882

## Lewis Foreman Day, "To Ladies and Amateurs"

According to historian Joellen Secondo, Lewis Foreman Day (1845–1910) was educated in France and Germany, "but his interest in design was provided by visits to the South Kensington Museum, London (now the Victoria & Albert Museum)"—the institution that was one of the fruits of the Great Exhibition of 1851. In the 1860s and 1870s, Day worked as a glass painter and designer, and, in 1880, started his own firm, for which he designed textiles, wallpapers, stained glass, embroidery, carpets, tiles, pottery, furniture, silver, jewelry, and book covers. In his numerous books and essays, Day advocated fine craftsmanship and promoted the merits of decorative designs based on natural forms. In these excerpts from his essay, "To Ladies and Amateurs," Day comments on the relative status of the decorative arts and fine arts, and explains why women were (as was commonly believed) unsuited for serious careers as designers and artists.[1]

Excerpted from Lewis Foreman Day, "To Ladies and Amateurs," in *Every-Day Art: Short Essays on the Arts Not Fine* (London: B. T. Batsford, 1882): 250–2, 254, 256, 260–262, 264–266.

[ . . . ]

The greatest art has always been of a decorative character; but let it suffice for the present to assert that decorative art is, as such, second to no other; that granted, we may admit that under the head of "decorative" are included also the lesser arts applied to industry. These arts have suffered from the slight esteem in which they have been held among us. "High art," so called, has been so far prejudicial to them that it has attracted, by its pretensions, the best of those whom nature had meant for decorators; and many a one who might perhaps in the natural direction of his own genius have risen to fame, has dissipated his talent in vain attempts to paint pictures. If high art were less high the art of every-day would be higher.

A most dangerous will-o'-the-wisp is high art to amateurs, and to lady amateurs in particular. It must be remembered that the signal success of certain lady artists is the result of a devotion to art, and a sacrifice to it, that amateurs are scarcely prepared to offer. How many even of those ladies who really love art would be willing to shut themselves out from household pleasures and from household cares, and devote some six or eight hours daily to the study of it? how many of them, even though they might be willing, would feel themselves justified in doing so? Those who clamour for women's rights are not yet in a majority; ladies are for the most part content with their privileges, none the less precious for the duties with which they are associated. Assuming that lady amateurs do not, as a class, think of materially altering their mode of life, but simply desire to occupy their leisure pleasurably, and at the same time not unprofitably, in the pursuit of art, it would be better for them, and for art too, that they should realise at the outset that, though they may easily paint such pictures as give satisfaction to their friends, it is improbable that the paintings of many of them will have any great value as art. The conditions of their life are against it. On the other hand, society is so constituted that there is every encouragement for the less ambitious arts in which they have hitherto distinguished themselves, and for some in which they have not as yet made very great progress.

The most obvious opportunity for the exercise of a woman's artistic faculty seems to lie in needlework. She may not compete favorably with professional men in the picture galleries, but in such delicate work as embroidery she has the game in her own hands. The needle was her sceptre from the first, and she has achieved with it royal results. Yet her sphere does not end there. Wherever there is question of taste, what might not woman's influence do for art? And how little it has actually accomplished!

[ . . . ]

There is here no thought of depreciating in any way the feminine capacity. More often than not a man's wife is his "better half" indeed, without suggestion of irony in the title. If man be the superior animal, it is mainly as animal that he is superior. Whether superior or inferior to him, woman is certainly different from man; her highest qualities are those in which man cannot compete with her, just as she cannot cope with him in things wherein his strength lies. With all the nattiness and delicacy which she brings to bear on decorative art, we miss largeness of treatment, breadth, originality, and self-restraint. The straight line, so needful in decoration, is hateful to her. The judicial faculty, on which (unrecognised) so much of taste depends, is not her *forte*.

[ . . . ]

The part that a lady can take in the execution of decorative work depends of course upon her artistic qualifications. There appears to be a notion prevalent that china-painting, panel-painting, and the like, are lesser arts that can be acquired in a few lessons, without previous training in art. Certainly a flat ornament is more easy to paint than a picture; but then the flat ornament has to be designed, and the art of design is not learnt in a day. There would be no difficulty in finding ladies well able to paint oak leaves; but most of them would find considerable difficulty in adapting them to decorative design. The truth, so obvious that one is half ashamed to have to reiterate it, is that only those who are prepared to work steadily and earnestly at the art they adopt, however small that art may be, are likely to produce anything in the least worth doing. The amateur needs to be advised that decoration is a much more serious matter than she imagines. [ . . . ]

One difficulty that ladies have to contend with in decoration is that what is most available, and most wanted, is bold work, large in design and treatment, whilst ladies lean rather towards refinement and finish than breadth. It is work, too, that is best done *in situ*, and a lady is not quite at home on the top of a scaffold. She has fuller opportunity for the exercise of her talent on panels, tiles, and all the smaller details of furniture, and these details can be executed conveniently and at leisure. The cabinet or sideboard is useful all the same, and is not unsightly, whilst the panels are yet unpainted; but the decoration of the walls of a room, which must be done quickly, is a tax upon the strength and endurance of the artist that few women can stand. [ . . . ] Ambition is not greatly to be encouraged in amateurs. It may safely be left to grow of itself with growing power. It is a pity that unprofessional effort is mainly directed towards the production of objects which only rare artistic excellence can make worth having. It is to be remembered that we judge more *useful* work with much greater leniency than that which has no other justification than beauty.

[ . . . ] In all respects the work of ladies would be more available in domestic decoration, if it were less lofty in its aim. The amateur burns always to do something of importance—figures probably, or at the very least flower-groups. But even if this ambition be warranted by ability, the occasion for a great deal of such prominent work seldom occurs in an ordinary living-room. There is, on the other hand, considerable scope for ornament of that more modest kind which is content to take its lowly place in the general effect.

Adaptation of the oak
to ornament.

[ . . . ]
The simple truth, as it seems to me, is that ladies seldom give sufficient
thought and study to decoration. If they have aptitude, they are too readily persuaded that they know all about it, when in reality their knowledge is rudimentary; they are too impatient, too ambitious, too little aware of the difficulties
before them, and of the limits of their ability. On the other hand, if they be
modest they are wanting in self-reliance, they do not believe enough in themselves, and they allow their feeling to be overruled by those who, knowing less,
talk more confidently. Needlework excepted, there is very little ladies' work done
that is of real value in decoration, yet there is scarcely a young housewife but
might learn to do good work, worth doing in the house, but which, failing her,
remains undone.
[ . . . ]

**N O T E S**

1. This introduction is adapted from Joellen Secondo, "Day, Lewis Foreman," *The Grove
   Dictionary of Art Online*, ed. L. Macy, <*http://www.groveart.com*>, (accessed 18 December
   2002).

# 1893

## Candace Wheeler, "Decorative and Applied Art"

Candace (Thurber) Wheeler (1827–1923), an American, was perhaps the first woman in the United States to run a successful design firm. Wheeler was committed to training women to earn their own livings by employing them in traditionally "feminine" craft enterprises, particularly needlework. To that end, Wheeler founded the Society of Decorative Art in 1877 and cofounded the New York Exchange for Woman's Work in 1878; both organizations were intended to promote the work of female craftspeople and artists. Wheeler and her female colleagues and employees designed technically and stylistically innovative textiles and embroideries for her decorating firm (Associated Artists, established 1882/1883) and for the firms that Wheeler cofounded with Louis Comfort Tiffany: Tiffany & Wheeler (established 1879) and Louis C. Tiffany & Company, Associated Artists (established 1881). Wheeler was responsible for the décor of the Woman's Building at the 1893 World's Columbian Exposition in Chicago; the following excerpts are from *Household Art*, the anthology of essays by female writers that she edited in the same year, which was available for sale in the library of the Woman's Building.[1]

Excerpted from Candace Wheeler, "Decorative and Applied Art," in *Household Art*, edited by Candace Wheeler (New York: Harper & Brothers, 1893): 198–204.

[ . . . ]

[ . . . ] **B**eauty of color and grace of line are qualities which are individual gifts, and serve to make the work of one artist more precious and attractive than that of another; but even these gifts must conform to laws, if we are to secure that conjunction which completes and perfects the most comprehensive beauty achieved by man—the beauty which becomes a permanent heritage of pleasurable sensation to the human race, and an absolute influence in its progress towards higher living.

This influence may seem a great deal to claim for art, but since the moral training of humanity is by means of its pleasures and its pains, no better teacher can be found than that which confers happiness by the gratification of the inherent and natural love of art; and hardly a greater good can be worked for mankind than the creation of universal and surrounding beauty. Decorative and applied art are of the utmost importance to mankind, since the one contributes to those monuments which excite the loftiest and most supreme satisfaction, and the other surrounds, or may surround, the individual with endless sources of pleasure and content. Applied art is to decorative art what the child is to the man. It is in short a consequence of the greater work, but it holds within itself the same obligation to the same laws. It is the application of knowledge and love of art to the implements and manufactures of the mechanic and manufacturer. It applies to things we may wear or use or handle, the small conveniences which are a part of our daily lives. It moulds the shape of the rude and common implement into grace, and invests it with interest and beauty. It puts art and *thought* into the things which surround us. It elevates our habits, and invests our customs with dignity, and is our unconscious teacher in beauty, grace, and truth. It fuses thought, sentiment, and feeling into the insensate matter of which these surroundings are composed, and performs the miracle of exciting in us an answering thought. It makes these things speak to us with a human voice, and express human thought as truly as a book may convey the thought of another mind to us; and in proportion as the thought is true, and the expression beautiful, are we benefitted [*sic*] or deteriorated by its proximity.

It is this domestic influence, if we may call it so, of applied art which makes its practice of true principles of importance to us. It is almost more necessary to the growth and culture of the every-day world that every-day art, the finish, proportion, and excellence of the things among which we live, and by which we live, should be perfect, and perfectly true to principles, than that we should have more or less frequent opportunities of studying the highest examples of human achievement. It is always a long step between us and them, even in comprehension; but the other lives with us, and is a part of our lives; it enters into our unconscious thoughts, and makes our judgment just and our knowledge enlightened. Applied art could do none of these things unless, in its best and purest practice, it followed the laws which govern decorative art, even to its utmost derivative. It must always and forever be mindful of its dependence and its meaning. It may be as beautiful as nature, and as harmonious as the truest chord upon the most perfect instrument, but its kind of beauty must be based upon the use of the thing to which it is applied, and its harmony be in accord with the purpose or necessity to which it is added. [ . . . ]

In the broad field of art applied to textiles and wall coverings there is room for profound study of the rules and philosophy of applied art, and the necessity of such study is apparent in the interior of almost every house, and in the materials shown in every shop window. It is a great mistake to suppose that in small things the rules of art, the philosophy of art, may be neglected. Small things cease to be unimportant if largely treated. The same kind of value may attach to a yard of muslin covered with beautiful and appropriate design, and treated with exhaustive knowledge and appreciation of color, as would belong to a picture by the same artist. It is a very common error to suppose that incomplete and inferior knowledge will suffice for the designer. Good design requires not only perfect observance of the fundamental law of appropriateness, but personal gifts of grace and composition, and an education which is not only technical, but special and literary. The designer should know the art of all nations and ages in design, not for imitation, but for cultivation. His compositions may and should be entirely uninfluenced by them in feeling, but he will have learned from them what is true or false in art, and to judge wisely of his own work. It is not to be supposed that the manufacturer should know what is absolutely best among the designs which he reproduces. He knows clearly the qualities which will appeal to the public, and except when a design is backed by a name which has influence with the buying public, and has gained its confidence, he will rarely accept a design which does not appeal to the popular taste by its color and sentiment. The enjoyment of fresh and positive coloring seems to be universal. There is also a universal liking for exact reproductions of familiar flowers, and as these two likings are inherent and spontaneous, the thoughtful designer will do well to add to his list of necessary requirements for a design, fresh and good color, and absolute truth in following natural forms. This is where Japanese design has obtained, and well deserves to obtain, world-wide popularity. Every flower or leaf or plant which appears in Japanese design is absolutely an individual specimen, true to its individualism as well as its species, and while there is little composition in the sense of large and regularly recurring groups or masses in Japanese design, the absolute truth and grace of drawing, and the unerring taste in *placing* ornament, has given Japanese art a foremost place in influence and favor in the world.

This truth to nature in representation does not by any means detract from composition in design, for there is abundant subject for composition in nature as well as for individual ornament. The important thing is to gather into design or into applied art all truth, all beauty, and all that will influence or elevate humanity; to be forever mindful of the dignity and value of art as a means of education and of happiness; and to be content with nothing less than the best, either as artist or possessor.

**NOTES**

1. Recent research has called into question many historians' long-standing beliefs about the dates and nature of Candace Wheeler's involvement with Tiffany & Company. This introduction is based on information presented in Amelia Peck and Carol Irish's book, *Candace Wheeler: The Art and Enterprise of American Design, 1875–1900* (New York: The Metropolitan Museum of Art and Yale University Press, 2001).

# 1897

## Henry van de Velde, "A Chapter on the Design and Construction of Modern Furniture"

Henry van de Velde (1863–1957), a Belgian painter, architect, and designer, is generally considered one of the originators of the Art Nouveau style, and was one of Europe's most prominent designers and theoreticians in the 1890s–1910s. Van de Velde promoted the ideas of William Morris, and used products from Morris & Co. as exemplars in his lectures at the University of Brussels in the 1890s.[1] In 1904, the Grand Duke of Saxe-Weimar appointed van de Velde head of the new Kunstgewerbeschule (arts and crafts school) in Weimar. Van de Velde remained in Germany until 1917, during which time he became a vocal member of the Deutscher Werkbund. In this 1897 essay, van de Velde expresses his wish to design for mass production, and to create products whose forms are "rational," "honest," "modern," and well suited to machine manufacture.

Reprinted from Henry van de Velde, "A Chapter on the Design and Construction of Modern Furniture," Pan (Berlin), vol. III (1897): 260–64, translated by Tim and Charlotte Benton, reprinted in *Form and Function: A Source Book for the History of Architecture and Design, 1890–1939,* edited by Tim and Charlotte Benton (London: Crosby Lockwood Staples in association with the Open University Press, 1975): 17–19. Reprinted by permission of Tim and Charlotte Benton.

**T**he nature of my entire industrial and ornamental production springs from the single source of reason, rationality in essence and appearance, and this is no doubt what accounts for my oddness and the peculiar position I occupy. Certainly I could scarcely have found a better means of being different, though evidently my aims go farther than that. We must endeavour to work out the foundations on which to build a new style and in my opinion the origin clearly lies in never creating anything which has no valid reason for existing, even with the almighty sanction of industry and the manifold consequences of its powerful machines.

But I could be prouder of the certainly far more individual principle of systematically avoiding designing anything that cannot be *mass-produced*. My ideal would be to have my projects executed a thousand times, though obviously not without strict supervision, because I know from experience how soon a model can deteriorate through dishonest or misguided handling until its effect is as worthless as the one it was destined to counteract. I can thus only hope to make my influence felt when more widespread industrial activity will allow me to live up to the maxim which has guided my social beliefs, namely that a man's worth can be measured by the number of people who have derived use and benefit from his life's work.

We can succeed in modernising the appearances of things by carrying out the simple intention to be strictly rational, by following the principle of rejecting without exception all forms and ornamentation which a modern factory could not easily manufacture and reproduce, by plainly stating the essential structure of every piece of furniture and object and by constantly bearing in mind that they must be easy to use. Is there anything which has been the object of keener striving for new forms than a hall-stand, a folding-table, or an armchair? And yet these articles simply show that new results can be obtained by using means and materials which are as old as the hills. And I must confess that my own means are the same as those which were used in the very early stages of popular arts and crafts. It is only because I understand and marvel at how simply, coherently and beautifully a ship, weapon, car, or wheelbarrow is built that my work is able to please the few remaining rationalists who realise that what has seemed odd to others has in fact been produced by following unassailable traditional principles, in other words unconditionally and resolutely following the functional logic of an article and being unreservedly honest about the materials employed, which naturally vary with the means of each.

## NOTES

1. Jane Block and Paul Kruty, "Van de Velde, Henry," *The Grove Dictionary of Art Online*, ed. L. Macy, <*http://www.groveart.com*>, (accessed 18 December 2002).

# 1899

## Thorstein Veblen, "Pecuniary Canons of Taste"

Although the American economist and social critic Thorstein Veblen (1857–1929) is perhaps best known today for his theory of "conspicuous consumption," in his influential 1899 book, *The Theory of the Leisure Class*, he also sought to explain, among other things, why so many people believed handcrafted objects to be more beautiful than mass-produced ones. Veblen's subject of inquiry was particularly relevant in an era in which many Arts and Crafts designers and theorists—following the lead of William Morris and John Ruskin, whom Veblen mentions by name—were attempting to promote handcraft as a viable, or at least socially preferable, alternative to machinofacture. In these selections from the chapter titled "Pecuniary Canons of Taste," Veblen argues that aesthetics are inextricably linked to monetary value. In contrast to most design theorists of the period, who argued that beauty was related to functionality, Veblen claimed that the more "wasteful and ill adapted to their ostensible use" most objects were, the more likely consumers were—perversely—to prefer them.

Excerpted from Thorstein Veblen, *The Theory of the Leisure Class: An Economic Study of Institutions* (1899; reprint, New York: Macmillan & Co., 1905): pp. 126–129, 130–131, 159–162.

[ . . . ]

[ . . . ] **The requirements of pecuniary decency have, to a very appreciable** extent, influenced the sense of beauty and of utility in articles of use or beauty. Articles are to an extent preferred for use on account of their being conspicuously wasteful; they are felt to be serviceable somewhat in proportion as they are wasteful and ill adapted to their ostensible use.

The utility of articles valued for their beauty depends closely upon the expensiveness of the articles. A homely illustration will bring out this dependence. A hand-wrought silver spoon, of a commercial value of some ten to twenty dollars, is not ordinarily more serviceable—in the first sense of the word—than a machine-made spoon of the same material. It may not even be more serviceable than a machine-made spoon of some "base" metal, such as aluminum, the value of which may be no more than some ten to twenty cents. The former of the two utensils is, in fact, commonly a less effective contrivance for its ostensible purpose than the latter. The objection is of course ready to hand that, in taking this view of the matter, one of the chief uses, if not the chief use, of the costlier spoon is ignored; the hand-wrought spoon gratifies our taste, our sense of the beautiful, while that made by machinery out of the base metal has no useful office beyond a brute efficiency. The facts are no doubt as the objection states them, but it will be evident on reflection that the objection is after all more plausible than conclusive. It appears (1) that while the different materials of which the two spoons are made each possesses beauty and serviceability for the purpose for which it is used, the material of the hand-wrought spoon is some one hundred times more valuable than the baser metal, without very greatly excelling the latter in intrinsic beauty of grain or colour, and without being in any appreciable degree superior in point of mechanical serviceability; (2) if a close inspection should show that the supposed hand-wrought spoon were in reality only a very clever imitation of hand-wrought goods, but an imitation so cleverly wrought as to give the same impression of line and surface to any but a minute examination by a trained eye, the utility of the article, including the gratification which the user derives from its contemplation as an object of beauty, would immediately decline by some eighty or ninety per cent, or even more; (3) if the two spoons are, to a fairly close observer, so nearly identical in appearance that the lighter weight of the spurious article alone betrays it, this identity of form and colour will scarcely add to the value of the machine-made spoon, nor appreciably enhance the gratification of the user's "sense of beauty" in contemplating it, so long as the cheaper spoon is not a novelty, and so long as it can be procured at a nominal cost.

The case of the spoons is typical. The superior gratification derived from the use and contemplation of costly and supposedly beautiful products is, commonly, in great measure a gratification of our sense of costliness masquerading under the name of beauty. Our higher appreciation of the superior article is an appreciation of its superior honorific character, much more frequently than it is an unsophisticated appreciation of its beauty. The requirement of conspicuous wastefulness is not commonly present, consciously, in our canons of taste, but it is none the less present as a constraining norm selectively shaping and sustaining our sense of what is beautiful, and guiding our discrimination with respect to what may legitimately be approved as beautiful and what may not.

[ . . . ]

The generalisation for which the discussion so far affords ground is that any valuable object in order to appeal to our sense of beauty must conform to the requirements of beauty and of expensiveness both. But this is not all. Beyond this the canon of expensiveness also affects our tastes in such a way as to inextricably blend the marks of expensiveness, in our appreciation, with the beautiful features of the object, and to subsume the resultant effect under the head of an appreciation of beauty simply. The marks of expensiveness come to be accepted as beautiful features of the expensive articles. They are pleasing as being marks of honorific costliness, and the pleasure which they afford on this score blends with that afforded by the beautiful form and colour of the object; so that we often declare that an article of apparel, for instance, is "perfectly lovely," when pretty much all that an analysis of the aesthetic value of the article would leave ground for is the declaration that it is pecuniarily honorific.

[ . . . ]

[ . . . ] The point of material difference between machine-made goods and the hand-wrought goods which serve the same purposes is, ordinarily, that the former serve their primary purpose more adequately. They are a more perfect product—show a more perfect adaptation of means to end. This does not save them from disesteem and depreciation, for they fall short under the test of honorific waste. Hand labour is a more wasteful method of production; hence the goods turned out by this method are more serviceable for the purpose of pecuniary reputability; hence the marks of hand labour come to be honorific, and the goods which exhibit these marks take rank as of higher grade than the corresponding machine product. Commonly, if not invariably, the honorific marks of hand labour are certain imperfections and irregularities in the lines of the hand-wrought article, showing where the workman has fallen short in the execution of the design. The ground of the superiority of hand-wrought goods, therefore, is a certain margin of crudeness. This margin must never be so wide as to show bungling workmanship, since that would be evidence of low cost, nor so narrow as to suggest the ideal precision attained only by the machine, for that would be evidence of low cost.

[ . . . ]

As has already been pointed out, the cheap, and therefore indecorous, articles of daily consumption in modern industrial communities are commonly machine products; and the generic feature of the physiognomy of machine-made goods as compared with the hand-wrought article is their greater perfection in workmanship and greater accuracy in the detail execution of the design. Hence it comes about that the visible imperfections of the hand-wrought goods, being honorific, are accounted marks of superiority in point of beauty, or serviceability, or both. Hence has arisen that exaltation of the defective, of which John Ruskin and William Morris were such eager spokesmen in their time; and on this ground their propaganda of crudity and wasted effort has been taken up and carried forward since their time. And hence also the propaganda for a return to the handicraft and household industry. So much of the work and speculations of this group of men as fairly comes under the characterisation here given would have been impossible at a time when the visibly more perfect goods were not the cheaper.

[ . . . ]

# 1901-1925

# 1901

## Frank Lloyd Wright, "The Art and Craft of the Machine"

Frank Lloyd Wright (1867–1959), one of the United States' foremost architects, was a theorist as well as a creator of buildings and furnishings. Like most designers and architects of his generation, he had been reared on the writings of John Ruskin and William Morris, and his early architectural and theoretical works, including his renowned "Prairie School" houses of the early 1900s, were clearly shaped in large part by the two Englishmen's ideals. However, in this well-known essay, Wright declared—in clear opposition to Morris's and Ruskin's sentiments—that the Machine (a word he deliberately capitalized) was an integral part of modern society that had the potential to do great good, both socially and artistically.

Excerpted from Frank Lloyd Wright, "The Art and Craft of the Machine," an address delivered to the Chicago Arts and Crafts Society, at Hull-House, March 6, 1901, and to the Western Society of Engineers, March 20, 1901, and reprinted in the *Catalogue of the Fourteenth Annual Exhibition of the Chicago Architectural Club* (Chicago: Chicago Architectural Club, 1901).

**A**s we work along our various ways, there takes shape within us, in some sort, an ideal—something we are to become—some work to be done. This, I think, is denied to very few, and we begin really to live only when the thrill of this ideality moves us in what we will to accomplish. In the years which have been devoted in my own life to working out in stubborn materials a feeling for the beautiful, in the vortex of distorted complex conditions, a hope has grown stronger with the experience of each year, amounting now to a gradually deepening conviction that in the Machine lies the only future of art and craft—as I believe, a glorious future; that the Machine is, in fact, the metamorphosis of ancient art and craft; that we are at last face to face with the machine—the modern Sphinx—whose riddle the artist must solve if he would that art live—for his nature holds the key. For one, I promise "whatever gods may be" to lend such energy and purpose as I may possess to help make that meaning plain; to return again and again to the task whenever and wherever need be; for this plain duty is thus relentlessly marked out for the artist in this, the Machine Age, although there is involved an adjustment to cherished gods, perplexing and painful in the extreme; the fire of many long-honored ideals shall go down to ashes to reappear, phœnix like, with new purposes.

The great ethics of the Machine are as yet, in the main, beyond the ken of the artist or student of sociology; but the artist mind may now approach the nature of this thing from experience, which has become the commonplace of his field, to suggest, in time, I hope, to prove, that the machine is capable of carrying to fruition high ideals in art—higher than the world has yet seen!

Disciples of William Morris cling to an opposite view. Yet William Morris himself deeply sensed the danger to art of the transforming force whose sign and symbol is the machine, and though of the new art we eagerly seek he sometimes despaired, he quickly renewed his hope.

He plainly foresaw that a blank in the fine arts would follow the inevitable abuse of new-found power, and threw himself body and soul into the work of bridging it over by bringing into our lives afresh the beauty of art as she had been, that the new art to come might not have dropped too many stitches nor have unraveled what would still be useful to her.

That he had abundant faith in the new art his every essay will testify.

That he miscalculated the machine does not matter. He did sublime work for it when he pleaded so well for the process of elimination its abuse had made necessary; when he fought the innate vulgarity of theocratic impulse in art as opposed to democratic; and when he preached the gospel of simplicity.

All artists love and honor William Morris.

He did the best in his time for art and will live in history as the great socialist, together with Ruskin, the great moralist: a significant fact worth thinking about, that the two great reformers of modern times professed the artist.

The machine these reformers protested, because the sort of luxury which is born of greed had usurped it and made of it a terrible engine of enslavement, deluging the civilized world with a murderous ubiquity, which plainly enough was the damnation of their art and craft.

It had not then advanced to the point which now so plainly indicates that it will surely and swiftly, by its own momentum, undo the mischief it has made, and the usurping vulgarians as well.

Nor was it so grown as to become apparent to William Morris, the grand democrat, that the machine was the great forerunner of democracy.

The ground plan of this thing is now grown to the point where the artist must take it up no longer as a protest: genius must progressively dominate the work of the contrivance it has created; to lend a useful hand in building afresh the "Fairness of the Earth."

That the Machine has dealt Art in the grand old sense a death-blow, none will deny.

The evidence is too substantial.

Art in the grand old sense—meaning Art in the sense of structural tradition, whose craft is fashioned upon the handicraft ideal, ancient or modern; an art wherein this form and that form as structural parts were laboriously joined in such a way as to beautifully emphasize the manner of the joining: the million and one ways of beautifully satisfying bare structural necessities, which have come down to us chiefly through the books as "Art."

For the purpose of suggesting hastily and therefore crudely wherein the machine has sapped the vitality of this art, let us assume Architecture in the old sense as a fitting representative of Traditional-art, and Printing as a fitting representation of the Machine.

What printing—the machine—has done for architecture—the fine art—will have been done in measure of time for all art immediately fashioned upon the early handicraft ideal.

[ . . . ]

And, invincible, triumphant, the machine goes on, gathering force and knitting the material necessities of mankind ever closer into a universal automatic fabric; the engine, the motor, and the battle-ship, the works of art of the century!

The Machine is Intellect mastering the drudgery of earth that the plastic art may live; that the margin of leisure and strength by which man's life upon the earth can be made beautiful, may immeasurably widen; its function ultimately to emancipate human expression!

It is a universal educator, surely raising the level of human intelligence, so carrying within itself the power to destroy, by its own momentum, the greed which in Morris' time and still in our own time turns it to a deadly engine of enslavement. The only comfort left the poor artist, side-tracked as he is, seemingly is a mean one; the thought that the very selfishness which man's early art idealized, now reduced to its lowest terms, is swiftly and surely destroying itself through the medium of the Machine.

The artist's present plight is a sad one, but may he truthfully say that society is less well off because Architecture, or even Art, as it was, is dead, and printing, or the Machine, lives?

Every age has done its work, produced its art with the best tools or contrivances it knew, the tools most successful in saving the most precious thing in the world—human effort. Greece used the chattel slave as the essential tool of its art and civilization. This tool we have discarded, and we would refuse the return of Greek art upon the terms of its restoration, because we insist now upon a basis of Democracy.

Is it not more likely that the medium of artistic expression itself has broadened and changed until a new definition and new direction must be given the art activity of the future, and that the Machine has finally made for the artist, whether he will yet own it or not, a splendid distinction between the Art of old and the Art to come? A distinction made by the tool which frees human labor, lengthens and broadens the life of the simplest man, thereby the basis of the Democracy upon which we insist.

[ . . . ]

The Art of old idealized a Structural Necessity—now rendered obsolete and unnatural by the Machine—and accomplished it through man's joy in the labor of his hands.

The new will weave for the necessities of mankind, which his Machine will have mastered, a robe of ideality no less truthful, but more poetical, with a rational freedom made possible by the machine, beside which the art of old will be as the sweet, plaintive wail of the pipe to the outpouring of full orchestra.

It will clothe Necessity with the living flesh of virile imagination, as the living flesh lends living grace to the hard and bony human skeleton.

The new will pass from the possession of kings and classes to the every-day lives of all—from duration in point of time to immortality.

This distinction is one to be felt now rather than clearly defined.

The definition is the poetry of this Machine Age, and will be written large in time; but the more we, as artists, examine into this premonition, the more we will find the utter helplessness of old forms to satisfy new conditions, and the crying need of the machine for plastic treatment—a pliant, sympathetic treatment of its needs that the body of structural precedent cannot yield.

To gain further suggestive evidence of this, let us turn to the Decorative Arts—the immense middle-ground of all art now mortally sickened by the Machine—sickened that it may slough the art ideal of the constructural art for the plasticity of the new art—the Art of Democracy.

Here we find the most deadly perversion of all—the magnificent prowess of the machine bombarding the civilized world with the mangled corpses of strenuous horrors that once stood for cultivated luxury—standing now for a species of fatty degeneration simply vulgar.

Without regard to first principles or common decency, the whole letter of tradition—that is, ways of doing things rendered wholly obsolete and unnatural by the machine—is recklessly fed into its rapacious maw until you may buy reproductions for ninety-nine cents at "The Fair"[1] that originally cost ages of toil and cultivation, worth now intrinsically nothing—that are harmful parasites befogging the sensibilities of our natures, belittling and falsifying any true perception of normal beauty the Creator may have seen fit to implant in us.

The idea of fitness to purpose, harmony between form and use with regard to any of these things, is possessed by very few, and utilized by them as a protest chiefly—a protest against the machine!

As well blame Richard Croker[2] for the political iniquity of America.

As "Croker is the creature and not the creator" of political evil, so the machine is the creature and not the creator of this iniquity; and with this difference—that the machine has noble possibilities unwillingly forced to degrada-

tion in the name of the artistic; the machine, as far as its artistic capacity is concerned, is itself the crazed victim of the artist who works while he waits, and the
artist who waits while he works.

There is a nice distinction between the two.

Neither class will unlock the secrets of the beauty of this time.

They are clinging sadly to the old order, and would wheedle the giant frame
of things back to its childhood or forward to its second childhood, while this
Machine Age is suffering for the artist who accepts, works, and sings as he
works, with the joy of the *here* and *now*!

We want the man who eagerly seeks and finds, or blames himself if he fails
to find, the beauty of this time; who distinctly accepts as a singer and a prophet;
for no man may work while he waits or wait as he works in the sense that
William Morris' great work was legitimately done—in the sense that most art
and craft of to-day is an echo; the time when such work was useful has gone.

Echoes are by nature decadent.

Artists who feel toward Modernity and the Machine now as William Morris
and Ruskin were justified in feeling then, had best distinctly wait and work
sociologically where great work may still be done by them. In the field of art
activity they will do distinct harm. Already they have wrought much miserable
mischief.

If the artist will only open his eyes he will see that the machine he dreads
has made it possible to wipe out the mass of meaningless torture to which
mankind, in the name of the artistic, has been more or less subjected since time
began; for that matter, has made possible a cleanly strength, an ideality and a
poetic fire that the art of the world has not yet seen; for the machine, the process
now smooth[e]s away the necessity for petty structural deceits, soothes this
wearisome struggle to make things seem what they are not, and can never be;
satisfies the simple term of the modern art equation as the ball of clay in the
sculptor's hand yields to his desire—comforting forever this realistic, brain-sick
masquerade we are wont to suppose art.

William Morris pleaded well for simplicity as the basis of all true art. Let
us understand the significance to art of that word—SIMPLICITY—for it is vital
to the Art of the Machine.

We may find, in place of the genuine thing we have striven for, an affecta-
tion of the naïve, which we should detest as we detest a full-grown woman with
baby mannerisms.

English art is saturated with it, from the brand-new imitation of the old
house that grew and rambled from period to period to the rain-tub standing
beneath the eaves.

In fact, most simplicity following the doctrines of William Morris is a
protest; as a protest, well enough; but the highest form of simplicity is not simple in the sense that the infant intelligence is simple—nor, for that matter, the
side of a barn.

A natural revulsion of feeling leads us from the meaningless elaboration of to-day to lay too great stress on mere platitudes, quite as a clean sheet of paper is a relief after looking at a series of bad drawings—but simplicity is not merely a neutral or a negative quality.

Simplicity in art, rightly understood, is a synthetic, positive quality, in which we may see evidence of mind, breadth of scheme, wealth of detail, and withal a sense of completeness found in a tree or a flower. A work may have the delicacies of a rare orchid or the stanch fortitude of the oak, and still be simple. A thing to be simple needs only to be true to itself in organic sense.

With this ideal of simplicity, let us glance hastily at a few instances of the machine and see how it has been forced by false ideals to do violence to this simplicity; how it has made possible the highest simplicity, rightly understood and so used. As perhaps wood is most available of all homely materials and therefore, naturally, the most abused—let us glance at wood.

Machinery has been invented for no other purpose than to imitate, as closely as possible, the wood-carving of the early ideal—with the immediate result that no ninety-nine cent piece of furniture is salable without some horrible botchwork meaning nothing unless it means that art and craft have combined to fix in the mind of the masses the old hand-carved chair as the *ne plus ultra*[3] of the ideal.

The miserable, lumpy tribute to this perversion which Grand Rapids[4] alone yields would mar the face of Art beyond repair; to say nothing of the elaborate and fussy joinery of posts, spindles, jig sawed beams and braces, butted and strutted, to outdo the sentimentality of the already over-wrought antique product.

Thus is the wood-working industry glutted, except in rarest instances. The whole sentiment of early craft degenerated to a sentimentality having no longer decent significance nor commercial integrity; in fact all that is fussy, maudlin, and animal, basing its existence chiefly on vanity and ignorance.

Now let us learn from the Machine.

It teaches us that the beauty of wood lies first in its qualities as wood; no treatment that did not bring out these qualities all the time could be plastic, and therefore not appropriate—so not beautiful, the machine teaches us, if we have left it to the machine that certain simple forms and handling are suitable to bring out the beauty of wood and certain forms are not; that all wood-carving is apt to be a forcing of the material, an insult to its finer possibilities as a material having in itself intrinsically artistic properties, of which its beautiful markings is one, its texture another, its color a third.

The machine, by its wonderful cutting, shaping, smoothing, and repetitive capacity, has made it possible to so use it without waste that the poor as well as the rich may enjoy to-day beautiful surface treatments of clean, strong forms that the branch veneers of Sheraton and Chippendale only hinted at, with dire extravagance, and which the middle ages utterly ignored.

The machine has emancipated these beauties of nature in wood; made it possible to wipe out the mass of meaningless torture to which wood has been subjected since the world began, for it has been universally abused and mal-treated by all peoples but the Japanese.

Rightly appreciated, is not this the very process of elimination for which Morris pleaded?

Not alone a protest, moreover, for the machine, considered only technically, if you please, has placed in artist hands the means of idealizing the true nature of wood harmoniously with man's spiritual and material needs, without waste, within reach of all.

[ . . . ]

**N O T E S**

1. The 1893 World's Columbian Exposition in Chicago; Wright detested its uniform, classiciz-ing architecture, feeling it was an inappropriate form of expression for the modern United States.

2. Richard Croker (1841–1922) was an Irish-born New York City politician who was a mem-ber of the corrupt "Tammany Hall" city government, and who became rich from the bribes and "protection" money he collected while in office.

3. Culmination or utmost limit.

4. Grand Rapids, Michigan, was the center of the U.S. furniture industry in the late nineteenth and early twentieth centuries.

# 1905

# Josef Hoffmann and Koloman Moser, "The Work-Program of the Wiener Werkstätte"

The Austrian architect-designers Josef Hoffmann (1870–1956) and Koloman Moser (1868–1918), both members of the Vienna Secession movement of the 1890s, cofounded the Wiener Werkstätte (Viennese Workshop; 1903–1932) with the industrialist and collector Fritz Wärndorfer, who provided financial backing for the endeavor.[1] Modeled on C. R. Ashbee's Guild of Handicraft (see next selection), the Wiener Werkstätte was an enterprise dedicated to realizing the ideas of John Ruskin and William Morris by producing exquisitely hand-crafted furnishings, decorative objects, textiles, jewelry, and bookbindings.[2]

Despite constant financial pressures, the members of the Wiener Werkstätte remained committed to the handcraft ideal long after the heyday of the Arts and Crafts movement.

Reprinted from Josef Hoffmann and Koloman Moser, *Katalog mit Arbeitsprogramm der Wiener Werkstätte* (Vienna, 1905), translated by Tim and Charlotte Benton, reprinted in *Form and Function: A Source Book for the History of Architecture and Design, 1890–1939*, edited by Tim and Charlotte Benton and Dennis Sharp (London: Crosby Lockwood Staples in association with the Open University Press, 1975): 36–37. Reprinted by permission of Tim and Charlotte Benton.

The boundless evil, caused by shoddy mass-produced goods and by the uncritical imitation of earlier styles, is like a tidal wave sweeping across the world. We have been cut adrift from the culture of our forefathers and are cast hither and thither by a thousand desires and considerations. The machine has largely replaced the hand and the business-man has supplanted the craftsman. To attempt to stem this torrent would seem like madness.

Yet for all that we have founded our workshop. Our aim is to create an island of tranquillity in our own country, which, amid the joyful hum of arts and crafts, would be welcome to anyone who professes faith in Ruskin and Morris. We are calling for all those who regard culture in this sense as valuable and we hope that the errors we are bound to commit will not dissuade our friends from lending their support.

We wish to create an inner relationship linking public, designer, and worker and we want to produce good and simple articles of everyday use. Our guiding principle is function, utility our first condition, and our strength must lie in good proportions and the proper treatment of material. We shall seek to decorate when it seems required but we do not feel obliged to adorn at any price. We shall use many semi-precious stones, especially in our jewellery, because in our eyes their manifold colours and ever-varying facets replace the sparkle of diamonds. We love silver and gold for their sheen and regard the lustre of copper as just as valid artistically. We feel that a silver brooch can have as much intrinsic worth as a jewel made of gold and precious stones. The merit of craftsmanship and artistic conception must be recognised once more and be valued accordingly. Handicrafts must be measured by the same standards as the work of a painter or sculptor.

We cannot and will not compete with cheap work, which has succeeded largely at the expense of the worker. We have made it our foremost duty to help the worker recover pleasure in his task and obtain humane conditions in which to carry it out, but this can only be achieved step by step.

In our leather-work and book-binding, just as in our other productions, we shall aim at providing good materials and technical finish. Decoration will obviously only be added when it does not conflict with the nature of the material and we shall make frequent and varied use of the different techniques of leather-inlay, embossing, hand gilding, plaiting and steeping.

The art of good binding has completely died out. Hollow backs, wire sewing, carelessly-cut, loosely-bound leaves and poor quality have become ineradicable. The manufactured so-called first edition, with its brightly printed jacket, is all that we have. The machines work away busily and swamp our bookshelves with faulty printed works and hold the record for cheapness. And yet any cultivated person ought to be ashamed of this material plenty, because he knows that on the one hand easy production means fewer responsibilities and on the other excess can only lead to superficiality. And how many of these books can we really call our own? Ought we not to possess them in their finest apparel, printed on the best paper and bound in the most beautiful leather? Have we so soon forgotten that the love with which a book is printed, put together and bound totally alters our relationship with it, that lasting acquaintance with beauty can only improve us? A book should be a work of art through and through and its merit be judged in those terms.

Our carpenters' workshops have always insisted upon the exactest and most reliable craftsmanship. But nowadays people have unfortunately grown so used to catch-penny trash that a piece of furniture executed even with a minimum of care seems quite out of reach. But it must be pointed out once and for all that we should have to assemble a pretty big house, not to mention everything inside it, if we were to equal the cost of building a railway sleeping-compartment, for example. This shows just how impossible it is to work out a sound basis for comparison. Only a hundred years ago, people were already paying hundreds of thousands for a period cabinet in a mansion, whereas today, when the most unexpected effects might be achieved if only the necessary commissions were forthcoming, they are inclined to reproach modern work with lacklustre inelegance. Reproductions of earlier styles can satisfy only the parvenu. The ordinary citizen of today, like the worker, must be proud and fully aware of his own worth and not seek to compete with other social stations which have accomplished their cultural task and are justified in looking back on an artistically splendid heritage. Our citizens have still far from carried out their artistic duties. Now it is their turn to do full justice to the new developments. Just striving to own pictures, however magnificent, cannot possibly suffice. As long as our towns, houses, rooms, cupboards, utensils, clothes, jewellery, language and feelings fail to express the spirit of the times in a clear, simple and artistic manner, we shall remain indefinitely far behind our ancestors and no pretence will conceal our lack. We should also like to draw attention to the fact that we too are aware that, under certain circumstances, an acceptable article can be made by mechanical means, provided that it bears the stamp of manufacture[3], but it is not our purpose to pursue that aspect yet. We want to do what the Japanese have always done, and no one could imagine machine-made arts and crafts in Japan. We shall try to accomplish what lies within our power, but our progress will depend on the encouragement of all our friends. We are not free to follow fancy. We stand with both feet in reality and await the commissions.

**NOTES**

1. Eduard F. Sekler, "Hoffmann, Josef," *The Grove Dictionary of Art Online,* ed. L. Macy, <*http://www.groveart.com*>, (accessed 18 December 2002).
2. Cynthia Prossinger, "Wiener Werkstätte," *The Grove Dictionary of Art Online,* ed. L. Macy, <*http://www.groveart.com*>, (accessed 22 December 2002).
3. Literally, "hand production" (as opposed to machinofacture).

# 1908

# C. R. Ashbee, *Craftsmanship in Competitive Industry*

The Englishman Charles Robert Ashbee (1863–1942) is best known today as the founder of the Guild of Handicraft, an idealistic Arts and Crafts business/community that he headed from 1888 until its 1907 closure due to insolvency. A jack-of-all-trades who trained as an architect but whose artistic fame rests largely on his metalwork, Ashbee, like so many of his contemporaries, was inspired by the writings and example of William Morris. *Craftsmanship in Competitive Industry* is Ashbee's narrative of the Guild of Handicraft's goals, successes, and failures.

Excerpted from C. R. Ashbee, *Craftsmanship In Competitive Industry: Being a Record of the Workshops of the Guild of Handicraft, and Some Deductions from their Twenty-One Years' Experience* (Campden [Gloucester] and London: Essex House Press, 1908): 5–7, 9–11, 15–18, 20.

The Arts and Crafts movement began with the object of making useful
things, of making them well and of making them beautiful; goodness
and beauty were to the leaders of the movement synonymous terms.

The attempt to carry through these principles has brought those who have
worked consistently at the details of their crafts face to face with a series of problems they never anticipated at the outset, and has made them, in the course of
the last 25 years, shape for themselves a view of life which differs from that generally held. This view may take now a political, now a social, now an æsthetic
form; it may or may not be directly practicable, but it claims to be based upon
experience, and to have a definite objective in modern English life and thought.

As far as an artist may have politics at all, I figure the outlook in England
to myself in the following formula. Our political theories are determined ultimately by the great economic factor of Industrial machinery. It is this that has
given us our great cities, our colonial expansion, the fact of our Imperialism, the
theory of our Free Trade. Industrial machinery is now finding its limitation, and
therefore a new political era is beginning. The signs of this are in the three
protests against the old order, which have cut completely across the old lines of
thought. The first protest is Socialism which says "Look what a fearful mess the
uncontrolled use of Industrial machinery has made of our civilization, we must
start sweeping things up from below, and get rid of the curse of cheap labour."
The second protest is Tariff Reform, which says "The Free Trade theory that
sacrifices everything to provide cheap food for our industrial centres, is out of
date, we must have a new fiscal system, so devised as to give expression to that
racial consciousness which our Colonial expansion has brought about. The standard of the English speaking people must be one standard." The third protest
against the Industrial system is the protest of the Arts and Crafts, the protest of
the individual, who says "What is all this worth after all, and where is it leading us? Neither your Socialism on the one hand, nor your expression of racial
consciousness on the other, is of any use unless you determine what is right and
what is wrong in your industrial production, unless you say what ought and
what ought not to be made. Let Socialism sweep up by all means, and let Fiscal
Reform tie the English people together and make their standard one, but we,
and Arts and Crafts, are here to determine what Standard is, to show it you in
product and producer alike; we are here to bring you back again to the realities
of life, to the use of the hand and the brain, of which your Industrial machinery has deprived over half your population."

Thus it comes that those men whose names are connected inseparably with
the Arts and Crafts, perhaps form part of that movement which is discrediting
conservative and liberal alike, which is giving to the English cities a consciousness, and making for the reform of Parliament; the movement by which a new
ideal is shaping in national education, an ideal higher than the petty sectarian-

ism of the last generation—the generation of the churches—and by which technical schools are springing up all over the country, and efforts are being made to get once more at the secret of the hand. [ . . . ] It is an idealistic movement, this of which they are part, and it is their function, the function of the Arts and Crafts, to express it, to be its plastic voice.

Through their workshops then, and the work of their hands, have they been brought step by step into touch with the great problems of English life, and arguing from their experience they do not accept the views usually taken by politicians and economists as to their solution. Thus it is usually held as an axiom that production on a large scale—through the factory system—is more economical than small production—the production of the hand or the domestic industry. It is held that because this has been shown to apply in competitive industry, that therefore it must be true nationally, that because it has been shown under a system of private enterprise how the hand and the domestic industry has been extinguished by the factory system, that therefore it must necessarily apply also to the whole community, that the saving must increase proportionately. The artists and the craftsmen deny that this is so, and they think it can be proved.

[ . . . ]

What I seek to show is that this Arts and Crafts movement, which began with the earnestness of the Pre-Raphaelite painters, the prophetic enthusiasm of Ruskin and the titanic energy of Morris, is not what the public has thought it to be, or is seeking to make it: a nursery for luxuries, a hothouse for the production of mere trivialities and useless things for the rich. It is a movement for the stamping out of such things by sound production on the one hand, & the inevitable regulation of machine production and cheap labour on the other. My thesis is that *the expensive superfluity and the cheap superfluity are one and the same thing*, equally useless, equally wasteful, & that both must be destroyed. The Arts and Crafts movement then, if it means anything, means Standard, whether of work or of life, the protection of Standard, whether in the product or in the producer, and it means that these two things must be taken together.

To the men of this movement, who are seeking to compass the destruction of the commercial system, to discredit it, undermine it, overthrow it, their mission is just as serious and just as sacred as was that of their great grandfathers who first helped raise it into being, and thought that they had built for it an abiding monument in a crystal palace of glass & iron.[1] They want to put into the place of the old order that is passing away, something finer, nobler, saner; they want to determine the limitations of the factory system, to regulate machinery, to get back to realities in labour and human life.

As for their own particular work, their buildings, their furniture, their metal work, their pottery, the things they make with their hands, they know that they can do these things if the community will only give them the opportunity. They want to be allowed to do them, to do good work & useful work, and in so doing

live the decent quiet lives of good citizens, they want to do this under conditions best suited to the work they offer, and the children—the young citizens
they bring up. They are not interested in the race for riches, they see something
better, on the other hand they do not see how their work,—the work of the Arts
and Crafts,—can be practised with the constant haunting fear of the workhouse
for themselves and their families. The work they have to do postulates time,
thought, technical skill and experiment, they cannot do it "to date," they often
cannot do it "to price." They consider that the mental vision of the Englishman
has been so deflected by the mechanical conditions of modern life, that he
unconsciously measures everything by a machine standard, and there are certain
things that cannot be so measured. The Arts and Crafts claim to be among such
things, just as the coming of seeds in the ground, the times and seasons of the
year and the changing of the character of youth. They are of the fundamental
necessities, they are among the basic educational needs of the community, and
the community must find a place for them and give those who practise them a
stable economic basis. Some of us indeed go further, and say that the proper
place for the Arts and Crafts is in the country, the place where the children
ought to be, in among the direct, elemental facts of life, and away from the complex, artificial and often destructive influences of machinery and the great town.
Some of us would hold that this in itself implies the need for regulating machinery with a direct ethical objective.

[ . . . ]

Those masters of craftsmanship, however, who look more deeply into the
purpose of the Arts and Crafts and the conditions of modern Industry in which
they are fulfilling themselves, know that their purpose is useful public service,
and that if this purpose be temporarily obscured, it will be made clear again;
that their purpose fundamentally is utility and utility of the best. Their mission
is to establish Standard; to determine the right and the wrong in commodities,
to say which of them are better produced by the hand than by the machine, to
say which are the things where individuality is a prime factor, which are the
things best made for their own sake, which best develope [sic] character and
invention in the maker.

[ . . . ]

[ . . . ] The approaching economic revolution in England will largely take
the form of a struggle between the Cities and the Parliament, the cities which
represent Democracy, & which are trying to get control of their own economic
environment, and Parliament which represents privilege, privilege as expressed
in land, capital, and the control of the means of production. In this struggle
there seems little room for the craftsman, and so it beho[o]ves him to carve out
a way for himself. I am in hopes that some of the experiences and some of the
suggestions in this book will help him towards doing this.

In so far then as the justification of the Arts & Crafts is the Standard they
set, the real want they fulfil, in so far must the craftsmen themselves come to be

more real and more direct in their hold on life, the men & women who practise craftsmanship must not be dependent on their craftsmanship alone. They
must be ready to take a hand at the elemental processes of life, work on the land,
cooking and baking, husbandry, the things of the house, the more direct things
that show what it is well to have and what it is better to do without, all those
things that imply a simpler living of life. The townsman of the future will I think
largely live out in the country, and he will have to do more with his hands than
he does now, perhaps he will bring with him what he has learnt in the town.
But to perfect and fulfil the life of Civic democracy, the lesson of the great town,
we must go beyond it, we must learn the lesson of the country also, the Arts &
Crafts must go "back to the land," they must in part at least be self supporting.
While on the one hand they must obtain a control over their own market, &
by collective action establish a limitation of machine production, they must on
the other hand become self dependent, at least in part, by a return to the direct
processes of husbandry, a return to the land. *The Arts and Crafts and the problem of the land in England, are complementary to each other.*

What I have endeavoured to set forth in this book is the practical effort of
a body of English craftsmen, who aided by a little group of capitalists, have
taken their labour, their skill and their traditions with them, packed up their kit
and gone off into the country to labour. How far they have succeeded or failed
it is not for me to say. The deductions I make are from their experience, and
indeed anything I may say is of value only in so far as their experience has tested
it. If it can be shown that they have succeeded in certain directions, it means
that others shall succeed also and go further; if they have failed it means nothing more than that for the time being the right way has not yet been found, and
that others will find it.

## Chapter II. The General Problem of the Guild of Handicraft and What It Has Tried to Do

The story of the Guild of Handicraft at the close of 20 years of life, or as some
will prefer to put it, at the commencement of its majority and a new phase of
its development, may be summed in a sentence. It has temporarily ruined itself
in an attempt to uphold Standard and humanize work; and to show, in other
words, that standard of workmanship and standard of life must be taken together
and that the one is dependent upon the other.

The wise, hard, shrewd business man will no doubt say—indeed I have
heard him say—"I told you so." But that scarce suffices as prophecy, and it lacks
definiteness. I propose in the following pages to show that the business man is
wrong; that his prediction is only partially true, that a great many things have
happened in the 20 years, that were undreamed of by him or us, at the outset;
that rapidly changing economic conditions have affected the whole problem of
the Guild of Handicraft and the Arts and Crafts movement of which it is an

expression; and that apart from its artistic product, in building, furnishing, silver, jewels & books, which we are here not called upon to judge, these being workshop matters and matters for the future, the Guild of Handicraft has arrived at certain social and economic results, which may claim to be of real value towards national life and towards those aspirations of labour and craftsmanship which will in the future largely help shape national life.

When we say that the Guild has ruined itself, we mean that as far as its legal position as a limited liability company is concerned it has gone as far as it can go in that direction, and that this chapter in its history ends at the close of the year 1907. The condition of limited liability has been an episode in the Guild's life, and the principles for which the Guild stands, will now have to develop in some other way in order to find their fulfilment. In plain business terms the Guild had dropped at the beginning of its twenty-first year and at the end of a period of acute commercial depression, a substantial sum of money, upwards of £6,000–£7,000, the money of its shareholders, many of whom are the workmen themselves, in the attempt to carry through certain principles of workmanship and life.

These principles may be briefly resumed. There should be under some collective grouping, a number of workmen practising different crafts, carrying out as far as possible their own designs, coming into direct contact with material, and so organised as to make it possible for the workmen to be wherever necessary in direct touch with the consumer.

The crafts were mainly those that had to do with Architecture and they were mainly handicrafts, that is to say machinery was not repudiated, but the idea was that in those cases where the hand was better used it should be used, and that the customer was not to be put off with the machine-made article on the score of cheapness, neatness or trade finish. Thus a timber plank, it was held, could be sawn by the circular saw [ . . . ], but should not be subsequently carved by machinery. A silver plate could be rolled by the mill, but the actual dish or cup should not be subsequently spun in the chuck [ . . . ]. In this we considered, and still do, that there lies a vital question of principle, affecting the whole future of the industries concerned, the life of the men engaged in them, and the arts and crafts which can and should grow out of them for the greater honour and beauty of national life.

In addition to these principles of right and wrong in craftsmanship and the use and abuse of machinery, the Guild went further. It laid down, and has consistently applied the principle, that the men themselves should hold shares and have an interest and stake in the concern, that personal interest must affect product, especially such product as has an intrinsic personal quality, and that through the men's appointed labour director they should have a voice in the management & policy of the business. It was even hoped at one time that the business might ultimately belong entirely to the men themselves.

Finally as the outcome of these principles, it was felt that for the sake of the work and the life growing out of it, some better conditions than those prevalent in a great city like London, or Birmingham, with their horrible workshop associations and the dreary confinement of their grey streets & houses, should be given a chance; and for this the move of the whole concern into the country— with some 150 men, women and children—was effected in the year 1902. For this move there were needed three things: enthusiasm, skill and money. The first two we had in abundance, the third we borrowed. [ . . . ]

[ . . . ]

**N O T E S**

1. This passage refers to Joseph Paxton's "Crystal Palace," which was built in Hyde Park, London, to house the Great Exhibition of 1851.

# 1909

## Filippo Tommaso Marinetti, "The Foundation and Manifesto of Futurism"

F. T. Marinetti (1876–1944) was an Italian avant-garde poet and theorist who founded the literary and artistic movement called Futurism. In his deliberately shocking writings and activities, Marinetti promoted speed, technology, youth, automobiles, airplanes, fascism, and war ("the world's only hygiene"), and called for the destruction of museums and libraries. Marinetti's figurative (and literal) embrace of the automobile in his narrative of the founding of Futurism signals the beginning of European avant-garde artists' and designers' sustained interest in the aesthetic and social possibilities of modern technology. The Futurist group grew to include artists, designers, and architects such as Giacomo Balla, Umberto Boccioni, Carlo Carrà, Fortunato Depero, Luigi Russolo, Antonio Sant'Elia, and Gino Severini.

Excerpted from "The Foundation and Manifesto of Futurism," in *Marinetti: Selected Writings,* by F. T. Marinetti, edited by R. W. Flint, translated by R. W. Flint and Arthur A. Coppotelli (New York: Farrar, Straus and Giroux, 1972): pp. 39–43 (originally published in *Le Figaro* [Paris], February 20, 1909, p. 1). Reprinted by permission of Farrar, Straus, and Giroux, LLC, and Middlesex University Press.

We had stayed up all night, my friends and I, under hanging mosque lamps with domes of filigreed brass, domes starred like our spirits, shining like them with the prisoned radiance of electric hearts. For hours we had trampled our atavistic ennui into rich oriental rugs, arguing up to the last confines of logic and blackening many reams of paper with our frenzied scribbling.

An immense pride was buoying us up, because we felt ourselves alone at that hour, alone, awake, and on our feet, like proud beacons or forward sentries against an army of hostile stars glaring down at us from their celestial encampments. Alone with stokers feeding the hellish fires of great ships, alone with the black specters who grope in the red-hot bellies of locomotives launched down their crazy courses, alone with drunkards reeling like wounded birds along the city walls.

Suddenly we jumped, hearing the mighty noise of the huge double-decker trams that rumbled by outside, ablaze with colored lights, like villages on holiday suddenly struck and uprooted by the flooding Po and dragged over falls and through gorges to the sea.

Then the silence deepened. But, as we listened to the old canal muttering its feeble prayers and the creaking bones of sickly palaces above their damp green beards, under the windows we suddenly heard the famished roar of automobiles.

"Let's go!" I said. "Friends, away! Let's go! Mythology and the Mystic Ideal are defeated at last. We're about to see the Centaur's birth and, soon after, the first flights of Angels! . . . We must shake the gates of life, test the bolts and hinges. Let's go! Look there, on the earth, the very first dawn! There's nothing to match the splendor of the sun's red sword, slashing for the first time through our millennial gloom!"

We went up to the three snorting beasts, to lay amorous hands on their torrid breasts. I stretched out on my car like a corpse on its bier, but revived at once under the steering wheel, a guillotine blade that threatened my stomach.

The raging broom of madness swept us out of ourselves and drove us through streets as rough and deep as the beds of torrents. Here and there, sick lamplight through window glass taught us to distrust the deceitful mathematics of our perishing eyes.

I cried, "The scent, the scent alone is enough for our beasts."

And like young lions we ran after Death, its dark pelt blotched with pale crosses as it escaped down the vast violet living and throbbing sky.

But we had no ideal Mistress raising her divine form to the clouds, nor any cruel Queen to whom to offer our bodies, twisted like Byzantine rings! There was nothing to make us wish for death, unless the wish to be free at last from the weight of our courage!

And on we raced, hurling watchdogs against doorsteps, curling them under our burning tires like collars under a flatiron. Death, domesticated, met me at every turn, gracefully holding out a paw, or once in a while hunkering down, making velvety caressing eyes at me from every puddle.

"Let's break out of the horrible shell of wisdom and throw ourselves like pride-ripened fruit into the wide, contorted mouth of the wind! Let's give ourselves utterly to the Unknown, not in desperation but only to replenish the deep wells of the Absurd!!"

The words were scarcely out of my mouth when I spun my car around with the frenzy of a dog trying to bite its tail, and there, suddenly, were two cyclists coming toward me, shaking their fists, wobbling like two equally convincing but nevertheless contradictory arguments. Their stupid dilemma was blocking my way—damn! Ouch! . . . I stopped short and to my disgust rolled over into a ditch with my wheels in the air. . . .

Oh! Maternal ditch, almost full of muddy water! Fair factory drain! I gulped down your nourishing sludge; and I remembered the blessed black breast of my Sudanese nurse. . . . When I came up—torn, filthy, and stinking—from under the capsized car, I felt the white-hot iron of joy deliciously pass through my heart!

A crowd of fishermen with handlines and gouty naturalists were already swarming around the prodigy. With patient, loving care those people rigged a tall derrick and iron grapnels to fish out my car, like a big beached shark. Up it came from the ditch, slowly, leaving in the bottom like scales its heavy framework of good sense and its soft upholstery of comfort.

They thought it was dead, my beautiful shark, but a caress from me was enough to revive it; and there it was, alive again, running on its powerful fins!

And so, faces smeared with good factory muck—plastered with metallic waste, with senseless sweat, with celestial soot—we, bruised, our arms in slings, but unafraid, declared our high intentions to all the *living* of the earth:

## MANIFESTO OF FUTURISM

1. We intend to sing the love of danger, the habit of energy and fearlessness.
2. Courage, audacity, and revolt will be essential elements of our poetry.
3. Up to now literature has exalted a pensive immobility, ecstasy, and sleep. We intend to exalt aggressive action, a feverish insomnia, the racer's stride, the mortal leap, the punch and the slap.
4. We say that the world's magnificence has been enriched by a new beauty; the beauty of speed. A racing car whose hood is adorned with great pipes, like serpents of explosive breath—a roaring car that seems to ride on grapeshot—is more beautiful than the *Victory of Samothrace*.[1]
5. We want to hymn the man at the wheel, who hurls the lance of his spirit across the Earth, along the circle of its orbit.
6. The poet must spend himself with ardor, splendor, and generosity, to swell the enthusiastic fervor of the primordial elements.

7. Except in struggle, there is no more beauty. No work without an aggressive character can be a masterpiece. Poetry must be conceived as a violent attack on unknown forces, to reduce and prostrate them before man.

8. We stand on the last promontory of the centuries!...Why should we look back, when what we want is to break down the mysterious doors of the Impossible? Time and Space died yesterday. We already live in the absolute, because we have created eternal, omnipresent speed.

9. We will glorify war—the world's only hygiene—militarism, patriotism, the destructive gesture of freedom-bringers, beautiful ideas worth dying for, and scorn for women.

10. We will destroy the museums, libraries, academies of every kind, will fight moralism, feminism, every opportunistic or utilitarian cowardice.

11. We will sing of great crowds excited by work, by pleasure, and by riot; we will sing of the multicolored, polyphonic tides of revolution in the modern capitals; we will sing of the vibrant nightly fervor of arsenals and shipyards blazing with violent electric moons; greedy railway stations that devour smoke-plumed serpents; factories hung on clouds by the crooked lines of their smoke; bridges that stride the rivers like giant gymnasts, flashing in the sun with a glitter of knives; adventurous steamers that sniff the horizon; deep-chested locomotives whose wheels paw the tracks like the hooves of enormous steel horses bridled by tubing; and the sleek flight of planes whose propellers chatter in the wind like banners and seem to cheer like an enthusiastic crowd.

It is from Italy that we launch through the world this violently upsetting, incendiary manifesto of ours. With it, today, we establish *Futurism* because we want to free this land from its smelly gangrene of professors, archaeologists, ciceroni,[2] and antiquarians. For too long has Italy been a dealer in secondhand clothes. We mean to free her from the numberless museums that cover her like so many graveyards.

Museums: cemeteries! . . . Identical, surely, in the sinister promiscuity of so many bodies unknown to one another. Museums: public dormitories where one lies forever beside hated or unknown beings. Museums; absurd abattoirs of painters and sculptors ferociously macerating each other with color-blows and line-blows, the length of the fought-over walls!

[ . . . ]

In truth I tell you that daily visits to museums, libraries, and academies (cemeteries of empty exertion, calvaries of crucified dreams, registries of aborted beginnings!) is, for artists, as damaging as the prolonged supervision by parents of certain young people drunk with their talent and their ambitious wills. When the future is barred to them, the admirable past may be a solace for the ills of the moribund, the sickly, the prisoner. . . . But we want no part of it, the past, we the young and strong *Futurists*!

So let them come, the gay incendiaries with charred fingers! Here they are! Here they are! . . . Come on! set fire to the library shelves! Turn aside the canals to flood the museums! . . . Oh, the joy of seeing the glorious old canvases bobbing adrift on those waters, discolored and shredded! . . . Take up your pickaxes, your axes and hammers, and wreck, wreck the venerable cities, pitilessly!

The oldest of us is thirty: so we have at least a decade for finishing our work. When we are forty, other younger and stronger men will probably throw us in the wastebasket like useless manuscripts—we want it to happen!

They will come against us, our successors, will come from far away, from every quarter, dancing to the winged cadence of their first songs, flexing the hooked claws of predators, sniffing doglike at the academy doors the strong odor of our decaying minds, which already will have been promised to the literary catacombs.

[ . . . ]

## NOTES

1. The *Victory* (or *Nike*) *of Samothrace* is an ancient (ca. 300–200 BCE) Greek marble sculpture of a winged female figure. It was excavated on the island of Samothrace in the mid-nineteenth century and taken to the Louvre in Paris.
2. Tour guides.

# 1910

# Adolf Loos, "Ornament and Crime"

The Austrian architect Adolf Loos (1870–1933) is probably as well known today for his essay, "Ornament and Crime," as he is for the innovative modernist structures he built after 1910, which include some of the first private residences made of reinforced concrete.[1] A harsh critic of the Vienna Secession, Loos traveled in the United States from 1893 to 1896, during which time he not only visited the World's Columbian Exposition of 1893, but also the new steel-frame "skyscrapers" being built in cities such as Chicago, New York, and Saint Louis. Although "Ornament and Crime" is often dated to 1908, the first date for which its existence can be verified is 1910.[2] In it, Loos argues that a civilization's "progress" can be measured by the degree to which it has spurned ornament.

Essay reproduced in its entirety from Adolf Loos, "Ornament and Crime," translated by Wilfried Wang, in *The Architecture of Adolf Loos: An Arts Council Exhibition*, edited by Yehuda Safran and Wilfried Wang (London: Arts Council of Great Britain, 1985): 100–103. Reprinted by permission of Yehuda Safran.

I n the womb the human embryo passes through all the development stages of the animal kingdom. At the moment of birth, human sensations are equal to those of a newborn dog. His childhood passes through all the transformations which correspond to the history of mankind. At the age of two, he sees like a Papuan, at four, like a Teuton, at six like Socrates, at eight like Voltaire. When he is eight years old, be becomes aware of violet, the colour which the eighteenth century had discovered, because before that the violet was blue and the purple snail red. Today the physicist points to colours in the sun's spectrum which already bear a name, whose recognition, however, is reserved for the coming generation.

The child is amoral. To us the Papuan is also amoral. The Papuan slaughters his enemies and devours them. He is no criminal. If, however, the modern man slaughters and devours somebody, he is a criminal or a degenerate. The Papuan tattoos his skin, his boat, his oar, in short, everything that is within reach. He is no criminal. The modern man who tattoos himself is a criminal or a degenerate. There are prisons where eighty percent of the inmates bear tattoos. Those who are tattooed but are not imprisoned are latent criminals or degenerate aristocrats. If a tattooed person dies at liberty, it is only that he died a few years before he committed a murder.

The urge to ornament one's face, and everything within one's reach[,] is the origin of fine art. It is the babble of painting. All art is erotic.

The first ornament that came into being, the cross, had an erotic origin. The first work of art, the first artistic action of the first artist daubing on the wall, was in order to rid himself of his natural excesses. A horizontal line: the reclining woman. A vertical line: the man who penetrates her. The man who created it felt the same urge as Beethoven, he experienced the same joy that Beethoven felt when he created the Ninth Symphony.

But the man of our time who daubs the walls with erotic symbols to satisfy an inner urge is a criminal or a degenerate. It is obvious that this urge overcomes man: such symptoms of degeneration most forcefully express themselves in public conveniences. One can measure the culture of a country to the degree to which its lavatory walls are daubed. With children it is a natural phenomenon: their first artistic expression is to scrawl on the walls erotic symbols. But what is natural to the Papuan and the child is a symptom of degeneration in the modern man. I have made the following observation and have announced it to the world:

*The evolution of culture is synonymous with the removal of ornament from objects of daily use.* I had thought to introduce a new joy into the world: but it has not thanked me for it. Instead the idea was greeted with sadness and despondency. What cast the gloom was the thought that ornament could no longer be produced. What! Are we alone, the people of the nineteenth century, are we no longer capable of doing what any Negro can do, or what people have been able to do before us?

Those objects without ornament, which mankind had created in earlier centuries, had been carelessly discarded and destroyed. We possess no carpenter's benches of the Carolingian period; instead any rubbish which had even the smallest ornament was collected, cleaned and displayed in ostentatious palaces that were built for them, people walked about sadly amongst the display cabinets. Every period had its style: why was it that our period was the only one to be denied a style? By 'style' was meant ornament. I said, 'weep not. Behold! What makes our period so important is that it is incapable of producing new ornament. We have out-grown ornament, we have struggled through to a state without ornament. Behold, the time is at hand, fulfilment awaits us. Soon the streets of the cities will glow like white walls! Like Zion, the Holy City, the capital of heaven. It is then that fulfilment will have come'.

But there are hob goblins who will not allow it to happen. Humanity is still to groan under the slavery of ornament. Man had progressed enough for ornament to no longer produce erotic sensations in him, unlike the Papuans, a tattooed face did not increase the aesthetic value, but reduced it. Man had progressed far enough to find pleasure in purchasing a plain cigarette case, even if it cost the same as one that was ornamented. They were happy with their clothes and they were glad that they did not have to walk about in red velvet trousers with gold braids like monkeys at a fun fair. And I said: 'Behold, Goethe's death chamber is more magnificent than all the pomp of the Renaissance, and a plain piece of furniture is more beautiful than all the inlaid and carved museum pieces. Goethe's language is more beautiful than all the ornaments of the shepherds of the Pegnitz'.

This was heard by the hob goblins with displeasure. The state, whose duty it is to impede people in their cultural development, took over the question of development and re-adoption of ornament and made it its own. Woe betide the state, whose revolutions are brought about by its privy councillors!

Soon one was to see a buffet introduced into the Viennese Museum of Applied Arts, which was called 'the pro[s]perous fish shoal', there was even a cupboard, which was given the trade name 'the cursed princess' or something similar, which referred to the ornament with which this unfortunate piece of furniture was covered. The Austrian state takes its task so seriously that it ensures that outdated footwear will not disappear from within the boundaries of the

Austro-Hungarian Empire. The state forces every cultivated twenty-year-old man to wear outdated footwear for three years (after all, every state proceeds on the assumption that a poorly developed population is more easily governed). Well, the epidemic of ornament is recognised by the state and is subsidised with government money. I, however, consider that to be a regressive. I will not subscribe to the argument that ornament increases the pleasure of the life of a cultivated person, or the argument which covers itself with the words: 'But if the ornament is beautiful! . . .' To me, and to all the cultivated people, ornament does not increase the pleasures of life. If I want to eat a piece of gingerbread I will choose one that is completely plain and not a piece which represents a baby in arms of a horserider, a piece which is covered over and over with decoration. The man of the fifteenth century would not understand me. But modern people will. The supporter of ornament believes that the urge for simplicity is equivalent to self-denial. No, dear professor from the College of Applied Arts, I am not denying myself! To me, it tastes better this way. The dishes of the past centuries which used decoration to make the peacocks, pheasants and lobsters appear more appetising produce the opposite effect on me. I look on such a culinary display with horror when I think of having to eat these stuffed animal corpses. I eat roast beef.

The immense damage and devastation which the revival of ornament has caused to aesthetic development could easily be overcome because nobody, not even the power of the state, can stop the evolution of humanity! It represents a crime against the national economy, and, as a result of it, human labour, money and material are ruined. Time cannot compensate for this kind of damage.

The rate of cultural development is held back by those that cannot cope with the present. I live in the year 1908, but my neighbour lives approximately in the year 1900, and one over there lives in the year 1880. It is a misfortune for any government, if the culture of its people is dominated by the past. The farmer from Kals lives in the twelfth century, and on the occasion of the Jubilee Procession, tribes walked past which even during the period of mass migration were thought to be backward. Happy is the country which does not have such backward-looking inhabitants. Happy is America! Even here we have people in the cities who are survivors from the eighteenth century, and who are appalled by a painting with violet shadows, because they cannot understand why the artist has used violet. To them, the pheasant which the cook has spent days preparing tastes better, and the cigarette case with Renaissance ornaments is more pleasing. And what is happening in the countryside? Clothes and household utensils belong to previous centuries. The farmer is no Christian, he is still a heathen.

Those who measure everything by the past impede the cultural development of nations and of humanity itself. Ornament is not merely produced by criminals, it commits a crime itself by damaging national economy and therefore its cultural development. Two people living side by side who have the same needs, the same demands on life, and the same income, but belong to different cultures, perceive the national economy differently. The result is that the man of the twentieth century becomes richer and the man of the eighteenth century becomes poorer. I assume that both their lifestyles reflect their different attitudes. The man of the twentieth century can satisfy his needs with a much smaller capital and can, therefore, set aside savings. The vegetable which is appetising to him is simply boiled in water and has butter spread over it. To the other man it will only taste good if honey and nuts are added to it and it has been cooked by someone for hours. Decorated plates are expensive, while white crockery, which is pleasing to the modern individual, is cheap. Whilst one person saves money, the other becomes insolvent. This is what happens to entire nations. Woe betide the nation that remains behind in its cultural development. The English become richer and we become poorer. . . .

In a highly productive nation ornament is no longer a natural product of its culture, and therefore represents backwardness or even a degenerative tendency. As a result, those who produce ornament are no longer given their due reward. We are aware of the conditions that exist in the wood carving and turning trades, the very low wages which are paid to the embroiderers and lace makers. The producer of ornament must work for twenty hours to obtain the same income of a modern labourer who works for eight hours. As a rule, ornament increases the price of the object. All the same there are occasions when an ornamented object is offered at half the price, despite the same material cost and production time, which works out to be three times longer as that of a plain unornamented object. The lack of ornament results in reduced working hours and an increased wage. The Chinese carver works sixteen hours, the American labourer works eight hours. If I pay as much for a plain box as I would for an ornamented one, then the difference is in working hours. And if there existed no ornament at all, a condition which might arise in millenia, man would only need to work four instead of eight hours, as the time spent on ornament represents half of today's working day.

Ornament is wasted manpower and therefore wasted health. It has always been like this. But today it also means wasted material, and both mean wasted capital.

As ornament is no longer organically related to our culture, it is also no longer the expression of our culture. The ornament that is produced today bears no relation to us, or to any other human or the world at large. It has no potential for development. What happened to Otto Eckmann's[3] ornaments, and those of Van de Velde? The artist always stood at the centre of humanity, full of power and health. The modern producer of ornament is, however, left behind or a pathological phenomenon. He disowns his own products after only three years. Cultivated people find them instantaneously intolerable, others become conscious of their intolerability after many years. Where are Otto Eckmann's products today? Where will Olbrich's[4] work be, ten years from now? Modern ornament has no parents and no offspring, it has no past and no future. Uncultivated people, to whom the significance of our time is a sealed book, welcome it with joy and disown it after a short while.

Today, mankind is healthier than ever before; only a few are ill. These few, however, tyrannise the worker, who is so healthy that he is incapable of inventing ornament. They force him to execute ornament which they have designed, in the most diverse materials.

The change in ornament implies a premature devaluation of labour. The worker's time, the utilised material is capital that has been wasted. I have made the statement: The form of an object should be bearable for as long as the object lasts physically. I would like to try to explain this: a suit will be changed more frequently than a valuable fur coat. A lady's evening dress, intended for one night only, will be changed more rapidly than a writing desk. Woe betide the writing desk that has to be changed as frequently as an evening dress, just because the style has become unbearable. Then the money that was spent on the writing desk will have been wasted.

This fact is well known to the Austrians who promote decoration and try to justify it by saying: 'A consumer who owns furnishings which become unbearable to him, after only ten years, and who is therefore forced to buy furniture every ten years, is preferable to one who only buys an object for himself once the old one can no longer be used. Industry demands it. Millions of people are employed because of this rapid change'. This appears to be the secret of the Austrian national economy; how often does one hear the words uttered on the oc[c]asion of the outbreak of a fire: 'Thank God: now there will be some work again'. I know a good remedy! Set a whole city on fire, set the entire Empire alight and everyone will wallow in money and wealth. Let us have furniture made which can be used for firewood after three years; let us have ironmongery which will have to be melted down after four years, as it is impossible to realise even a tenth of the original labour and material costs at the pawn-brokers, and we will become richer and richer.

The loss not only hits the consumer; it hits primarily the producer. Today, decorated objects, which, thanks to progress, have become separated from the realm of ornamentation[,] imply wasted labour and materials. If all objects were to last as long in aesthetic terms as they did physically, the consumer could pay a price for them which would enable the labourer to earn more money and work shorter hours. I would gladly pay forty crowns for my boots even though I could obtain boots for ten crowns at another store. But in every trade which languishes under the tyranny of the ornamentalists, neither good nor bad work is valued. Labour suffers because no one is prepared to pay for its true value.

Thank goodness that this is the case, because these ornamented objects are only bearable in the shabbiest execution. I recover from the news of a fire more rapidly if I hear that only worthless rubbish was burnt. I can be happy about the junk in the Künstlerhaus (the Municipal art gallery in Vienna), as I know that they put on exhibitions in a few days which are pulled down in one. But the flinging of gold coins instead of pebbles, the lighting of a cigarette with a banknote, the pulverisation and drinking of a pearl appear unaesthetic.

Ornamented objects appear truly unaesthetic if they have been executed in the best material, with the highest degree of meticulous detail, and if they have required a long production time. I cannot plead innocence for having been the first to call for quality labour, but not for this kind of work.

The modern man who holds ornament sacred as the sign of artistic achievement of past epochs will immediately recognise the tortured, laboriously extracted and pathological nature of modern ornament. Ornament can no longer be borne by someone who exists at our level of culture.

It is different for people and nations who have not reached this level.

I preach to the aristocrats, I mean the individuals who stand at the pinnacle of humanity and who nevertheless have the deepest understanding for the motivations and privations of those who stand further below. The Kafir who weaves fabric according to a specific order which only appears when one unravels it, the Persian who ties his carpets, the Slovak farmer's wife who embroiders her lace, the old lady who makes beautiful things with glass, beads and silk; all these he understands very well. The aristocrat lets them have their own way; he knows that they are sacred hours in which they work. The revolutionary would come and say 'it is all nonsense'. As he would pull the old lady away from the roadside shrine and say to her: 'There is no God'. But the atheist amongst the aristocrats lifts his hat as he walks past a church.

My shoes are covered all over with ornaments, which result from notches and holes: work which the cobbler carried out and which he was not paid for. I go to the cobbler and say to him: 'For a pair of shoes you are asking thirty crowns. I will pay you forty crowns'. By doing this I have made him happy and he will thank me for it by the work and materials which will not bear any relation in terms of quality to the extra amount. He is happy because rarely does fortune enter his house and he has been given work by a man who understands him, who appreciates his work and who does not doubt his honesty. He already imagines the finished pair in front of him. He knows where the best leather is to be found today, he knows which worker he will entrust with the shoes, and that they will display notches and holes, as many as there is space for on an elegant pair of shoes. And now I say: 'But there is one condition which I have. The shoes must be completely smooth.' By that, I have plunged him from the height of happiness to the depths of Tartarus. He has less work to do, I have robbed him of all pleasures.

I preach to the aristocrats. I allow decoration on my own body, if it provides a source of pleasure for my fellow men. Then they are also my pleasures. I suffer the ornament of the Kafir, that of the Persian, that of the Slovak farmer's wife, the ornaments of my cobbler, because they all have no other means of expressing their full potential. We have our culture which has taken over from ornament. After a day's trouble and pain, we go to hear Beethoven or Wagner. My cobbler cannot do that. I must not rob him of his pleasures as I have nothing else to replace them with. But he who goes to listen to the Ninth Symphony and who then sits down to draw up a wallpaper pattern, is either a rogue or a degenerate.

The absence of ornament has raised the other arts to unknown heights. Beethoven's symphonies would never have been written by a man who walked around in silk, velvet and lace. The person who runs around in a velvet suit is no artist but a buffoon or merely a decorator. We have become more refined, more subtle. Primitive men had to differentiate themselves by various colours, modern man needs his clothes as a mask. His individuality is so strong that it can no longer be expressed in terms of items of clothing. The lack of ornament is a sign of intellectual power. Modern man uses the ornament of past and foreign cultures at his discretion. His own inventions are concentrated on other things.

## NOTES

1. Yehuda Safran, "Loos, Adolf," *The Grove Dictionary of Art Online*, ed. L. Macy, <*http://www.groveart.com*>, (accessed 22 December 2002).

2. B. Rukschio, "Ornament und Mythos," *Ornament und Askese*, ed. A. Pfahigan (Vienna, 1985), p. 57f, cited in Yehuda Safran, "Loos, Adolf," *The Grove Dictionary of Art Online*, ed. L. Macy, <*http://www.groveart.com*>, (accessed 22 December 2002).

3. The German artist and designer Otto Eckmann (1865–1902) worked in the Jugendstil mode.

4. The Austrian architect and designer Josef Maria Olbrich (1867–1908) was a member of the Vienna Secession and designed its exhibition building.

# 1911

## Hermann Muthesius, "Aims of the Werkbund"

The German architect and critic Hermann Muthesius (1861–1927) was one of
the founders of the Deutscher Werkbund (1907–1934), an organization of
architects, craftspeople, designers, and businesspeople that attempted to raise
the quality of German manufactures by defining industrial, craft, and aesthetic
standards. The other founding members of the group were Peter Behrens,
Heinrich Tessenow, Fritz Schumacher, and Theodor Fischer.[1]

From Hermann Muthesius, "Aims of the Werkbund," an address given at the annual
meeting of the Deutscher Werkbund in Dresden, 1911; quoted from the *Jahrbuch
des Deutschen Werkbundes* (Jena: E. Diederichs, 1912), translated by Michael
Bullock, reprinted in *Programs and Manifestoes on 20th-Century Architecture,* by
Ulrich Conrads (Copyright © 1964 by Verlag Ullstein GmbH, Frankfurt/M-Berlin;
English translation copyright © 1970 Lund Humphries, London, and the Massachusetts Institute of Technology, Cambridge, Mass.): 26–27. Reprinted by permission of MIT Press.

To help form recover its rights must be the fundamental task of our era;
in particular it must be the content of any work of artistic reform
embarked upon today. The fortunate progress of the arts and crafts movement,
which has given new shape to the interior decoration of our rooms, breathed
fresh life into handicrafts and imparted fruitful inspiration to architecture, may
be regarded as only a minor prelude to what must come. For in spite of all we
have achieved we are still wading up to our knees in the brutalization of forms.
If proof is needed, we have only to observe the fact that our country is being
covered daily and hourly with buildings of the most inferior character, unwor-
thy of our age and calculated to speak to posterity all too eloquently of our
epoch's lack of culture. What sense is there in speaking of a success so long as
this is still the case? Is there a more accurate testimony to a nation's taste than
the buildings with which it fills its streets and populated areas? What would it
mean, compared with this, if we could prove that today the energies required
for decent architectural constructions are available and that these energies have
simply not been able to get to grips with the tasks? Precisely the fact that they

have not got to grips with the tasks characterizes the cultural situation of our day. The very fact that thousands and thousands of our people not merely pass by this crime against form unperturbed, but as the employers of architects contribute to its multiplication by choosing unsuitable advisers, is unmistakable proof of the abysmal condition of our sense of form and hence of our artistic culture in general.

The Deutscher Werkbund was founded in years when a closing of the ranks of all those struggling for better things was made necessary by the violent assaults of their opponents. Its years of struggle for its principles are now over. The ideas it existed to propagate are no longer contradicted by anyone; they enjoy universal acceptance. Does this mean that its existence is now superfluous? One might think so if one were to consider only the narrower field of applied art. But we cannot rest content with having put cushions and chairs in order; we must think further. In truth the Deutscher Werkbund's real work is only now beginning, with the dawning of the era of peace. And if up to now the idea of quality has held first place in the Werkbund's work we can already observe today that, as far as technique and material are concerned, the sense of quality in Germany is in the process of rapidly improving. Yet even this success is far from completing the Werkbund's task. Far more important than the material aspect is the spiritual; higher than purpose, material, and technique stands form. Purpose, material, and technique might be beyond criticism, yet without form we should still be living in a crude and brutal world. Thus we are ever more clearly confronted by the far greater, far more important task of reviving intellectual understanding and reanimating the architectonic sense. For its architectonic culture is and remains the true index of a nation's culture as a whole. If a nation produces good furniture and good light fittings, but daily erects the worst possible buildings, this can only be a sign of heterogeneous, unclarified conditions, conditions whose very inconsistency is proof of the lack of discipline and organization. Without a total respect for form, culture is unthinkable, and formlessness is synonymous with lack of culture. Form is a higher spiritual need to the same degree that cleanliness is a higher bodily need. Crudities of form cause the really cultivated man an almost physical pain; in their presence he has the same feeling of discomfort produced by dirt and a bad smell. But as long as a sense of form has not been developed in the cultured members of our nation to the same level of intensity as their need for clean linen, we are still far removed from conditions which could in any way be compared with epochs of high cultural achievement.

## NOTES

1. Julius Posener, "Muthesius, Hermann," *Grove Dictionary of Art Online*, ed. L. Macy, <*http://www.groveart.com*>, (accessed 23 December 2002).

# 1911

# Frederick Winslow Taylor, *The Principles of Scientific Management*

The American engineer Frederick Winslow Taylor (1856–1915) was the inventor of "scientific management" (often called simply "Taylorism"), a theory of efficiency that has been applied to nearly every realm of human endeavor. Taylor's method involved conducting detailed time-and-motion studies of workers who were deemed to be very efficient at their tasks, then searching for ways to eliminate unnecessary motions or moments of idleness from their work. By altering one factor at a time (such as the length of a shovel handle, or the size of its blade) and measuring the effects on worker productivity, Taylor claimed to be able to define the "one best way" of performing a given task. His theories were extraordinarily influential in the manufacturing arena, but also had many applications for product design, and served as one impetus for the development of the field of ergonomics.

Excerpted from Frederick Winslow Taylor, *The Principles of Scientific Management* (1911; reprint, New York and London: Harper & Brothers Publishers, 1923): 64–72.

O ne of the important objects of this paper is to convince its readers that every single act of every workman can be reduced to a science. With the hope of fully convincing the reader of this fact, therefore, the writer proposes to give several more simple illustrations from among the thousands which are at hand.

For example, the average man would question whether there is much of any science in the work of shoveling. Yet there is but little doubt, if any intelligent reader of this paper were deliberately to set out to find what may be called the foundation of the science of shoveling, that with perhaps 15 to 20 hours of thought and analysis he would be almost sure to have arrived at the essence of this science. On the other hand, so completely are the rule-of-thumb ideas still dominant that the writer had never met a single shovel contractor to whom it had ever even occurred that there was such a thing as the science of shoveling. This science is so elementary as to be almost self-evident.

For a first-class shoveler there is a given shovel load at which he will do his biggest day's work. What is this shovel load? Will a first-class man do more work per day with a shovel load of 5 pounds, 10 pounds, 15 pounds, 20, 25, 30, or 40 pounds? Now this is a question which can be answered only through carefully made experiments. By first selecting two or three first-class shovelers, and paying them extra wages for doing trustworthy work, and then gradually varying the shovel load and having all the conditions accompanying the work carefully observed for several weeks by men who were used to experimenting, it was found that a first-class man would do his biggest day's work with a shovel load of about 21 pounds. For instance, that this man would shovel a larger tonnage per day with a 21-pound load than with a 24-pound load or than with an 18-pound load on his shovel. It is, of course, evident that no shoveler can always take a load of exactly 21 pounds on his shovel, but nevertheless, although his load may vary 3 or 4 pounds one way or the other, either below or above the 21 pounds, he will do his biggest day's work when his average for the day is about 21 pounds.

The writer does not wish it to be understood that this is the whole of the art or science of shoveling. There are many other elements, which together go to make up this science. But he wishes to indicate the important effect which this one piece of scientific knowledge has upon the work of shoveling.

At the works of the Bethlehem Steel Company, for example, as a result of this law, instead of allowing each shoveler to select and own his own shovel, it became necessary to provide some 8 to 10 different kinds of shovels, etc., each one appropriate to handling a given type of material; not only so as to enable the men to handle an average load of 21 pounds, but also to adapt the shovel to several other requirements which become perfectly evident when this work is studied as a science. A large shovel tool room was built, in which were stored not only shovels but carefully designed and standardized labor implements of all kinds, such as picks, crowbars, etc. This made it possible to issue to each workman a shovel which would hold a load of 21 pounds of whatever class of material they were to handle: a small shovel for ore, say, or a large one for ashes. Iron ore is one of the heavy materials which are handled in a works of this kind, and rice coal, owing to the fact that it is so slippery on the shovel, is one of the lightest materials. And it was found on studying the rule-of-thumb plan at the Bethlehem Steel Company, where each shoveler owned his own shovel, that he would frequently go from shoveling ore, with a load of about 30 pounds per shovel, to handling rice coal, with a load on the same shovel of less than 4 pounds. In the one case, he was so overloaded that it was impossible for him to do a full day's work, and in the other case he was so ridiculously underloaded that it was manifestly impossible to even approximate a day's work.

Briefly to illustrate some of the other elements which go to make up the science of shoveling, thousands of stop-watch observations were made to study just how quickly a laborer, provided in each case with the proper type of shovel, can push his shovel into the pile of materials and then draw it out properly loaded. These observations were made first when pushing the shovel into the body of the pile. Next when shoveling on a dirt bottom, that is, at the outside edge of the pile, and next with a wooden bottom, and finally with an iron bottom. Again a similar accurate time study was made of the time required to swing the shovel backward and then throw the load for a given horizontal distance, accompanied by a given height. This time study was made for various combinations of distance and height. With data of this sort before him, coupled with the law of endurance described in the case of the pig-iron handlers, it is evident that the man who is directing shovelers can first teach them the exact methods which should be employed to use their strength to the very best advantage, and can then assign them daily tasks which are so just that the workman can each day be sure of earning the large bonus which is paid whenever he successfully performs this task.

There were about 600 shovelers and laborers of this general class in the yard of the Bethlehem Steel Company at this time. These men were scattered in their work over a yard which was, roughly, about two miles long and half a mile wide. In order that each workman should be given his proper implement and his proper instructions for doing each new job, it was necessary to establish a detailed system for directing men in their work, in place of the old plan of handling them in large groups, or gangs, under a few yard foremen. As each workman came into the works in the morning, he took out of his own special pigeonhole, with his number on the outside, two pieces of paper, one of which stated just what implements he was to get from the tool room and where he was to start to work, and the second of which gave the history of his previous day's work; that is, a statement of the work which he had done, how much he had earned the day before, etc. Many of these men were foreigners and unable to read and write, but they all knew at a glance the essence of this report, because yellow paper showed the man that he had failed to do his full task the day before, and informed him that he had not earned as much as $1.85 a day, and that none but high-priced men would be allowed to stay permanently with this gang. The hope was further expressed that he would earn his full wages on the following day. So that whenever the men received white slips they knew that everything was all right, and whenever they received yellow slips they realized that they must do better or they would be shifted to some other class of work.

Dealing with every workman as a separate individual in this way involved the building of a labor office for the superintendent and clerks who were in charge of this section of the work. In this office every laborer's work was planned out well in advance, and the workmen were all moved from place to place by the clerks with elaborate diagrams or maps of the yard before them, very much as chessmen are moved on a chess-board, a telephone and messenger system having been installed for this purpose. In this way a large amount of the time lost through having too many men in one place and too few in another, and through waiting between jobs, was entirely eliminated. Under the old system the workmen were kept day after day in comparatively large gangs, each under a single foreman, and the gang was apt to remain of pretty nearly the same size whether there was much or little of the particular kind of work on hand which this foreman had under his charge, since each gang had to be kept large enough to handle whatever work in its special line was likely to come along.

When one ceases to deal with men in large gangs or groups, and proceeds to study each workman as an individual, if the workman fails to do his task, some competent teacher should be sent to show him exactly how his work can best be done, to guide, help, and encourage him, and, at the same time, to study his possibilities as a workman. So that, under the plan which individualizes each workman, instead of brutally discharging the man or lowering his wages for failing to make good at once, he is given the time and the help required to make him proficient at his present job, or he is shifted to another class of work for which he is either mentally or physically better suited.

All of this requires the kindly cooperation of the management, and involves a much more elaborate organization and system than the old-fashioned herding of men in large gangs. This organization consisted, in this case, of one set of men, who were engaged in the development of the science of laboring through time study, such as has been described above; another set of men, mostly skilled laborers themselves, who were teachers, and who helped and guided the men in their work; another set of toolroom men who provided them with the proper implements and kept them in perfect order, and another set of clerks who planned the work well in advance, moved the men with the least loss of time from one place to another, and properly recorded each man's earnings, etc. And this furnishes an elementary illustration of what has been referred to as cooperation between the management and the workmen.

The question which naturally presents itself is whether an elaborate organization of this sort can be made to pay for itself; whether such an organization is not top-heavy. This question will best be answered by a statement of the results of the third year of working under this plan.

|  | Old Plan | New Plan Task Work |
|---|---|---|
| The number of yard laborers was reduced from between . . . . | 400 & 600 down to about | 140 |
| Average number of tons per man per day . . . . . . . . . . . . . | 16 | 59 |
| Average earnings per man per day . . . . . . . . . . . . . . . . | $1.15 | $1.88 |
| Average cost of handling a ton of 2240 lbs. . . . . . . . . . . | $0.072 | $0.033 |

And in computing the low cost of $0.033 per ton, the office and tool-room expenses, and the wages of all labor superintendents, foremen, clerks, time-study men, etc., are included.

During this year the total saving of the new plan over the old amounted to $36,417.69, and during the six months following, when all of the work of the yard was on task work, the saving was at the rate of between $75,000 and $80,000 per year.

Perhaps the most important of all the results attained was the effect on the workmen themselves. A careful inquiry into the condition of these men developed the fact that out of the 140 workmen only two were said to be drinking men. This does not, of course, imply that many of them did not take an occasional drink. The fact is that a steady drinker would find it almost impossible to keep up with the pace which was set, so that they were practically all sober. Many, if not most of them, were saving money, and they all lived better than they had before. These men constituted the finest body of picked laborers that the writer has ever seen together, and they looked upon the men who were over them, their bosses and their teachers, as their very best friends; not as nigger drivers, forcing them to work extra hard for ordinary wages, but as friends who were teaching them and helping them to earn much higher wages than they had ever earned before. It would have been absolutely impossible for any one to have stirred up strife between these men and their employers. And this presents a very simple though effective illustration of what is meant by the words "prosperity for the employé, coupled with prosperity for the employer," the two principal objects of management. It is evident also that this result has been brought about by the application of the four fundamental principles of scientific management.

[ . . . ]

# 1914

## Hermann Muthesius and Henry van de Velde, Statements from the Werkbund Conference of 1914

By 1915, the Deutscher Werkbund boasted nearly 2000 members, including groups as diverse in purpose as the Wiener Werkstätte and the Allgemeines Elektricitäts Gesellschaft (AEG; the German version of General Electric).[1] In a heated set of exchanges at the 1914 Werkbund Conference in Cologne,

Hermann Muthesius (1861–1927; see introduction to "Aims of the Werk-bund") and Henry van de Velde (1863–1957; see introduction to "A Chapter on the Design and Construction of Modern Furniture") debated the purposes and goals of the Werkbund. Muthesius, representing the concerns of many businessmen and industrial designers, argued in favor of *Typisierung*, the standardization of industrial forms for mass production. Van de Velde, representing the concerns of many of the artists and crafts workers who were Werkbund members, argued, in contrast, that beauty could not be achieved through standardization (which he equated with sterilization).

Hermann Muthesius and Henry van de Velde, Statements from the Werkbund Conference of 1914 (quoted from *Bauwelt 27* (Berlin: Ullstein, 1962): 770f., translated by Michael Bullock, in *Programs and Manifestoes on 20th-Century Architecture*, by Ulrich Conrads (Copyright ©1964 by Verlag Ullstein GmbH, Frankfurt/M-Berlin; English translation copyright ©1970 Lund Humphries, London, and the Massachusetts Institute of Technology, Cambridge, Mass.): 28–31. Reprinted by permission of MIT Press.

1. Architecture, and with it the whole area of the Werkbund's activities, is pressing towards standardization, and only through standardization can it recover that universal significance which was characteristic of it in times of harmonious culture.

2. Standardization, to be understood as the result of a beneficial concentration, will alone make possible the development of a universally valid, unfailing good taste.

3. As long as a universal high level of taste has not been achieved, we cannot count on German arts and crafts making their influence effectively felt abroad.

4. The world will demand our products only when they are the vehicles of a convincing stylistic expression. The foundations for this have now been laid by the German movement.

5. The creative development of what has already been achieved is the most urgent task of the age. Upon it the movement's ultimate success will depend. Any relapse and deterioration into imitation would today mean the squandering of a valuable possession.

6. Starting from the conviction that it is a matter of life and death for Germany constantly to ennoble its production, the Deutscher Werkbund, as an association of artists, industrialists, and merchants, must concentrate its attention upon creating the preconditions for the export of its industrial arts.

7. Germany's advances in applied art and architecture must be brought to the

attention of foreign countries by effective publicity. Next to exhibitions the most obvious means of doing this is by periodical illustrated publications.

8. Exhibitions by the Deutscher Werkbund are only meaningful when they are restricted radically to the best and most exemplary. Exhibitions of arts and crafts abroad must be looked upon as a national matter and hence require public subsidy.

9. The existence of efficient large-scale business concerns with reliable good taste is a prerequisite of any export. It would be impossible to meet even internal demands with an object designed by the artist for individual requirements.

10. For national reasons large distributive and transport undertakings whose activities are directed abroad ought to link up with the new movement, now that it has shown what it can do, and consciously represent German art in the world.

*Hermann Muthesius*


1. So long as there are still artists in the Werkbund and so long as they exercise some influence on its destiny, they will protest against every suggestion for the establishment of a canon and for standardization. By his innermost essence the artist is a burning idealist, a free spontaneous creator. Of his own free will he will never subordinate himself to a discipline that imposes upon him a type, a canon. Instinctively he distrusts everything that might sterilize his actions, and everyone who preaches a rule that might prevent him from thinking his thoughts through to their own free end, or that attempts to drive him into a universally valid form, in which he sees only a mask that seeks to make a virtue out of incapacity.

2. Certainly, the artist who practises a 'beneficial concentration' has always recognized that currents which are stronger than his own will and thought demand of him that he should acknowledge what is in essential correspondence to the spirit of his age. These currents may be very manifold; he absorbs them unconsciously and consciously as general influences; there is something materially and morally compelling about them for him. He willingly subordinates himself to them and is full of enthusiasm for the idea of a new style *per se*. And for twenty years many of us have been seeking forms and decorations entirely in keeping with our epoch.

3. Nevertheless it has not occurred to any of us that henceforth we ought to try to impose these forms and decorations, which we have sought or found, upon others as standards. We know that several generations will have to work upon what we have started before the physiognomy of the new style is established, and that we can talk of standards and standardization only after the passage of a whole period of endeavours.

4. But we also know that as long as this goal has not been reached our endeav-

ours will still have the charm of creative impetus. Gradually the energies, the gifts of all, begin to combine together, antitheses become neutralized, and at precisely that moment when individual strivings begin to slacken, the physiognomy will be established. The era of imitation will begin and forms and decorations will be used, the production of which no longer calls for any creative impulse: the age of infertility will then have commenced.

5. The desire to see a standard type come into being before the establishment of a style is exactly like wanting to see the effect before the cause. It would be to destroy the embryo in the egg. Is anyone really going to let themselves be dazzled by the apparent possibility of thereby achieving quick results? These premature effects have all the less prospect of enabling German arts and crafts to exercise an effective influence abroad, because foreign countries are a jump ahead of us in the old tradition and the old culture of good taste.

6. Germany, on the other hand, has the great advantage of still possessing gifts which other, older, wearier peoples are losing: the gifts of invention, of brilliant personal brainwaves. And it would be nothing short of castration to tie down this rich, many-sided, creative élan so soon.

7. The efforts of the Werkbund should be directed toward cultivating precisely these gifts, as well as the gifts of individual manual skill, joy, and belief in the beauty of highly differentiated execution, not toward inhibiting them by standardization at the very moment when foreign countries are beginning to take an interest in German work. As far as fostering these gifts is concerned, almost everything still remains to be done.

8. We do not deny anyone's good will and we are very well aware of the difficulties that have to be overcome in carrying this out. We know that the workers' organization has done a very great deal for the workers' material welfare, but it can hardly find an excuse for having done so little towards arousing enthusiasm for consummately fine worksmanship in those who ought to be our most joyful collaborators. On the other hand, we are well aware of the need to export that lies like a curse upon our industry.

9. And yet nothing, nothing good and splendid, was ever created out of mere consideration for exports. Quality will not be created out of the spirit of export. Quality is always first created exclusively for a quite limited circle of connoisseurs and those who commission the work. These gradually gain confidence in their artists; slowly there develops first a narrower, then a national clientele, and only then do foreign countries, does the world slowly take notice of this quality. It is a complete misunderstanding of the situation to make the industrialists believe that they would increase their chances in the world market if they produced *a priori* standardized types for this world market before these types had become well tried common property at home. The wonderful works being exported to us now were none of them originally created for export: think of Tiffany glasses, Copenhagen porcelain, jewellery by Jensen, the books of Cobden-Sanderson, and so on.

10. Every exhibition must have as its purpose to show the world this native quality, and it is quite true that the Werkbund's exhibitions will have meaning only when, as Herr Muthesius so rightly says, they restrict themselves radically to the best and most exemplary.

*Henry van de Velde*

### N O T E S

1. Iain Boyd White, "Deutscher Werkbund," *Grove Dictionary of Art Online*, edited by L. Macy, <*http://www.groveart.com*>, (accessed 24 December 2002).

# 1919

## Christine Frederick, "The Labor-Saving Kitchen"

Christine Frederick (1883–1970), an American who applied the lessons of scientific management to the operation of the household, was an important early twentieth-century theorist of home economics and consumer marketing. Her books *Household Engineering* (1919) and *Selling Mrs. Consumer* (1929) were widely known; *Household Engineering*, in particular, had a marked impact on European avant-garde kitchen design. Envisioning the physical environment of the home like an assembly line in a factory (whose "products" in this case included nutritious meals and clean sheets rather than Model Ts), Frederick attempted to design environments and procedures that would maximize the homemaker's investment of time, energy, and money. In these excerpts from *Household Engineering*, Frederick, using her famed "before" and "after" floor plans, discusses the characteristics of a well-designed kitchen. In addition, she outlines some of the factors she believed homemakers should consider before purchasing new appliances for the home. (Her emphasis on comfort in use and ease of cleaning predates by at least a decade most designers' and manufacturers' widespread interest in these issues.)

Excerpted from Christine Frederick, *Household Engineering: Scientific Management in the Home* (Chicago: American School of Home Economics, 1920): pp. 19–25, 99–100, 104–106.

# The Labor-Saving Kitchen

When we estimate the time consumed in all the various tasks of the home, cleaning, cooking, serving meals, laundry, etc., we find that about 70 per cent of the housekeeper's day is spent in and about the kitchen. It is therefore clear that any plan for a reorganization of the work of the home on a more efficient basis must begin with a careful study of present kitchen conditions and methods of work.

[ . . . ]

The first step towards reducing time spent in the kitchen is to have a kitchen small and compact, without loosely connected pantries and cupboards. The small kitchen costs less to build, but even more important to the worker, the small kitchen saves steps by concentrating the working processes. It should be slightly oblong, or almost square[,] as this shape permits the most step-saving arrangement of the main equipment.

[ . . . ]

When we study the steps entailed in food preparation, we find that work in the kitchen does not consist of independent, separate acts, but of a series of inter-related processes. No matter whether we are serving a six-course formal luncheon, or a simple family breakfast, each act in food preparation is part of a distinct process. There are just two of these processes: (1) PREPARING FOOD, and (2) CLEARING AWAY. Each of them has (or should have) definite, distinct steps, as we see if we analyze our work from the time preparation of food is started to the moment when the last dish is washed and laid away.

The steps in the preparing process are:

(1)  Raw materials taken from storage, refrigerator or pantry to
(2)  Preparing surface where they are beaten, mixed, or put in condition to place on
(3)  Cooking surface or in cooking device. When finished, placed on
(4)  Serving surface (table or tray) on which hot food is laid and given final touches before being sent to the table.

In other words, we (1) COLLECT, (2) PREPARE, (3) COOK, and (4) SERVE food materials according to these definite steps, even with so simple a task as boiling an egg.

The steps in the clearing away process are:

(1)  Remove soiled dishes and utensils from dining-room.
(2)  Stack and scrape them to right of sink.
(3)  Wash, drain and wipe.
(4)  Lay away in respective closets and shelves.

LATER VIEW OF APPLECROFT COUNTRY KITCHEN.
Cooking cabinet, stove and serving table in sequence, permitting step-saving food preparation.

In other words, we (1) REMOVE, (2) SCRAPE, (3) WASH, and (4) LAY AWAY dishes and utensils according to these definite steps, in this definite order at every meal.

It therefore follows that the equipment connected with these two processes and their respective chain of steps should be arranged in a corresponding order. *This principle of arranging and grouping equipment to meet the actual order of work is the basis of kitchen efficiency.*

[ . . . ]

If the storage, stove, tables, sinks, etc., are arranged after this fundamental order, the work will proceed in a progressive, step-saving track, or "routing," as the efficiency engineer calls work which proceeds in a consecutive, orderly manner. If the equipment is not arranged on this principle, the result will be cross-tracking, useless steps and waste[d] energy in all kitchen work. On pages 22 and 23 [page 95 of this book] are given two diagrams which clearly illustrate the efficient versus the drudgifying kitchen arrangement.

[ . . . ]

## Helpful Household Tools

[ . . . ]

[ . . . ] In the United States, according to estimates, only 8 percent of all families employ even one servant permanently. This means that 92 percent of homemakers are performing their own household tasks. It is to this class of women who are actively concerned in the work of the home that the labor-saver and improved modern tool most appeal. The homemaker's time and effort are worth conserving by every means. She should therefore, be eager to buy and use all the household tools which will save her strength and time and liberate her from household drudgery.

## Need of Mechanical Knowledge

While some women are "handy" with tools, the fact remains that most women are unfamiliar with the different principles involved in mechanical tools and devices. The boy almost unconsciously absorbs knowledge about gears, motors, force pumps, turbines, etc., in his daily work and play, but the girl neglects handling or learning about tools, believing it unnecessary or possibly unfeminine.

The homemaker, however, needs a most thorough knowledge of the principles of applied mechanics. Even many a good course in school physics unfortunately leaves a student with but little practical knowledge applied to the tools and equipment to be found in every kitchen and home. The more a woman knows about tools the more intelligent she will be as a buyer. Such knowledge will save her from the useless expense of buying worthless equipment, and make her more interested in purchasing the good tools and high-class equipment which will help greatly in saving time and labor.

[ . . . ]

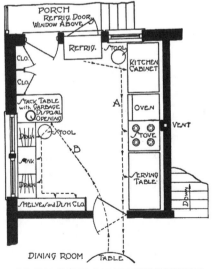

EFFICIENT GROUPING OF KITCHEN EQUIPMENT
A. Preparing route.   B. Clearing away route.

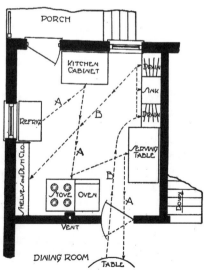

BADLY GROUPED KITCHEN EQUIPMENT

## Comfort in Use Essential

Very often a device which fulfils other conditions mentioned above fails in the small but essential point of comfort in use. This is especially true of handles, levers, etc., which either by their shape, finish, or point of attachment prove uncomfortable when used in the hands of the worker. There is the case of a breadmaker with the leverage applied at the top of the pail; otherwise a fine labor-saver, it requires an awkward arm motion which would not be the case if the leverage were applied at the base and side of the pail as indeed it is, in another make. The handles of many egg-beaters, mashers, spoons, etc., are not shaped for the comfort of the hand, although there are others on the market which do offer this point of comfort. Sometimes the handle is too short or too long, flat instead of rounded. Or a lever would be easier to operate if several inches longer, and many other instances occur where the small but important points of comfort are not considered.

## Device Should Be Well Finished

Frequently the lack of a well-finished surface, or poor construction spoils an otherwise good tool. An excellent dish drainer with a tray of galvanized iron is on the market, but the edges of the lower pan are so imperfectly soldered and so rough that the hand continually becomes scratched while working near it. Again, the hinges of a fine fireless cooker were found to be so jagged that as the cooker set out in the room, the worker tore her apron upon it every time she passed quickly. This detail of finishing should not have been overlooked in such a high-priced device, nor indeed in any other. The interior of kitchen cabinets, the trays of gas ranges, the seams and handles of many other utensils, especially those made of wire, tin or galvanized iron, are all places for the housewife's careful inspection before purchase.

## Ease in Care and Cleaning

"Is this device easy to wash and keep clean?" is another important question which should be asked previous to buying. Too frequently the time and difficulty of washing and keeping a tool in good condition is entirely overlooked. Many devices have complicated parts, gears, beaters, adjustable cutters, etc. Now, the question of how long it takes to wash and assemble these parts after use must be considered, *because this time really forms part of the total time that the device is being used.* [ . . . ]

It should be firmly remembered that no device should take longer to clean and adjust than the time it saves by its increased efficiency over some other method—otherwise, it ceases to be a labor-saver and must be justified on some other grounds. [ . . . ]

[ . . . ]

# 1919

# Walter Gropius, "Program of the Staatliche Bauhaus in Weimar"

As did his contemporaries Adolf Meyer, Ludwig Mies van der Rohe, and Le Corbusier, the German architect and designer Walter Gropius (1883–1969) worked for a time in Peter Behrens's Berlin architecture and design firm. He left Behrens's office in 1910, joined the Deutscher Werkbund in 1911, and built the famed Fagus Factory at Alfeld in 1911–13. After returning from service in World War I, he became the head of the Kunstschule and Kunstgewerbeschule in Saxony (formerly directed by Henry van de Velde), which he merged into the institution known as the Staatliche Bauhaus, Weimar. Gropius served as director of the Bauhaus from 1919 to 1928; when the Bauhaus moved to Dessau in 1925, he designed its new facilities. (The Bauhaus moved again in 1932 to Berlin, where the Nazis closed it in 1933.) The title page of Gropius's program for the Bauhaus, which was printed as a four-page leaflet in April 1919, featured Lyonel Feininger's cubist/expressionist woodcut *Cathedral of Socialism*—a fitting symbol of the institution's guild-inspired educational system, emphasis on architecture, and political ideals.

Reprinted in its entirety from Walter Gropius, "Program of the Staatliche Bauhaus in Weimar," translated by Wolfgang Jabs and Basil Gilbert, in *Bauhaus: Weimar Dessau Berlin Chicago,* by Hans Wingler (originally published in German as *Das Bauhaus* [Cologne: Verlag Gebr. Rasch & Co., 1962]; English adaptation copyright ©1969 by The Massachusetts Institute of Technology): 31–33. Reprinted by permission of MIT Press.

The ultimate aim of all visual arts is the complete building! To embellish buildings was once the noblest function of the fine arts; they were the indispensable components of great architecture. Today the arts exist in isolation, from which they can be rescued only through the conscious, cooperative effort of all craftsmen. Architects, painters, and sculptors must recognize anew and learn to grasp the composite character of a building both as an entity and in its separate parts. Only then will their work be imbued with the architectonic spirit which it has lost as "salon art."

The old schools of art were unable to produce this unity; how could they, since art cannot be taught. They must be merged once more with the workshop. The mere drawing and painting world of the pattern designer and the applied artist must become a world that builds again. When young people who take a joy in artistic creation once more begin their life's work by learning a trade, then the unproductive "artist" will no longer be condemned to deficient artistry, for their skill will now be preserved for the crafts, in which they will be able to achieve excellence.

Architects, sculptors, painters, we all must return to the crafts! For art is not a "profession." There is no essential difference between the artist and the craftsman. The artist is an exalted craftsman. In rare moments of inspiration, transcending the consciousness of his will, the grace of heaven may cause his work to blossom into art. But proficiency in a craft is essential to every artist. Therein lies the prime source of creative imagination. Let us then create a new guild of craftsmen without the class distinctions that raise an arrogant barrier between craftsman and artist! Together let us desire, conceive, and create the new structure of the future, which will embrace architecture and sculpture and painting in one unity and which will one day rise toward heaven from the hands of a million workers like the crystal symbol of a new faith.

*Walter Gropius*

## Program of the Staatliche Bauhaus in Weimar

The Staatliche Bauhaus resulted from the merger of the former Grand-Ducal Saxon Academy of Art with the former Grand-Ducal Saxon School of Arts and Crafts in conjunction with a newly affiliated department of architecture.

### AIMS OF THE BAUHAUS

The Bauhaus strives to bring together all creative effort into one whole, to reunify all the disciplines of practical art—sculpture, painting, handicrafts, and the crafts—as inseparable components of a new architecture. The ultimate, if distant, aim of the Bauhaus is the unified work of art—the great structure—in which there is no distinction between monumental and decorative art.

The Bauhaus wants to educate architects, painters, and sculptors of all levels, according to their capabilities, to become competent craftsmen or independent creative artists and to form a working community of leading and future artist-craftsmen. These men, of kindred spirit, will know how to design buildings harmoniously in their entirety—structure, finishing, ornamentation, and furnishing.

## PRINCIPLES OF THE BAUHAUS

Art rises above all methods; in itself it cannot be taught, but the crafts certainly can be. Architects, painters, and sculptors are craftsmen in the true sense of the word; hence, a thorough training in the crafts, acquired in workshops and in experimental and practical sites, is required of all students as the indispensable basis for all artistic production. Our own workshops are to be gradually built up, and apprenticeship agreements with outside workshops will be concluded.

The school is the servant of the workshop, and will one day be absorbed in it. Therefore there will be no teachers or pupils in the Bauhaus but masters, journeymen, and apprentices.

The manner of teaching arises from the character of the workshop:

Organic forms developed from manual skills.

Avoidance of all rigidity; priority of creativity; freedom of individuality, but strict study discipline.

Master and journeyman examinations, according to the Guild Statutes, held before the Council of Masters of the Bauhaus or before outside masters.

Collaboration by the students in the work of the masters.

Securing of commissions, also for students.

Mutual planning of extensive, Utopian structural designs—public buildings and buildings for worship—aimed at the future. Collaboration of all masters and students—architects, painters, sculptors—on these designs with the object of gradually achieving a harmony of all the component elements and parts that make up architecture.

Constant contact with the leaders of the crafts and industries of the country. Contact with public life, with the people, through exhibitions and other activities.

New research into the nature of the exhibitions, to solve the problem of displaying visual work and sculpture within the framework of architecture.

Encouragement of friendly relations between masters and students outside of work; therefore plays, lectures, poetry, music, costume parties. Establishment of a cheerful ceremonial at these gatherings.

### RANGE OF INSTRUCTION

Instruction at the Bauhaus includes all practical and scientific areas of creative work.

A. Architecture,

B. Painting,

C. Sculpture

including all branches of the crafts.

Students are trained in a craft (1) as well as in drawing and painting (2) and science and theory (3).

1. Craft training—either in our own, gradually enlarging workshops or in outside workshops to which the student is bound by apprenticeship agreement—includes:

a) sculptors, stonemasons, stucco workers, woodcarvers, ceramic workers, plaster casters,
b) blacksmiths, locksmiths, founders, metal turners,
c) cabinetmakers,
d) painter-and-decorators, glass painters, mosaic workers, enamelers,
e) etchers, wood engravers, lithographers, art printers, enchasers,
f) weavers.

Craft training forms the basis of all teaching at the Bauhaus. Every student must learn a craft.

2. Training in drawing and painting includes:
a) free-hand sketching from memory and imagination,
b) drawing and painting of heads, live models, and animals,
c) drawing and painting of landscapes, figures, plants, and still lives,
d) composition,
e) execution of murals, panel pictures, and religious shrines,
f) design of ornaments,
g) lettering,
h) construction and projection drawing,
i) design of exteriors, gardens, and interiors
j) design of furniture and practical articles.

3. Training in science and theory includes:
a) art history—not presented in the sense of a history of styles, but rather to further active understanding of historical working methods and techniques,
b) science of materials,
c) anatomy—from the living model,
d) physical and chemical theory of color,
e) rational painting methods,
f) basic concepts of bookkeeping, contract negotiations, personnel,
g) individual lectures on subjects of general interest in all areas of art and science.

### DIVISIONS OF INSTRUCTION

The training is divided into three courses of instruction:
  I. course for apprentices
  II. course for journeymen,
  III. course for junior masters.

The instruction of the individual is left to the discretion of each master within the framework of the general program and the work schedule, which is revised every semester.

In order to give the students as versatile and comprehensive a technical and artistic training as possible, the work schedule will be so arranged that every architect, painter, and sculptor-to-be is able to participate in part of the other courses.

**ADMISSION**
Any person of good repute, without regard to age or sex, whose previous education is deemed adequate by the Council of Masters, will be admitted, as far as space permits. The tuition fee is 180 marks per year (It will gradually disappear entirely with increasing earnings of the Bauhaus). A nonrecurring admission fee of 20 marks is also to be paid. Foreign students pay double fees. Address inquiries to the Secretariat of the Staatliche Bauhaus in Weimar.

*April 1919.*
*The administration of the Staatliche Bauhaus in Weimar:*
*Walter Gropius*

# 1922

## Theo van Doesburg, "The Will to Style"

The Dutch painter, designer, architect, and theorist Theo van Doesburg (1883–1931) was the founder, in 1917, of the avant-garde magazine *De Stijl.* De Stijl—which in English means "style," or, more literally, "*the* style"—was also the name adopted by a group of like-minded artists, designers, and architects that included van Doesburg, the painters Piet Mondrian and Bart van der Leck, and the architects Gerrit Rietveld and J. J. P. Oud. Although he worked as a Dadaist at times, in much of his work, van Doesburg was concerned with the rational, essential, and universal aspects of art and life (in contrast to Dada's engagement with the irrational, the absurd, and the contingent). In these selections from a 1922 lecture, van Doesburg describes the characteristics of what he calls "the new style."

Theo van Doesburg, "The Will to Style," text of a lecture given at Jena, Weimar, and Berlin, in *De Stijl,* edited by Hans L. C. Jaffe (London: Thames & Hudson, ©1970): 148, 155–156, 159, 161–163. Reprinted by permission of Thames & Hudson.

[ . . . ]

I n politics, as in art, only collective solutions can have decisive significance.
[ . . . ]

Where these two lines of development (the technical and the artistic) meet in our age the application of the machine to the new style is a matter of course. The machine is the purest example of balance between the static and the dynamic, between intellect and instinct. If culture in the broadest sense really means independence of nature, it is no wonder that the machine takes pride of place in the concept of cultural style. The machine is the supreme example of intellectual discipline. Materialism, as a philosophy of life and art, considered hand craftsmanship to be the purest expression of the soul.

The new spiritual philosophy of art not only saw at once its limitless potentialities for artistic expression. For a style which is no longer concerned with the production of individual pictures, ornaments or private houses, but makes a collective assault on whole districts of cities, skyscraper blocks and airports, with due consideration of the economic circumstances—for such a style there can be no question of employing hand craftsmanship. The machine is all-important here: hand craftsmanship is appropriate to an individualistic view of life which has been overtaken by progress. Hand craftsmanship, in the age of materialist philosophy, debased man to a machine; the machine, used properly in the service of cultural construction, is the only means of bringing about the converse: social liberation. This is by no means to say that mechanical production is the only requirement for creative perfection. A prerequisite for the correct use of machines is not quantity alone but, above all, quality. To serve artistic ends the use of machines must be governed by the artistic consciousness.

The needs of our age, both ideal and practical, demand constructive certainty. Only the machine can provide this constructive certainty. The new potentialities of the machine have given rise to an aesthetic theory appropriate to our age, which I have had occasion to call the 'mechanical aesthetic'. [ . . . ] The style which we are approaching will be, above all, a style of liberation and vital repose. This style, far removed from romantic vagueness, from decorative idiosyncrasy and animal spontaneity, will be a style of heroic monumentality (example: American grain silo). I should like to call this style, in contrast to all the styles of the past, the style of the perfect man, that is, the style in which the great opposites are reconciled. All the things which were known as magic, the spirit, love, etc., will be made real by it. [ . . . ]

Let me give you some examples of the characteristics of the new style in apposition [sic] to those of the old.

Certainty instead of uncertainty.

Openness instead of enclosure.

Clarity instead of vagueness.
Religious energy instead of faith and religious authority.
Truth instead of beauty.
Simplicity instead of complexity.
Relationship instead of form.
Synthesis instead of analysis.
Logical construction instead of lyrical constellation.
Mechanization instead of manual work.
Plastic form instead of imitation and decorative ornamentation.
Collectivism instead of individualism, etc.

The urge to establish the new style is seen in numerous phenomena. Not only in painting, sculpture and architecture, in literature, jazz and the cinema, but most significantly of all in purely utilitarian production.
[ . . . ]

In all these objects (whether iron bridges, railway engines, cars, telescopes, farmhouses, aeroplane hang[a]rs, chimneys, skyscrapers, or children's toys) we can see the urgings of the new style. They show exactly the same endeavour as the new creations in the realm of art to express the truth of the object in clarity and purity of form. So it is not surprising that the beauty of machinery is the very core of inspiration for the newest generation of artists.
[ . . . ]

[ . . . S]implicity, clarity and vital repose are the most important rules for the creation of monumental synthesis. The same concepts are expressed by this Rietveld armchair, whose simple construction gives harmonious shape to the function of sitting. [ . . . ]
[ . . . ]

What I have shown here to be the beginnings of Neoplasticism in art and technology has nothing to do with expressionistic anarchy. In the face of aggressive impulses, the new style requires a synthesis which transcends individuality, a harmonious union of all the arts. [ . . . ]

The demand for this monumental synthesis, using purely artistic means, was first made by the group of Dutch artists known as the De Stijl group [ . . . ].

This merging of art and life signifies nothing less than the spiritual reconstruction of Europe.
[ . . . ]

# 1922

## Alexander Rodchenko and Varvara Stepanova, "Program of the First Working Group of Constructivists"

The Russian artist, designer, and architect Alexander Rodchenko (1891–1956) and the Lithuanian/Russian artist and designer Varvara Stepanova (1894–1958), who were husband and wife, were founding members of the First Working Group of Constructivists. This group, created in 1921 at Inkhuk, the Institute of Artistic Culture in Moscow, was dedicated to promoting the values of Communism by rejecting fine art in favor of the more "productive" or "constructive" fields of design, architecture, and agitational propaganda (or "agitprop"). This selection, the first Russian-language version of their manifesto, was originally published in Moscow in August, 1922.

Reprinted in its entirety from Alexander Rodchenko and Varvara Stepanova, "Programme of the First Working Group of Constructivists," *Ermitazh* no. 13 (August 1922): 3–4, translated by Christina Lodder for the Open University, 1983, and reprinted in *Art in Theory 1900–1990: An Anthology of Changing Ideas,* edited by Charles Harrison and Paul Wood (Oxford, U.K. and Cambridge, U.S.A.: Blackwell, 1992): 317–8. Reprinted by permission of Blackwell Publishing.

The Group of Constructivists has set itself the task of finding *the communistic expression of material structures.*

In approaching its task the group insists on the need to synthesize the ideological aspect with the formal for the real transference of laboratory work on to the rails of practical activity.

Therefore, at the time of its establishment, the group's programme in its ideological aspect pointed out that:

1. Our sole ideology is scientific communism based on the theory of historical materialism.

2. The theoretical interpretation and assimilation of the experience of Soviet construction must impel the group to turn away from experimental activity 'removed from life' towards real experimentation.

3. In order to master the creation of practical structures in a really scientific and disciplined way the Constructivists have established three disciplines: *Tectonics, Faktura* and *Construction.*

   A. Tectonics or the tectonic style is tempered and formed on the one hand from the properties of communism and on the other from the expedient use of industrial material.

   B. *Faktura* is the organic state of the worked material or the resulting new state of its organism. Therefore, the group considers that *faktura* is material consciously worked and expediently used, without hampering the construction or restricting the tectonics.

   C. Construction should be understood as the organizational function of Constructivism.

If tectonics comprises the relationship between the ideological and the formal which gives unity to the practical design, and *faktura* is the material, the Construction reveals the very process of that structuring.

In this way the third discipline is the discipline of the realization of the design through the use of the worked material.

*The Material.* The material as substance or matter. Its investigation and industrial application, properties and significance. Furthermore, time, space, volume, plane, colour, line and light are also material for the Constructivists, without which they cannot construct material structures.

## The Immediate Tasks of the Group

1. In the ideological sphere:
   - To prove theoretically and practically the incompatibility of aesthetic activity with the functions of intellectual and material production.
   - The real participation of intellectual and material production as an equal element in the creation of communist culture.
2. In the practical sphere:
   - To publish a statement.
   - To publish a weekly paper, VIP [*Vestnik Intellektual'nogo Proizvodstva; The Herald of Intellectual Production*].
   - To print brochures and leaflets on questions relating to the activities of the group.
   - To construct designs.
   - To organize exhibitions.
   - To establish links with all the Production Boards and Centres of that unified Soviet machine which in fact practically shapes and produces the emergent forms of the communist way of life.
3. In the agitational sphere:
   - The Group declares uncompromising war on art.
   - It asserts that the artistic culture of the past is unacceptable for the communistic forms of Constructivist structures.

# 1923

## Le Corbusier, "Eyes Which Do Not See: Automobiles"

Le Corbusier ("The Raven") is the assumed name of the Swiss/French architect and designer Charles-Edouard Jeanneret (1887–1965), who was indubitably one of the twentieth century's most influential theorists and practitioners of architecture. His bold statement in *Towards a New Architecture* (1923) that a house is a "machine for living in" was widely quoted; the phrase described well the avant-garde houses he designed in the 1910s and 1920s, which, by the bourgeois standards of the day were stark, sparsely furnished, and more reminiscent of industrial than domestic spaces. Le Corbusier also wrote about decorative arts and product design; in this passage from *Towards a New Architecture*, he relates standardization in automobile design to standardization in architecture (using the Parthenon as his prime example).

Excerpted from Le Corbusier, *Towards a New Architecture*, translated by Frederick Etchells (1923; English translation, New York: Payson & Clarke, 1927): 127, 129, 131, 133–148.

**W**e must aim at the *fixing of standards* in order to face the problem of perfection.

*The Parthenon is a product of selection applied to a standard.*

*Architecture operates in accordance with standards.*

*Standards are a matter of logic, analysis and minute study: they are based on a problem which has been well "stated."*

*A standard is definitely established by experiment.*

DELAGE, 1921

*If the problem of the dwelling or the flat were studied in the same way that a chassis is, a speedy transformation and improvement would be seen in our houses. If houses were constructed by industrial mass-production, like chassis, unexpected but sane and defensible forms would soon appear, and a new æsthetic would be formulated with astonishing precision.*

There is a new spirit: it is a spirit of construction and of synthesis guided by clear conception.

Programme of *l'Esprit Nouveau.*
No. 1. October 1920.

It is necessary to press on towards the establishment of *standards* in order to face the problem of *perfection.*
The Parthenon is a product of selection applied to an established standard. Already for a century the Greek temple had been standardized in all its parts.

PAESTUM, 600-550 B.C.

THE PARTHENON, 447-434 B.C.

When once a standard is established, competition comes at once and violently into play. It is a fight; in order to win you must do better than your rival *in every minute point,* in the run of the whole thing and in all the details. Thus we get the study of minute points pushed to its limits. Progress.
A standard is necessary for order in human effort.

HUMBER, 1907

DELAGE, "GRAND-SPORT," 1921

A standard is established on sure bases, not capriciously but with the surety of something intentional and of a logic controlled by analysis and experiment.
All men have the same organism, the same functions.
All men have the same needs.

The social contract which has evolved through the ages fixes standardized classes, functions and needs producing standardized products.

The house is a thing essential to man.

Painting is a thing essential to man since it responds to needs of a spiritual order, determined by the standards of emotion.

All great works of art are based on one or other of the great standards of the heart: *Œdipus, Phaedra,* the *Enfant Prodigue,* the Madonnas, *Paul et Virginie,* Philemon and Baucis, the *Pauvre Pêcheur,* the *Marseillaise, Madelon vient nous verser à boire.* . . .

HISPANO-SUIZA, 1911. OZENFANT COACHWORK                     BIGNAN-SPORT 1921

The establishment of a standard involves exhausting every practical and reasonable possibility, and extracting from them a recognized type conformable to its functions, with a maximum output and a minimum use of means, workmanship and material, words, forms, colours, sounds.

The motor-car is an object with a simple function (to travel) and complicated aims (comfort, resistance, appearance), which has forced on big industry the absolute necessity of standardization. All motor-cars have the same essential arrangements. But, by reason of the unceasing competition between the innumerable firms who make them, every maker has found himself obliged to get to the top of this competition and, over and above the standard of practical realization, to prosecute the search for a perfection and a harmony beyond the mere practical side, a manifestation not only of perfection and harmony, but of beauty.

Here we have the birth of style, that is to say the attainment, universally recognized, of a state of perfection universally felt.

The establishment of a standard is developed by organizing rational elements, following a line of direction equally rational. The form and appearance are in no way preconceived, *they are a result*; they may have a strange look at first sight. Ader made a "Bat," but it did not fly; Wright and Farman set themselves the problem of sustaining solid bodies in air, the result was jarring and disconcerting, but it flew. The standard had been fixed. Practical results followed.

The first motor-cars were constructed, and their bodies built, on old lines.

This was contrary to the necessities of the displacement and rapid penetration of a solid body. The study of the laws of penetration fixed the standard, a standard which has evolved in accordance with two different aims: speed, the greater mass in front (sporting bodies); comfort, the main bulk at the back (saloon). In either case there is no longer anything in common with the ancient carriage with its slow displacement.

Civilizations advance. They pass through the age of the peasant, the soldier and the priest and attain what is rightly called culture. Culture is the flowering of the effort to select. Selection means rejection, pruning, cleansing; the clear and naked emergence of the Essential.

THE PARTHENON
*Little by little the Greek temple was formulated, passing from construction to Architecture. One hundred years later the Parthenon marked the climax of the ascending curve.*

From the primitiveness of the Early Christian chapel, we pass to *Notre Dame* of Paris, the *Invalides*, the *Place de la Concorde*. Feeling has been clarified and refined, mere decoration set aside and proportion and scale attained, an advance has been made; we have passed from the elementary satisfactions (decoration) to the higher satisfactions (mathematics).

If Breton cupboards still remain in Brittany, it is because the Bretons have continued there, very remote and very stable, fully occupied in their fishing and cattle breeding. It is not seemly that a gentleman of good standing should sleep on a Breton bed in his Paris mansion; it is not seemly that a gentleman who owns a saloon car should sleep in a Breton bed, and so on. We have only to get a clear idea of this and to draw the logical conclusion. To own together a large car and a Breton bed is quite usual, I am sorry to say.

Everybody asserts with conviction and enthusiasm: "The motor-car marks the style of our epoch!" but the Breton bed is sold and manufactured every day by the antique dealers.

THE PARTHENON

*Each part is decisive and marks the highest point in precision and executi
proportion is clearly written therein.*

TRIPLE HYDROPLANE CAPRONI

*Showing how plastic organisms are created in response to a well-stated problem.*

Let us display, then, the Parthenon and the motor-car so that it may be clear that it is a question of two products of selection in different fields, one of which has reached its climax and the other is evolving. That ennobles the automobile. And what then? Well, it remains to use the motor-car as a challenge to our houses and our great buildings. It is here that we come to a dead stop. "Rien ne va plus." Here we have no Parthenons.

CAPRONI-EXPLORATION

*Poetry lies not only in the spoken or written word. The poetry of facts is stronger still. Objects which signify something and which are arranged with talent and with tact create a poetic fact.*

The standard of the house is a question of a practical and constructive order. I have attempted to set it forth in the preceding chapter on airplanes.

The standard of furniture is in its full flood of experiment among the makers of office furniture and trunks, clock-makers and so on. We have only to follow this path: a task for the engineer. And all the humbug talked about the unique object, the precious "piece," rings false and shows a pitiful lack of understanding of the needs of the present day: a chair is in no way a work of art; a chair has no soul; it is a machine for sitting in.

Art, in a highly cultivated country, finds its means of expression in pure art, a concentrated thing free from all utilitarian motives—painting, literature, music.

Every human manifestation involves a certain quantum of interest and particularly so in the æsthetic domain; this interest may be of an order dealing with the senses or of an intellectual order. Decoration is of a sensorial and elementary order, as is colour, and is suited to simple races, peasants and savages. Harmony and proportion incite the intellectual faculties and arrest the man of culture. The peasant loves ornament and decorates his walls. The civilized man wears a well-cut suit and is the owner of easel pictures and books.

Decoration is the essential overplus, the quantum of the peasant; and proportion is the essential overplus, the quantum of the cultivated man.

In architecture, the quantum of interest is achieved by the grouping and proportion of rooms and furniture; a task for the architect. And beauty? This is an imponderable which cannot function except in the actual presence of its primordial bases: the reasonable satisfaction of the mind (utility, economy); after that, cubes, spheres, cylinders, cones, etc. (sensorial). Then . . . the imponderable, the relationships which create the imponderable: this is genius, inventive genius, plastic genius, mathematical genius, this capacity for achieving order and unity by measurement and for organizing, in accordance with evident laws, all those things which excite and satisfy our visual senses to the fullest degree.

Then there arise those multifarious sensations, which evoke all that a highly cultivated man may have seen, felt and loved; which release, by means he cannot escape, vibrations he has already experienced in the drama of life: nature, men, the world.

BELLANGER. SALOON

In this period of science, of strife and drama in which the individual is violently tossed about at every moment, the Parthenon appears to us as a living work, full of grand harmonies. The sum of its inevitable elements gives the measure of the degree of perfection to which man can attain when he is absorbed in a problem definitely stated. The perfection in this case is so much outside the normal, that our apprehension of the Parthenon can only correspond nowadays with a very limited range of sensation, and, unexpectedly enough, with sensations of a mechanical kind; its correspondence is rather with those huge impressive machines with which we are familiar and which may be considered the most perfect results of our present-day activities, the only products of our civilization which have really "got there."

VOISIN. SPORTS TORPEDO, 1921

*It is a simpler matter to form a judgment on the clothes of a well-dressed man than on those of a well-dressed woman, since masculine costume is standardized. It is certain that Phidias was at the side of Ictinos and Kallicrates in building the Parthenon, and that he dominated them, since all the temples of the time were of the same type, and the Parthenon surpasses them all beyond measure.*

*The cone which gives the best penetration is the result of experiment and calculation, and this is confirmed by natural creations such as fishes, birds, etc. Experimental application : the dirigible, racing car.*

IN SEARCH OF A STANDARD

THE PARTHENON

*Phidias in building the Parthenon did not work as a constructor, engineer or designer. All these elements already existed. What he did was to perfect the work and endue it with a noble spirituality.*

Phidias[1] would have loved to have lived in this standardized age. He would have admitted the possibility, nay the certainty of success. His vision would have seen in our epoch the conclusive results of his labours. Before long he would have repeated the experience of the Parthenon.

Architecture is governed by standards. Standards are a matter of logic, analysis and precise study. Standards are based on a problem which has been well stated. Architecture means plastic invention, intellectual speculation, higher mathematics. Architecture is a very noble art.
Standardization is imposed by the law of selection and is an economic and social necessity. Harmony is a state of agreement with the norms of our universe. Beauty governs all; she is of purely human creation; she is the overplus necessary only to men of the highest type.

But we must first of all aim at the setting up of standards in order to face the problem of perfection.

**NOTES**

1.  Phidias was the ancient Greek sculptor in charge of the Parthenon's sculptural program, and, according to Plutarch, was the overseer of the entire Periclean Acropolis project. Fred S. Kleiner, Christin J. Mamiya, and Richard G. Tansey, *Gardner's Art Through the Ages*, 11th edition (Fort Worth: Harcourt College Publishers, 2001), p. 128.

# 1925

## Helen Appleton Read, "The Exposition in Paris"

The American critic Helen Appleton Read (1897–1974) was a student of the painter Robert Henri at the Art Students' League in New York, but is best known as a writer on European and American modern art and architecture. She reported on a number of international expositions in American publications, and during the 1930s conducted a survey of art in United States federal buildings. In these excerpts from a two-part article in *International Studio*, Read discusses the architecture and design displayed in Paris at the influential 1925 *Exposition Internationale des Arts Décoratifs et Industriels Modernes* (International Exposition of Modern Decorative and Industrial Arts). The 1925 Exposition is generally considered the birthplace of the style now called "Art Deco" (which at the time was simply called "modern" or "*moderne*").

Excerpted from Helen Appleton Read, "The Exposition in Paris," parts I and II, *International Studio* (November and December 1925): 93–96 and 161–162.

LA PORTE D'HONNEUR, EXPOSITION DES ARTS DECORATIFS, PARIS

**W**hen Cézanne uttered his historic dictum that all form could be reduced to the cone, the cylinder and the cube, the corner stone was laid for a movement which had its fullest expression in the international *Exposition des Arts Décoratifs* in Paris. Cézanne's esthetique, the credo of modern art, was developed simultaneously with the age of scientific research and the glorification of the machine. Both of these are determining factors in the development of the new *décor*. It was, however, due to Cézanne's pronouncement that we substituted the philosophy of the angle for the curve, that we came to see that the intersection of two planes might be as beautiful as the relation of two colors, and that beauty was as existent in mere mass and proportion as in ornamented shapes. It is due to this that we have learned that designs whose inspirations are the clean lines of the machine may be quite as beautiful as those deriving from animal, human or flower forms. To have absorbed consciously or not this esthetique is a necessary perquisite [sic] to an enjoyment and appreciation of the new note for which the international *Exposition des Arts Décoratifs* stood sponsor.

International by courtesy rather than by fact, for although the nations of the world were invited to join with France to make this a twentieth-century convention of the decorative arts, twenty-six of them accepting, it is after all primarily a French exhibition. France alone is comprehensively represented; it is her exhibits which constitute the major interest and major part of this great dedication of a modern *décor.* Interesting as are many of the foreign pavilions, they can in no way be said to represent their countries, since they show a limited selection representing not so much the country as the special tastes and opinions of a committee, whose judgment in the case of the Italian, the English and the Austrian was, to say the least, doubtful. While on the other hand the French exhibit represents the nation's output, good, bad and indifferent. All had a chance to show—the artists, designers, students and manufacturers of *industries de luxe*—provided that they complied with the requisite of admission which stated that only those exhibits which were not dependent upon the art of the past would be admitted.

The Exposition marks the coming of age of a new *décor.* It differs from any expositions of the past, which have come about with clockwork regularity to celebrate a nation's progress in art and industry—a Wembley, a Pan-American or a San Franciscan—in that it is a setting up of new standards, not a perfecting or adapting of the old. It is a definite break with the past.

[ . . . ]

But the new *décor* does not merely set up new standards for old and ask us to accept them as authentic. It follows as closely the fundamental laws of esthetics as the most traditional and proves again that if harmony of line and proportion is preserved it matters not a jot whether it takes the form geometric, or of lilies. Gone are the time honored motives of the lotus and the *fleur de lis,* the Doric column and the Gothic arch. In their place we are asked to see as beautiful and decorative, angles and geometric designs; instead of ornamentation, flat surfaces and proportioned masses. Gone is all carving and superimposed decoration; interest and variety must depend upon the application of color and flat design, or the quality of beauty existing in the unadorned material.

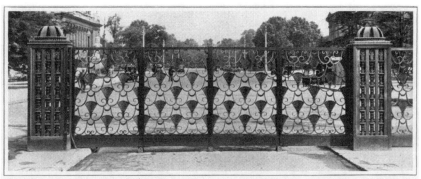

WROUGHT IRON GRILLE OF THE PORTE D'HONNEUR                    BY EDGAR BRANDT

It is characteristic of the new *décor* that the nature of the material is at all times respected and is allowed to dictate its treatment. Wood is wood, iron iron; the bad taste that invariably ensues when the attempt is made to give the quality of one material to another, to make wood look [like] iron or marble like lace, is avoided.

[ . . . ]

The note of the Exposition is set from the moment one enters the wrought-iron gateway of the *Porte d'Honneur* executed by the celebrated *ferronier* Edgar Brandt, whose talent has done so much to add beauty and distinction to the architectural exhibits.[1] From this point of vantage the Exposition can be seen at a glance, its cubist shapes and futurist colors stretching away across the Alexander Bridge to the great dome of Les Invalides, looking like nothing so much as a Picasso abstraction.

[ . . . ]

PAVILLION DE L'INTRANSIGEANT

This universal tendency towards simplicity of outline should be of the greatest interest to the American designer if he will recognize that this is the fundamental note. All design in this country is governed by the factor of whether or not it can be reproduced in mass production. It costs no more to get out a good design than it does a bad one, and the fact that the best designs of the new decor are the simplest to the point of being geometric makes them so much the more easy to put upon the market.

[ . . . ]

COSTUMED WOODEN MANNIQUINS IN THE PAVILLON DE ELÉGANCE

## NOTES

1. *Porte d'Honneur* means "Door (or Entrance) of Honor"; a *ferronier* is an ironworker.

# 1926-1950

# 1928

## Henry Ford, "Machinery, The New Messiah"

The American automobile manufacturer Henry Ford (1863–1947) was something of a messiah figure himself; he was undoubtedly one of the most powerful and influential persons of his time. He founded the Ford Motor Company in 1902, and, in 1908, began production of the Model T, nearly 17,000,000 of which were sold worldwide over the next nineteen years. (In 1927 the Model T was replaced, due to lagging sales, with the more stylish Model A.) The organization, appearance, and management of the Ford factories, where the modern assembly line was born in 1913, was the subject of sustained public interest. Ford's introduction of an eight-hour, $5.00 workday in 1914—in an industry in which the standard shift was nine hours and the average daily pay $2.34[1]— was the kind of innovative business practice for which Ford was renowned. (The $5.00 workday was fairly clearly an implementation of Frederick Winslow Taylor's theories of compensation for "good" employees; only those workers whose workplace performance and home lives were deemed acceptable by Ford's Sociological Department qualified for the higher wage.)[2] In these excerpts from a rather wide-ranging 1928 essay in the magazine *The Forum*, Ford discusses machinery in American society, the maintenance of the human body, and the relation of home life to industry.

Excerpted from Henry Ford, "Machinery, the New Messiah," *The Forum* (March 1928): 359–364.

[ . . . ]

The great problem in the home to-day is that there is too much drudgery there. Although a man's actual working hours a week have decreased, hardly anything has been done to eliminate the fundamental drudgery of housekeeping; there has been no decrease in the hours of wives. Well, the modern young woman who maintains a household and brings up several children is going to change this. She is refusing the drudgery. What you call "the indifference of the young" in this respect is simply a coming event casting its shadow before. They have refused household drudgery, and as a consequence it will disappear.

There is some machinery to use in the kitchen to-day. We have the vacuum cleaner, the various electric appliances, the electric washing machine, the electric ice boxes; but most of it is still too expensive. We must find some way to reduce the cost and some way to lighten the other labors of women. [ . . . ]

[ . . . ]

Food is one of the most important commodities with which we have to deal. I am becoming more convinced every day that we should spend more time in the study of food and how to eat it. Most of us eat too much. We eat the wrong kind of food at the wrong time and ultimately suffer for it. We must find a better way to feed ourselves and provide our bodies with what they need for replenishment and growth. Hitherto, we have spent more time in studying methods of repairing machinery and of renewing mechanisms than we have in studying this fundamental problem of human life. Of course, much has been done by our dietetists, but they have only scratched the surface. One does not have to be a food faddist to be interested in the subject.

Although the normal average life of human beings has been almost doubled in the last fifty years, I feel sure that we shall find means of renewing the human body so that men will retain their health, vitality, and mental keenness for many years longer. Take Edison, for example; to-day he is just as keen mentally as he ever was. There is every reason to believe that we should be able to renew our human bodies in the same manner as we renew a defect in a boiler. Not so long ago we found that our boilers were being discarded because in one or two spots corrosion had set in and weakened the surface.

We had some research work done on the problem and soon found a way to renew this metal at the point of expected failure, so that it was just as good as new. The boiler was put back into operation stronger, if anything, than when it was first installed. [ . . . ]

The point is, if there is enough thinking done along this line, there is no reason why we could not do the same with the human body.

[ . . . ]

Anything that interferes with our ability to think clearly, lead healthy, normal lives, and do our work well will ultimately be discarded, either as an economic handicap or from a desire for better personal health. Tobacco is a narcotic which is exacting a heavy toll from our present generation. No one smokes in the Ford industries. Tobacco is not a good thing for industry nor for the individual.

The coming of prohibition has put more of the workman's money into savings banks and into his wife's pocketbook. He has more leisure to spend with his family. The family life is healthier. Workmen go out of doors, go on picnics, have time to see their children and play with them. They have more time to see more, do more—and, incidentally, they buy more. This stimulates business and *increases prosperity*, and in the general economic circle the money passes through industry again and back into the workman's pocket. It is a truism that what benefits one is bound to benefit all, and labor is coming to see the truth of this more every day.

Human demands are increasing every day and the needs for their gratification are increasing also. This is as it should be. Gradually, under the benign influence of American industry, wives are released from work, little children are no longer exploited; and, given more time, they both become free to go out and find new products, new merchants and manufacturers who are supplying them. Thus business grows. Thus we see the close relation which home life bears to industry. The prosperity of one is the prosperity of the other. In reality, all problems may be resolved into one great one. The parts are all interrelated one with another. The solution of one helps in the solution of another, and so on.

Machinery is accomplishing in the world what man has failed to do by preaching, propaganda, or the written word. The airplane and radio know no boundary. They pass over the dotted lines on the map without heed or hindrance. They are binding the world together in a way no other systems can. The motion picture with its universal language, the airplane with its speed, and the radio with its coming international programme—these will soon bring the whole world to a complete understanding. Thus may we vision a United States of the World. Ultimately, it will surely come!

[ . . . ]

**N O T E S**

1. "Ford, Henry," *Encyclopædia Britannica*, <*http://www.britannica.com/eb/article?eu=117255*>, (accessed 22 December 2002).
2. Terry Smith, *Making the Modern: Industry, Art, and Design in America* (Chicago: University of Chicago Press, 1993): 47.

# 1930

## *Fortune,* "Color in Industry"

*Fortune* magazine was founded by the American Henry Luce (1898–1967), who also published *Time* and *Life* magazines. *Fortune* was a business publication aimed at sophisticated leaders of industry; its $1.00-per-copy price tag, a hefty sum during the lean years of the Great Depression, kept its readership exclusive and helped to defray the expense of the numerous full-color illustrations that graced its pages. *Fortune* prided itself on providing well-written and well-researched reports—accompanied by exceptional photography and artwork—on the latest developments in industry. This anonymous essay from the very first issue of *Fortune* discusses the importance of color in product design.

---

Excerpted from "Color in Industry," *Fortune* (February 1930): 85–86. Reprinted by permission of *Fortune*.

---

Consider, for a moment, a red bed. Red is a common color and a bed is a fundamental article of furniture. Yet the combination of the two had, until very recently, almost a startling effect. Grandmother, perhaps, would have thought a red bed immoral. Mother would have considered it at least peculiar. Nearly anyone in, say, 1920, would have expected to find only a Red in a red bed.

Yet, within the past five or six years, thousands of red beds have blossomed in corresponding thousands of American bedrooms. Also have arrived blue beds, green beds, yellow beds, purple beds, mauve beds, and blue, green, yellow, purple and mauve bedspreads to cover them. There is now nothing startling about color in the bedroom—although architecture remains drably monotone. For during the past few years a great pail has up-ended itself over the American scene, has splashed our household goods and gods with a rich, warm stream of flat, bright color.

Remember, for contrast's sake, the home of 1920 and of 1925. Here there were chiefly natural colors. Kitchen and bathroom were a porcelain and surgical white. Furniture was in natural wood tints, surfaced with colorless finish. The stove was black. Faucets were metallic. Things were, so to speak, as God made them—each object deriving its color from the material of which it was fashioned. Even the family car was black, or some dull, dark color allied to blackness. In the nursery, perhaps, Junior possessed and treasured a blue horse. Only in the nursery, however, was such a contradiction of nature permissible.

Turn now to the thoroughly painted home of 1928. Here so utilitarian an object as a sink was purchased from a color range of T'äng Red, Orchid of Vincennes, Royal Copenhagen Blue, Ivoire de Medici, St. Porchaire Brown, Rose du Barry, Ionian Black, Clair de Lune Blue, Ming Green and Meissen White. In the cellar stood a Redflash Boiler, more crimson than the flames in the adjacent furnace. On the door of the orange refrigerator was perched a bright green parrot. Not only the dishes, but the pots and pans were decked in bright gay tints and tones. A green-tiled bathroom was set off with green tub, green towels and, monstrously enough, green toilet paper. For afternoon tea there were blue glasses and a yellow cloth. A yellow alarm clock—a cherry garbage can—a scarlet typewriter—surfaces had turned suddenly into palettes. Nor had such staples as chairs, desks and tables missed submergence in color's rising tide. As for automobiles—the autumn woods showed no more varied or more brilliant plumage.

The aesthetic value of all this decoration was, in many instances, open to question and, in its more extreme vagaries, color suffered from the fevered and fleeting qualities of a fad. Yet in a country so long committed to the proposition that where there is beauty there is decadence, the acceptance of color was undoubtedly significant from the standpoint of old traditions being abandoned and old suppressions being released.

[ . . . ]

# 1930

## Sigmund Freud, *Civilization and Its Discontents*

The Austrian Sigmund Freud (1856–1939), the founder of the field of psychoanalysis, wrote as provocatively about human society as he did about the human mind. In his 1930 book, *Civilization and Its Discontents*, he compared the cultural development of civilizations to the psychic development of individuals. Freud's comments about the roles of technology and hygiene in human societies are particularly fascinating, given the dramatic increases in the levels of both during his lifetime. (The theory of antisepsis, for example, which was developed during Freud's childhood, became universally accepted in the early twentieth century.)

[ . . . ]

During the last few generations mankind has made an extraordinary advance in the natural sciences and in their technical application and has established his control over nature in a way never before imagined. The single steps of this advance are common knowledge and it is unnecessary to enumerate them. Men are proud of those achievements, and have a right to be. But they seem to have observed that this newly-won power over space and time, this subjugation of the forces of nature, which is the fulfilment of a longing that goes back thousands of years, has not increased the amount of pleasurable satisfaction which they may expect from life and has not made them feel happier. From the recognition of this fact we ought to be content to conclude that power over nature is not the *only* precondition of human happiness, just as it is not the *only* goal of cultural endeavour; we ought not to infer from it that technical progress is without value for the economics of our happiness. One would like to ask: is there, then, no positive gain in pleasure, no unequivocal increase in my feeling of happiness, if I can, as often as I please, hear the voice of a child of mine who is living hundreds of miles away or if I can learn in the shortest possible time after a friend has reached his destination that he has come through the long and difficult voyage unharmed? Does it mean nothing that medicine has succeeded in enormously reducing infant mortality and the danger of infection for women in childbirth, and, indeed, in considerably lengthening the average life of a civilized man? And there is a long list that might be added to benefits of this kind which we owe to the much-despised era of scientific and technical advances. But here the voice of pessimistic criticism makes itself heard and warns us that most of these satisfactions follow the model of the 'cheap enjoyment' extolled in the anecdote—the enjoyment obtained by putting a bare leg from under the bed-clothes on a cold winter night and drawing it in again. If there had been no railway to conquer distances, my child would never have left his native town and I should need no telephone to hear his voice; if travelling across the ocean by ship had not been introduced, my friend would not have embarked on his sea-voyage and I should not need a cable to relieve my anxiety about him. What is the use of reducing infantile mortality when it is precisely that reduction which imposes the greatest restraint on us in the begetting of children, so that, taken all round, we nevertheless rear no more children than in the days before the reign of hygiene, while at the same time we have created difficult conditions for our sexual life in marriage, and have probably worked against the beneficial effects of natural selection? And, finally, what good to us is a long life if it is difficult and barren of joys, and if it is so full of misery that we can only welcome death as a deliverer?

It seems certain that we do not feel comfortable in our present-day civilization, but it is very difficult to form an opinion whether and in what degree men of an earlier age felt happier and what part their cultural conditions played in the matter. [ . . . ]

It is time for us to turn our attention to the nature of this civilization on whose value as a means to happiness doubts have been thrown. We shall not look for a formula in which to express that nature in a few words, until we have learned something by examining it. We shall therefore content ourselves with saying once more that the word 'civilization' describes the whole sum of the achievements and the regulations which distinguish our lives from those of our animal ancestors and which serve two purposes—namely to protect men against nature and to adjust their mutual relations. [ . . . ]

[ . . . ] We recognize as cultural all activities and resources which are useful to men for making the earth serviceable to them, for protecting them against the violence of the forces of nature, and so on. As regards this side of civilization, there can be scarcely any doubt. If we go back far enough, we find that the first acts of civilization were the use of tools, the gaining of control over fire and the construction of dwellings. Among these, the control over fire stands out as a quite extraordinary and unexampled achievement, while the others opened up paths which man has followed ever since, and the stimulus to which is easily guessed. With every tool man is perfecting his own organs, whether motor or sensory, or is removing the limits to their functioning. Motor power places gigantic forces at his disposal, which, like his muscles, he can employ in any direction; thanks to ships and aircraft neither water nor air can hinder his movements; by means of spectacles he corrects defects in the lens of his own eye; by means of the telescope he sees into the far distance; and by means of the microscope he overcomes the limits of visibility set by the structure of his retina. In the photographic camera he has created an instrument which retains the fleeting visual impressions, just as a gramophone disc retains the equally fleeting auditory ones; both are at bottom materializations of the power he possesses of recollection, his memory. With the help of the telephone he can hear at distances which would be respected as unattainable even in a fairy tale. Writing was in its origin the voice of an absent person; and the dwelling-house was a substitute for the mother's womb, the first lodging, for which in all likelihood man still longs, and in which he was safe and felt at ease.

[ . . . ] Man has, as it were, become a kind of prosthetic God. When he puts on all his auxiliary organs he is truly magnificent; but those organs have not grown on to him and they still give him much trouble at times. Nevertheless, he is entitled to console himself with the thought that this development will not come to an end precisely with the year 1930 A.D. Future ages will bring with them new and probably unimaginably great advances in this field of civilization and will increase man's likeness to God still more. But in the interests of our investigations, we will not forget that present-day man does not feel happy in his Godlike character.

We recognize, then, that countries have attained a high level of civilization if we find that in them everything which can assist in the exploitation of the earth by man and in his protection against the forces of nature—everything, in short, which is of use to him—is attended to and effectively carried out. [...] We [also] require civilized man to reverence beauty wherever he sees it in nature and to create it in the objects of his handiwork so far as he is able. But this is far from exhausting our demands on civilization. We expect besides to see the signs of cleanliness and order. We do not think highly of the cultural level of an

English country town in Shakespeare's time when we read that there was a big dung-heap in front of his father's house in Stratford; we are indignant and call it 'barbarous' (which is the opposite of civilized) when we find the paths in the Wiener Wald[1] littered with paper. Dirtiness of any kind seems to us incompatible with civilization. We extend our demand for cleanliness to the human body too. We are astonished to learn of the objectionable smell which emanated from the *Roi Soleil*;[2] and we shake our heads on the Isola Bella[3] when we are shown the tiny wash-basin in which Napoleon made his morning toilet. Indeed, we are not surprised by the idea of setting up the use of soap as an actual yardstick of civilization. The same is true of order. It, like cleanliness, applies solely to the works of man. But whereas cleanliness is not to be expected in nature, order, on the contrary, has been imitated from her. [ . . . ]

Beauty, cleanliness and order obviously occupy a special position among the requirements of civilization. No one will maintain that they are as important for life as control over the forces of nature or as some other factors with which we shall become acquainted. And yet no one would care to put them in the background as trivialities. That civilization is not exclusively taken up with what is useful is already shown by the example of beauty, which we decline to omit from among the interests of civilization. The usefulness of order is quite evident. With regard to cleanliness, we must bear in mind that it is demanded of us by hygiene as well, and we may suspect that even before the days of scientific prophylaxis the connection between the two was not altogether strange to man. Yet utility does not entirely explain these efforts; something else must be at work besides. [ . . . ]

[ . . . ] The development of civilization appears to us as a peculiar process which mankind undergoes, and in which several things strike us as familiar. We may characterize this process with reference to the changes which it brings about in the familiar instinctual dispositions of human beings, to satisfy which is, after all, the economic task of our lives. A few of these instincts are used up in such a manner that something appears in their place which, in an individual, we describe as a character-trait. The most remarkable example of such a process is found in the anal erotism of young human beings. Their original interest in the excretory function, its organs and products, is changed in the course of their growth into a group of traits which are familiar to us as parsimony, a sense of order and cleanliness—qualities which, though valuable and welcome in themselves, may be intensified till they become markedly dominant and produce what is called the anal character. How this happens we do not know, but there is no doubt about the correctness of the finding. Now we have seen that order and cleanliness are important requirements of civilization, although their vital necessity is not very apparent, any more than their suitability as sources of enjoyment. At this point we cannot fail to be struck by the similarity between the process of civilization and the libidinal development of the individual. Other instincts [besides anal erotism] are induced to displace the conditions for their satisfaction, to lead them into other paths. In most cases this process coincides with that of the *sublimation* (of instinctual aims) with which we are familiar, but in some it can be differentiated from it. Sublimation of instinct is an especially conspicuous feature of cultural development; it is what makes it possible for higher psychical activities, scientific, artistic or ideological, to play such an important part in civilized life. If one were to yield to a first impression, one would say that sublimation is a vicissitude which has been forced upon the instincts entirely by civilization. But it would be wiser to reflect upon this a little longer. In the third place, finally, and this seems the most important of all, it is impossible to overlook the extent to which civilization is built up upon a renunciation of instinct, how much it presupposes precisely the non-satisfaction (by suppression, repression or some other means?) of powerful instincts. This 'cultural frustration' dominates the large field of social relationships between human beings. As we already know, it is the cause of the hostility against which all civilizations have to struggle. It will also make severe demands on our scientific work, and we shall have much to explain here. It is not easy to understand how it can become possible to deprive an instinct of satisfaction. Nor is doing so without danger. If the loss is not compensated for economically, one can be certain that serious disorders will ensue.

[ . . . ]

## NOTES

1. The woods around Vienna.
2. The "Sun King," Louis XIV of France (1643–1715), who was reputed to have bathed only twice in his life, both times on doctor's orders.
3. An island in Lake Maggiore, Italy.

# 1932

# Earnest Elmo Calkins, "What Consumer Engineering Really Is"

Earnest Elmo Calkins (1868–1964), head of the New York advertising firm Calkins and Holden, was probably the single most prominent American advertiser of the 1920s and 1930s. He and his partner Ralph Holden billed their firm as a "modern" ad agency, emphasizing the importance of good design in print advertisements, packaging, and promotional materials. Calkins wrote extensively about advertising and product design, and promoted "artificial obsolescence" as an answer both to the economic woes of the Great Depression and to the question of how to increase Americans' standard of living (artificial obsolescence, of course, was a strategy that came under fire in subsequent years for being wasteful and environmentally irresponsible). In these excerpts from the introduction to *Consumer Engineering,* a book written by industrial designers Roy Sheldon and Egmont Arens, Calkins argues in favor of this "new business science," whose task was to ensure that Americans consumed as many products as the factories could make.

Excerpted from Earnest Elmo Calkins, "What Consumer Engineering Really Is," the introduction to *Consumer Engineering,* by Roy Sheldon and Egmont Arens (Copyright ©1932 by Harper and Brothers; copyright © renewed 1952 by Roy Sheldon and Egmont Arens): 1, 4–8, 13–14. Reprinted by permission of Harper-Collins Publishers, Inc.

The newest business tool to receive a definite name is what has come to be known as consumer engineering. Briefly it is shaping a product to fit more exactly consumers' needs or tastes, but in its widest sense it includes any plan which stimulates the consumption of goods.

[ . . . ]

This was the situation in 1929. The making and selling of goods had reached a maximum pitch of efficiency. We were riding on a high wave of prosperity. Suddenly the nation received a shock. The collapse of the stock market stunned everybody. It paralyzed the spirit of free spending that had prevailed for several years.

Many stopped buying while still able financially to continue, and many are still able but restrained by fear and misplaced thrift. The sudden cessation of buying slowed up the entire industrial machine. Retail storekeepers curtailed orders to factories. Factories cut down production, reduced wages, laid off men, still further reducing the number of customers for goods. In a comparatively short time, with all the resources of the country still intact, we had depression. There were no longer enough buyers for the large quantities of goods we had learned to make and distribute so abundantly.

[ . . . ]

Strange as it may seem, a definite program for adapting goods to the needs and desires of the people who buy them is a comparatively new thing. In the early days the manufacturer decided what he would make, what color or design, how large the unit of quantity, every detail. There it was. The consumer could take it or leave it. Goods were not intelligently adapted to their markets even in those days, and certainly have not been coordinated with the changing habits of the people. The revolution in everyday living in the years since the war has been amazing. The manufacturers of some goods have kept pace with it, but the majority have ignored it. Take so simple a matter as the hunger for color and design in old familiar standardized articles that has arisen no one knows how. Note how successfully a few manufacturers have catered to this budding sense of beauty and made their products newly acceptable. It is going on all around you. Heaters, bathtubs, linoleums, kitchen ware, fountain pens, and typewriters. If you could put them beside the ugly counterparts of yesterday you would be astonished at the improvement. Sensing this growing demand for better taste in machine-made products is one of the earlier and simpler forms of consumer engineering.

[ . . . ]

Obsoletism is another device for stimulating consumption. The element of style is a consideration in buying many things. Clothes go out of style and are replaced long before they are worn out. That principle extends to other products—motor-cars, bathrooms, radios, foods, refrigerators, furniture. People are persuaded to abandon the old and buy the new to be up-to-date, to have the right and correct thing. Does there seem to be a sad waste in the process? Not at all. Wearing things out does not produce prosperity, but buying things does. Thrift in the industrial society in which we now live consists of keeping all the factories busy. Any plan which increases the consumption of goods is justifiable if we believe that prosperity is a desirable thing. If we do not, we can turn back the page to earlier and more primitive times when people got along with little and made everything last as long as possible. We have built up a complicated industrial machine and we must go on with it, or throw it into reverse and go backward.

"In the light of all the facts, which seem inescapable," says Robert P. Scripps, editorial director of the Scripps-Howard newspapers, "this conclusion seems inevitable: that unless we are going to break up the machines, put the scientists in jail, and generally try to make our clocks run in reverse, the only balance to increase potential per-capita production can be increased per-capital spending, or leisure, or a combination of both."

[ . . . ]

We have seen in a comparatively short time a complete reversal of much of the garnered economic wisdom of the centuries. Many of the old copy-book maxims have been scrapped. We have learned that prosperity lies in spending, not in saving. For years we thought that low-cost labor increased the profits of manufacture. Now we know that highly paid labor produces greater profits, and the highly paid laborers furnish the customers. The increased profits come from increased production made possible by increased consumption. With his wages and his dividends the workman buys more goods, products of his own and other factories, a cooperative arrangement of the highest potential significance. *Any interruption of this perfect balance is the concern of the whole industry, for it means that the supply of consumers is threatened.* We engineered an adequate supply of goods. We can engineer an adequate supply of customers. Unemployment means underconsumption, and underconsumption means the consumer is not buying. The cause may be that the goods are obsolete, or merely that the consumer has no money, but it is the duty of the consumer engineer to find the cause and remedy it. "Overproduction," says Henry Ford, "means something out of date."

[ . . . ]

Consumer engineering is the new business science. Some would call it Direction of Distribution, but that does not go far enough. I prefer the term that suggests the scientific approach. Distribution once meant merely getting the goods stocked in the retail store. Today our thinking has advanced to that point where by distribution we mean actually in the hands of the consumers. But even that is too static for this rapid-paced age. Are the consumers consuming them fast enough? Goods fall into two classes, those we use, such as motor-cars or safety razors, and those we use *up*, such as toothpaste or soda biscuit. Consumer engineering must see to it that we use *up* the kind of goods we now merely use. Would any change in the goods or the habits of people speed up their consumption? Can they be displaced by newer models? Can artificial obsolescence be created? Consumer engineering does not end until we can consume all we can make.

[ . . . ]

# 1934

## Alfred H. Barr, Jr. and Philip Johnson, *Machine Art*

The American art historian Alfred H. Barr, Jr. (1902–1981) was the director of the Museum of Modern Art, New York, from its founding in 1929 to his retirement in 1967. Few other curators have had so profound an influence on—or so powerful a hand in shaping the direction of—the history of art. In the groundbreaking 1934 show, *Machine Art*, Philip Johnson (1906– ), the curator of the Department of Architecture, exhibited functional industrial products such as ball bearings, springs, and propellers alongside "machine age" decorative arts. The purpose of the exhibition was apparently to foster what Barr called in the foreword an "appreciation of their beauty in the platonic sense."

Excerpted and reprinted by permission from *Machine Art,* ©1934 The Museum of Modern Art, New York (references omitted).

## Technical and Material Beauty.

In addition to perfection of shape and rhythm, beauty of surface is an important aesthetic quality of machine art at its best. Perfection of surface is, of course, made possible by the refinement of modern materials and the precision of machine manufacture. A watch spring is beautiful not only for its spiral shape but also for its bright steel surface and its delicately exact execution.

Machine art, devoid as it should be of surface ornament, must depend upon the sensuous beauty of porcelain, enamel, celluloid, glass of all colors, copper, aluminum, brass and steel. The circles and spheres of a ball bearing (No. 50) are greatly enhanced by the contrasting surfaces of brushed steel races, shining polished steel balls, and brass carriers.

## Visual Complexity.

The beauty in machine art as in all art varies in relation but not in proportion to its complexity. A watch crystal, perfect though it may be, is too simple a form to hold our visual interest for long. A printing press, on the other hand, is too complicated an arrangement of shapes for the human eye to enjoy aesthetically. Moderately simple machine compositions such as the door of a wall safe (No. 91) or the microscope (No. 314) or our classical example, the ball bearing (No. 50) prove more satisfactory.

## Function.

A knowledge of function may be of considerable importance in the visual enjoyment of machine art, though Plato might have considered such knowledge an impurity. Mechanical function and utilitarian function—"how it works" and "what it does"—are distinct problems, the former requiring in many cases a certain understanding of mechanics, the latter, of practical use. Whoever understands the dynamics of pitch in propeller blades (No. 41) or the distribution of forces in a ball bearing (No. 50) so that he can participate imaginatively in the action of mechanical functions is likely to find that this knowledge enhances the beauty of the objects. In the same way, using or understanding the use of, the calipers (No. 294), the retort (No. 394), or the rotary floor polisher (No. 71) is likely to increase their aesthetic value.

Fortunately the functional beauty of most of the objects is not obscure and in any case, so far as this exhibition is concerned, appreciation of their beauty in the platonic sense is more important.

[ . . . ]

*A. H. B., Jr.*

[ . . . ]

## The Scope of the Exhibition

The Exhibition contains machines, machine parts, scientific instruments and objects useful in ordinary life. There are no purely ornamental objects; the useful objects were, however, chosen for their aesthetic quality. Some will claim that usefulness is more important than beauty, or that usefulness makes an object beautiful. This Exhibition has been assembled from the point of view that though usefulness is an essential, appearance has at least as great a value.

The Exhibition cannot be exhaustive. The very number of useful objects and machines made it impossible even to cover the whole field in making the choices. Exigencies of space prohibited many large items. Inaccessibility prevented choosing items locally distributed in the Far and Middle West. Yet the Exhibition tries to be representative. Some fields, the kitchen and the laboratory, for example, are more fully present than others. This is because the nineteenth century did not consider these objects worthy of decorative treatment.

For the convenience of the reader and the visitor to the Exhibition, the list of objects is divided according to use into six categories.

1. **Industrial units:** Machines and machine parts: springs, insulators, cable sections, propeller blades, etc.
2. **Household and office equipment:** Sink, furnace, bathroom cabinets, dishwasher, carpet sweeper and business machines.
3. **Kitchenware**
4. **House furnishings and accessories:** Objects used in daily life: tableware, vases and bowls, smoking accessories, lighting fixtures, and furniture.
5. **Scientific instruments:** Precision, optical, drafting and surveying instruments.
6. **Laboratory glass and porcelain:** Beakers, hydrometer jars, petri dishes and boiling flasks.

*[P. J.]*

# 1934

## Norman Bel Geddes, "Streamlining"

The American Norman Bel Geddes's (1893–1958) first claim to fame was as a designer of innovative stage sets; however, he also worked in the fields of illustration, interior design, exhibition design, and, most notably, industrial design. Like Buckminster Fuller, in the 1930s, Bel Geddes produced many plans and predictions for future products, transportation forms, and technologies, a number of which have been—albeit in slightly altered form—realized over the course of the twentieth century. In the 1930s, Bel Geddes was a major proponent of streamlining, and in these excerpts from his 1934 *Atlantic Monthly* article on that subject, he examined its origins, applications, and possibilities.

Excerpted from Norman Bel Geddes, "Streamlining," *Atlantic Monthly* (November 1934): 553, 556–8. Reprinted by permission of the Estate of Edith Luytens Bel Geddes.

Originally, the word 'streamline' was a term of hydrodynamics. About the year 1909 the science of aerodynamics borrowed it to describe smooth flow of air as well as the form of a body which would move through air with a minimum of resistance. For some years 'streamline' in its aerodynamic sense enjoyed honorable obscurity in the physics laboratory and the shop talk of engineers. Last year, however, advertising copy writers seized upon it as a handy synonym for the word 'new,' using it indiscriminately and often inexactly to describe automobiles and women's dresses, railroad trains and men's shoes. Into such general use has the word come that it is, perhaps, time to examine its meaning and its implications.

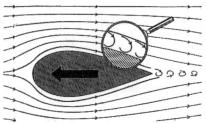

Fig. 1—The boundary layer follows the form of a streamlined body

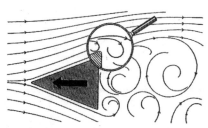

Fig. 2 — The boundary layer breaks away from a non-streamlined body

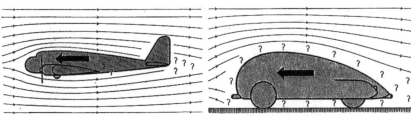

Fig. 3 — Airplane streamlining is very effective. There are few places where the flow pattern is uncertain

Fig. 4 — The ground effect makes the flow pattern around a motor car a matter of conjecture at best

The truth of the matter is that very little is known about streamlining. Most of the popular explanations have treated it as though the facts were established and accepted, and in this respect some technical treatises have not been without fault. Streamlining as a science has not yet really been born. Its practical development in aeronautics has been highly effective, but not understood. In other fields, both in theory and in practice, it is still in embryo.

[ . . . ]

In spite of the hiatus here and there in the theory, parasite drag in the airplane has been eliminated to an amazing degree by the empirical method, and airplane streamlining can be considered to be approaching practical perfection. In 1918 a 400-horsepower motor drove a plane at 125 miles per hour. To-day the equivalent power in a comparable plane would produce a speed of perhaps 200 miles per hour.

In the scientific sense, streamlining, so highly developed in the airplane, has made but little progress in the motor car, the railroad train, and the steamship, all of which stand to gain in efficiency, riding comfort, and economy when drag is reduced. Though streamline attempts have been made in several trains and motor cars, their influence on drag is open to question. In the American mass-production automotive fields, only the Chrysler and De Soto can be considered as pointing toward authentic streamline form. Nevertheless the significance of these two cars lies not in their streamline efficiency but in the foresight and courage shown by Walter P. Chrysler in departing abruptly from traditional attitudes of appearance. What the scientifically streamlined automobile will look like can merely be assumed within fairly broad limits, but it will certainly bear little resemblance to the car of to-day. The weaning of public taste from its illogical prejudices in the matter of appearance is paving the way for whatever form will best meet the automobile's requirements.

It has become fashionable of late to predict what streamlining will do for the motor car and the train. Unusually high speeds have been foreseen and practically no fuel consumption at all. While it is perfectly reasonable to expect a great deal from streamlining, the fact remains that its possibilities in the automobile and the train have been viewed through glasses made rose-color by the experience of aeronautics. Because of two factors not encountered in the free flight of an airplane, present knowledge does not assure us that the airplane's great success in overcoming parasite drag will be easily repeated in a vehicle moving in contact with the ground. [ . . . ]

[ . . . ]

From the technical point of view, then, streamlining of the motor car must reduce resistance to the air, both head-on and from the side, and must maintain present stability or improve it. The first and simplest step, and the one which is now under way, is the elimination of protuberances—headlights, fenders, door hinges, spare tires. Clean continuous lines from front to rear would aid in reaching all the objectives. The second and certainly equally important step is the development of the form. It is probable that this form will be a compromise, for it is extremely unlikely that any single solution can ideally satisfy all requirements. More than that cannot intelligently be said at the present time, nor can the form be foretold until the advent of sound data specific to the motor car, or until theory becomes more complete.

The technical requirements are not the only ones, however, and it is to be expected that further compromises will be necessary to provide convenience and comfort—two factors that are becoming increasingly important as the car ceases to be an article of sporting equipment and takes its place with the stove and the toothbrush as a normal commodity. [ . . . ]

[ . . . ]

# 1935

## Marcy Babbitt, "As a Woman Sees Design: An Interview with Belle Kogan"

Little is known about Marcy Babbitt—she seems not to have published extensively in the 1930s—but the subject of her article, the Russian-born American Belle Kogan (1902–2000), was one of the first women to adopt the new title of "industrial designer."[1] After designing metalwork for the Quaker Silver Company in the 1920s, she opened her own design firm in 1931 in New York City; her clients included Red Wing Pottery, Bausch and Lomb, Boonton Molding, Libbey Glass, and Dow Chemical.[2] In this interview, Kogan outlines some of the design possibilities of plastics, and comments on the roles and responsibilities of the industrial designer.

Excerpted from Marcy Babbitt, "As a Woman Sees Design: An Interview with Belle Kogan," *Modern Plastics*, vol. 13, no. 4 (December 1935): 16–17, 49, 51. Reprinted by permission of *Modern Plastics*, a publication of Chemical Week Associates, Inc.

"**I**n plastics the manufacturer has a material with tremendous possibilities," says Miss Kogan. "It is still in the active process of growth and development, but is rapidly gaining its stride. It is a material which no manufacturer, if he be alert and watchful of his competition, can afford to overlook. Radios, clocks, dishes, jewelry—all being developed in plastics today—have an enormous significance.

"Laboratory staffs and engineers are working toward a greater perfection of materials and compositions; for a finer classification of types of plastics; for a more practical and workable substance for molding and shaping larger sizes. It is inevitable that in the near future the world of manufacture will engage in a huge business of plastics—a business unconceived ten or even five years ago.

"But the thing which needs most to be understood by the manufacturer—particularly at this stage of our commercial development—is that the sale of any product is greatly determined by the reaction of the feminine consumer."

In considering the marketing and merchandising of any commodity, the modern manufacturer is confronted with the problem of pleasing the American housewife. Thirty million women—all potential customers—constituting practically the entire buying structure of the nation—comprise a force which cannot or should not be disregarded. The tastes of the American woman, her reaction to color and form, are of vital importance to the manufacturer.

And to those manufacturers who are using or who are planning to use plastics in the production of commodities, the feminine viewpoint is one to be studied closely, to be understood, to be coddled. Objects are being produced now in plastics which demand improved design before they can enjoy a wider consumer acceptance. Other things cry out for creation, which have not yet been conceived by any manufacturer.

No matter what the object is—whether an article already in manufacture or one soon to be produced—it must be styled for its appeal to women if the manufacturer wants a sales success. Articles manufactured in mass production for a popular priced market demand a knowledge of feminine buying psychology.

Today there is probably no one group more keenly alive to the caprices and demands of the buying public as industrial designers[.] The designer's viewpoint, therefore, is a valuable one from the basis of manufacture as well as from the basis of merchandising and selling. It is a broad conception of consumer[s'] desire.

"The women of today," says Miss Kogan, "those who belong to the middle classes (and these are the women who comprise the greatest group of consumers) want attractive things, things which are smart and things which are new. They are still interested in keeping up with the "Joneses." Items, to be readily accept-able[,] cannot, however, be too extreme in design. Such items do not fit into the average home, decorated as it is, with objects which are not too modern or severe in color or form.

"In designing for mass production, the designer must be aware of two things. First, he or she must know who the ultimate consumer is likely to be. Secondly, in designing for a popular priced market, there must be a realization of the limit to what can be done with color and form, and the designer must confine his designs within these limitations. Designs must be practical, not only for satisfactory manufacture, but practical from the standpoint of their utilitarian appeal to the public."

In questioning Miss Kogan as to her definition of the word "practical," she said: "Any device which will help a manufacturer to sell more goods can be defined as 'practical'."

[ . . . ]

As an artist, Miss Kogan is naturally sensitive to color and form. She deplores each error of design where plastics are misused. "It is most unfortunate, indeed, that manufacturers fail to take full advantage of plastic materials in creating new designs. There is too strong a tendency to imitate the materials used previously or at least to imitate their form and design. It should be realized that with new materials which can be so cleverly molded and machined, new forms are not only possible but are to be desired, and we must try to discover these new applications," she declares.

[ . . . ]

In spite of an occasional impatience with what she considers "lost opportunities" in plastic design, Miss Kogan believes the plastic field has gone through a relatively short period of bad design. There has been very little static acceptance of the material, both from a design and a manufacturing viewpoint. In general, both designer and manufacturer have felt that with a new material they must do new and interesting things. The host of articles on the market today, which employ plastics in an ingenious and clever manner, are witness to the excellent treatment given to the material.

[ . . . ]

NOTES

1. No entries appear under the name Marcy Babbitt in the *Industrial Arts Index*, the *Art Index*, or the *Reader's Guide to Periodical Literature* during the 1930s.

2. Ella Howard and Eric Setliff, "In a Man's World: Women Industrial Designers," in *Women Designers in the USA, 1900–2000: Diversity and Difference*, edited by Pat Kirkham (New Haven: Yale University Press/Bard Graduate Center, 2000): 271–3.

# 1936

## *Fortune,* "What Man Has Joined Together . . ."

This anonymous essay from the American magazine *Fortune* (see the introduction to "Color in Industry," 1930) challenged the widespread notion that the "Plastic Age" had arrived. Its writer explored the reasons for the popularity of plastics in some industries and their lack of impact in others, claiming—somewhat surprisingly—that ultimately plastics had failed to live up to their promise.

Excerpted from "What Man Has Joined Together . . . ," *Fortune* (March 1936): 69, 149–150. Reprinted by permission of *Fortune.*

O nly God can make a tree—and for that matter, until half a century ago, the divine monopoly on primary substances was almost universal. Man had learned how to make a great number of *things*, but for his solid materials he was mostly dependent on such natural products as stone, wood, and the metals. One outstanding exception to this rule was glass, a material of primary character altogether different in kind and function from the materials that went into it. And there were a few other such. But, by and large, industry was tied to the earth's apron strings and had never dreamed of creating a material world of its own.

[ . . . ]

The synthetic plastic, therefore, is a glamorous substance and a tribute to the powers of man. In the light of it the layman has been taught to believe that an age of plastics is at hand. There is a widespread impression that plastics have been making phenomenal industrial progress; that they are about to supersede glass, wood, porcelain, rubber, and even metal; that, in short, instead of being conditioned by the demands of industry, they have reached a point where they themselves can condition those demands. [ . . . ]

[ . . . ]

Now in spite of their remarkable depression record, plastics, as we have already said, have fallen far short of the future that was predicted for them by the prophets of the Plastic Age. Perhaps the prophets were too sanguine, or perhaps the manufacturers have not made the most of their opportunities; no one knows because an appraisal has never been made. Why, for instance, is a lamp globe or a scale housing made of a plastic while a typewriter chassis and most doorknobs are not? Why are gears for machinery only *sometimes* made of plastic? Are plastics, in their various branches, universal materials capable of displacing all others?

One cannot hope to answer these questions while the industry is so young. One can, however, lay down some generalities. When a plastic is substituted for some other material it is always for one of three reasons: (1) it may possess physical properties, other than color, that make it practically indispensable almost regardless of relative cost, as with most of the electrical applications of the phenolics; (2) it may be cheaper than the material it replaces, as with the Celluloid toilet sets in the place of ivory or amber; (3) it may have some desirable qualities, such as color, lightness, finish, nonconductivity of electricity, or, as with dentures, [non]conductivity of heat that make it preferable even at a fractionally higher cost but not beyond a certain differential.

When, on the other hand, an article which obviously *might* be made of plastics is not, there are also three broad reasons: (1) greater cost without countervailing advantages over the traditional material, as with a filing cabinet or a desk; (2) mechanical limitations which may be absolute, as is the present impossibility of molding a turret top for an automobile, or relative, as in the case of the typewriter frame, which could be made of a plastic if the advantages in so doing justified reëngineering the typewriter so that its frame would be sufficiently simple to be a moldable piece; and (3) the remoteness of most of the manufacturers of plastic materials from the ultimate user of plastic objects, which inhibits promotion and sales. An ideal article for plastics is the doorknob, but the hardware and lock industries have such big investments in machinery for metal doorknobs that they will not change, and there is little that the plastics manufacturer can do about it.

Among the properties of plastics that make them preferable to other materials but not indispensable, color comes first. But no industrial revolution is going to be based on color alone. The reason that the future looks bright for cellulose acetate is because it not only takes color but it also has wide fabricating possibilities. Its invasion of the automotive field illustrates the substitution of a plastic for another material even though it costs more, mainly because it looks better. [ . . . ]

Styling, next to color, is another quality that opens up markets to plastics even though at higher cost. And here even the serious-minded molded phenolics get their share of benefit. For example, during the depression manufacturers of toilet goods and cosmetics turned to dressing up their packaging for greater sales appeal, with plastic bottle tops to take the place of tin and cork. Drug manufacturers started the ball rolling by using molded phenolics for their closures, although Durez and Bakelite bottle tops then cost four times as much as metal.

Finally there are those applications in which plastics, once perhaps only better than something else, have become indispensable or irreplaceably superior.

They include, for example, automobile distributor heads, radio parts, telephone receivers, and the like. Eliminate molded phenolics, bring back hard rubber in their place, and you would have a regression in automotive and electrical technology. In the same way urea, which is today simply a desirable material for scale housings, may be irreplaceable tomorrow in the scale industry.

Plastics are not even potentially a universal material, and a Plastic Age, in the sense that we have had a Steel Age, is more or less of a myth. Given a little time, however, the semblance of it may come about.

# 1940

## Harold Van Doren, "The Designer's Place in Industry"

Harold Van Doren (1895–1957), an American, was profiled in a February, 1934 *Fortune* magazine article—along with luminaries such as Walter Dorwin Teague, Raymond Loewy, and Henry Dreyfuss—as a promising member of the "new" profession of industrial design. In 1940, Van Doren published what was probably the first textbook on industrial design *per se*. In these excerpts from the beginning pages of that book, Van Doren outlines some of the qualities he believed to be characteristic of a good industrial designer.

Excerpted from Harold Van Doren, *Industrial Design: A Practical Guide* (New York: McGraw-Hill, 1940): 16–17, 22, 26–7. Reprinted by permission of McGraw-Hill.

I f appearance design is really important to the scheme of things industrial, just where does the designer fit into that scheme and what is his relative importance? What should be his precise relationship to the various departments of the business he is serving? And how will he function within the existing framework of industry?

Art, even combined with mechanical ingenuity and merchandising spark, is still suspect with some hard-boiled businessmen. It smacks of afternoon tea and Greenwich Village. Unfortunately there has been just enough slapdash superficiality masquerading as industrial design to give credence to their patently unjust conclusion that the entire brotherhood is a pack of incompetents.

It may be a matter of years before the designer will find his proper level in the kingdom of commerce. To picture him as the savior of industry, the fair-haired boy with the magic wand who can always make sales curves hit the ceiling, is just as false as the opposite extreme. Somewhere between the two he will find his eventual place.

Once the industrial designer had made a dent on industry, it was perhaps only natural for him to exaggerate his own importance in the scheme of things. Indeed, one might almost say that he would not be a good designer unless he had that sort of excited enthusiasm that makes salesmen sell and designers create. But in sober moments he must have realized that, important as his contribution might seem to him, its relative importance might not be so great. As a rule the artist is, and should be, only one of the gears in the train that includes management, sales promotion, advertising, engineering, research—all those departments making up the complex mechanism of modern commerce.

[ . . . ]

A designer with the multiple gifts of artistic ability, mechanical sense, and merchandising wits may become indispensable to his client if these talents are permitted full scope. He should be careful, however, not to overestimate his importance by taking the attitude that appearance and appearance alone is of value. The best designed product in the world cannot be sold without clever promotion, nor will it make a profit for its sponsor if it lacks sound engineering and has been made by uneconomical factory methods.

[ . . . ]

At his best, the designer is an animator, a builder of enthusiasm in others. He is prodigal of ideas and if one proves too costly or impractical he has another on the tip of his tongue or the point of his pencil. He is resourceful; he is familiar with the standard processes of manufacture and can always see ways of improving a product within the framework of merchandising necessity, present equipment, and reasonable cost. He is creative without being crackbrained. He is practical without being timid. He knows how to work with others, meeting executives on an equal footing and still gaining the confidence of the man on the bench.

He brings to his client a broader design point of view than a man can have when burdened with the responsibilities of everyday operation. He fully acknowledges the superior technical knowledge of the men in the client's organization. He cannot and does not presume, of course, to tell them how to do things which they have learned through years of research and experience. But, through his varied contacts, he may contribute a helpful knowledge of materials and methods gained in the plants of other clients.

Although the best industrial designer must have a genuine flair for the mechanical, he is and should be primarily an artist. The belief, however, that all artists are temperamental is pure myth. They are no more so, and probably no less, than men and women in any other walk of life. Business executives are sometimes as touchy, inconsistent, and emotionally unstable as any opera singer. Crack salesmen, too, are notoriously mercurial—up one day and down the next. I know a brilliant engineer who resigns about once a week because of some fancied slight, then has to be cajoled out of his fit of sulks and coaxed back to his desk.

Industrial designers who take their work seriously cannot afford to play the prima donna. The successful ones work ten hours a day and throw in holidays for good measure. A few years ago our organization designed a line of machine tools to be presented at a trade show, working on a schedule figured almost to the hour. Every step of the way we kept abreast of the engineers, and twice we had to wait for them to catch up.

The designer who neither overestimates nor undervalues his importance is the one who will best serve industry. And the business man who realizes the importance of design and knows how to get the best value for his design expenditure is, other things being equal, the man who sells the most products.

# 1941

## Eliot Noyes, *Organic Design in Home Furnishings*

The American architect, designer, curator, and critic Eliot Noyes (1910–1977) was, at various times in his life, a member of the Cambridge, Massachusetts architectural firm of Walter Gropius and Marcel Breuer; an employee of the design office of Norman Bel Geddes; the first curator of the Department of Industrial Design at the Museum of Modern Art, New York (1939–1946); and the head of his own design firm (established 1947).[1] Noyes and the graphic designer Paul Rand were largely responsible in the 1950s and 1960s for creating IBM's distinctive corporate style in architecture, products, and graphics; Noyes's ubiquitous "Selectric" typewriter of 1961 is one of the iconic designs of its era. While design curator at the MoMA, Noyes organized a furniture design competition that traveled to locations such as Kaufmann's Department Store in Pittsburgh (see introduction to Edgar Kaufmann, jr., "What is Modern Design?"). The winners of the competition, who included Charles and Ray Eames and Eero Saarinen, had their works exhibited in the 1941 MoMA show, "Organic Design in Home Furnishings." These excerpts are from Noyes's introduction to its catalog.

Excerpted from Eliot Noyes, "A Note on the Competition," reprinted by permission from *Organic Design in Home Furnishings* (©1941 The Museum of Modern Art, New York): 4.

The wonders of modern mechanism, we all know, have wrought much more than a change in our habits of life. Economics and politics and the fate of nations in war and peace are all affected by the vast recent changes in the equipment of man.

In some respects, however, we foolishly flatter ourselves. We are not as modern as we think. In private, at home, most of us still live in the clutter of inheritance from the nineteenth century. Much of this out-of-date and rigidified furniture is no longer in tune with today's esthetic requirements, and is certainly far from suitable to our needs. Through design inertia, modern mass manufacture has simply seized upon and lifelessly repeated many weary old styles that are often neither beautiful nor practical.

Obviously the forms of our furniture should be determined by our way of life. Instead, for the most part, we have had to adapt ourselves uncomfortably and unreasonably to what has happened to be manufactured. For several years the Museum of Modern Art has been studying this problem in order to foster a collaboration between designer, manufacturer, and merchant, to fill this strange gap in the conveniences for modern existence.

On the first of October, 1940, the Museum's Department of Industrial Design inaugurated an inter-American competition for the design of furniture, fabrics, and lamps. The purpose of the contest was to discover good designers and engage them in the task of creating a better environment for today's living. Twelve important stores in major cities throughout the United States sponsored the competition and offered contracts with manufacturers as prizes to the winners, whose names appear at the beginning of the book.

A separate division of the competition was established for entrants from the other American republics [ . . . ].

Under the supervision of the Museum, contracts with manufacturers were arranged for all of the first prize winners and for some of those who had received honorable mention. During the process of manufacture, the original drawings were used as the basis for larger groups of furniture, and a number of the competition winners were asked to design additional pieces to fill out these groups. And as the purpose of the competition was to select designers rather than individual pieces, arrangements were made in some cases for a winner to develop designs for production in a category other than the one in which he had received an award. All pieces were produced as closely as possible in accordance with the original designs, and modified only when necessitated by the process of manufacture.

A significant innovation was that, in the case of chairs by Saarinen and Eames, a manufacturing method never previously applied to furniture was employed to make a light structural shell consisting of layers of plastic glue and wood veneer molded in three-dimensional forms. It should be born[e] in mind, however, that the theoretical or experimental aspects of design were necessarily limited by the existing facilities of the collaborating manufacturers.

Most of the designs in production are illustrated on the following pages. As this exhibition opens at the Museum of Modern Art, the furniture which has been produced through this project is being offered for sale by the sponsoring stores, some of which have arranged special displays designed by competition winners. It is expected that other distributors will join the project at a later date.

### NOTES

1. Walter Smith, "Noyes, Eliot," *The Grove Dictionary of Art Online*, ed. L. Macy, <*http://www .groveart.com*>, (accessed 23 December 2002).

# 1950

## Edgar Kaufmann, jr., *What Is Modern Design?*

The American architectural historian, curator, and critic Edgar Kaufmann, jr. (1910–1989; he preferred the "jr." uncapitalized) was a scion of the family that owned Kaufmann's Department Store in Pittsburgh, Pennsylvania. Kaufmann's father, Edgar Sr., commissioned Frank Lloyd Wright to design the Bear Run, Pennsylvania, house called "Fallingwater" (1934–39), probably at the urging of his son (who was briefly a member Wright's Taliesin Fellowship in 1934–35). In 1940 Kaufmann became a curator in the industrial design department at the Museum of Modern Art, New York, and directed the department from 1946 to 1948, at which time it merged with the architecture department under the leadership of Philip Johnson.[1] Kaufmann was the force behind the MoMA's influential "Good Design" exhibitions of 1950–55, which were co-sponsored by the Merchandise Mart in Chicago. Their aim was to promote good design—and good consumer taste—in everyday household objects and furnishings.

Excerpted from Edgar Kaufmann, jr., *What is Modern Design?* Reprinted by permission from *What is Modern Design?* (©1950 The Museum of Modern Art, New York): 5–9.

## What Is Design?

Who can resist looking into a lighted window at night?—a glimpse of a strange room, someone's home, a way of life grasped in a flash. That glance is intensely revealing precisely because a way of life is seen in the things people live with and the way they assemble them. Through the things we choose, design becomes the expression of ourselves.

But the things we choose are already designed, and often we pick them because of their design. For the time being, let us disregard design's other aspects. *Here design will mean conceiving and giving form to objects used in everyday life.*

### Design Is Expressive

Design in this sense is related to many other human activities, engineering and art in particular. Politics, economics, philosophy and science affect design and the way we look at it. That is to say, design is a central human activity, interlocked with everything people do. Hence its exceptional capacity to epitomize the character of an age and of the people who create it.

### Design Can Be Beautiful

Today, as always, people take pride in making and owning the best design of their times; not merely because design will carry the story of today into the future—their pride is one aspect of a deep, abiding pleasure which people derive from design. For design can do more than reveal the character of an age, it can be beautiful.

### Design Is Different from Art and Engineering

Art, of course, can soar higher, it is able to explore and express freely man's spirit. Engineering, in its single-minded devotion to efficiency, may reach a perfection incidentally so beautiful that design and even art are influenced. These are two special kinds of achievement, and each has its devotees.

[ . . . ]

## How Modern Design Developed

*Modern design is the planning and making of objects suited to our way of life, our abilities, our ideals.* It began a century ago when creative and perceptive people reacted to the vast problems posed by technological change and mass production. Modern design, in a steady development since then, has taken on a number of outward forms. Along with examples of current products some of the less familiar forms are pictured here, whenever these older works have present-day significance.

## Twelve Precepts of Modern Design

Out of a hundred years of development certain precepts have emerged and endured. They are generally conceded to be:

1. Modern design should fulfill the practical needs of modern life.
2. Modern design should express the spirit of our times.
3. Modern design should benefit by contemporary advances in the fine arts and pure sciences.
4. Modern design should take advantage of new materials and techniques and develop familiar ones.
5. Modern design should develop the forms, textures and colors that spring from the direct fulfillment of requirements in appropriate materials and techniques.
6. Modern design should express the purpose of an object, never making it seem to be what it is not.
7. Modern design should express the qualities and beauties of the materials used, never making the materials seem to be what they are not.
8. Modern design should express the methods used to make an object, not disguising mass production as handicraft or simulating a technique not used.
9. Modern design should blend the expression of utility, materials and process into a visually satisfactory whole.
10. Modern design should be simple, its structure, evident in its appearance, avoiding extraneous enrichment.
11. Modern design should master the machine for the service of man.
12. Modern design should serve as wide a public as possible, considering modest needs and limited costs no less challenging than the requirements of pomp and luxury.

## Modern Design Is a Necessity

Modern design has become a broad, powerful movement which includes work from all over the world, wherever men try to find the appropriate constructions and character for the things required in life today.

In this highly industrialized world where democratic societies are engaged in a formidable struggle to survive, life clearly has less and less resemblance to earlier times. Designs made now in mimicry of past periods or remote ways of life ('authentic Chippendale reproductions,' or 'Chinese modern'), cannot be considered as anything more than embarrassing indications of a lack of faith in our own values.

A well-established home in this country today has many requirements which were never envisaged in the designs of the past or of other civilizations. Our requirements cannot be fitted into their designs without inconvenience to ourselves and disregard for the fine accomplishments of other peoples. Modern life demands modern design. Not because it is cheaper to acquire or less work for housekeepers than 'period styles' (though sometimes these advantages are found), but because modern design is made to suit our own special needs and expresses our own spirit.

## Modern Design Makes Use of Good Ideas out of the Past

Now, as in the past, mere novelty is no key to good design. We use certain articles constantly whose forms have scarcely changed for two hundred years. Most of them have to do with eating—flatware, china and glass. Until modern designers develop fundamental improvements on them we shall pay tribute to the competence of the past in this field.

## Artificial Changes of Style

In contrast to this conservative area of modern design, there exists in commerce an organized procedure to make some things appear 'out-of-date' after a season or a year. This may well stimulate trade; but in design it affects only superficial details and is more likely to confuse or distort basic values than to forward them.

## Handicraft and Modern Design

There is another special condition which affects modern design. Handicraft and made-to-order design both have dwindled with the development of mass production. They have acquired the value of rarity and are prized for qualities that machine products cannot show: individuality and a warm human touch. As a means of experiment and of making preliminary models for the machine, handicraft has also proven its value in a whole new area of work.

## Modern Design Is Part of a Democratic Life

But the biggest problems of modern design lie in satisfying the wants of a new kind of public. The average person now has needs and tastes molded by his status as a free individual in an industrialized world. Despite elaborate specialization our technologies have a uniform direction: our activities focus increasingly on individuals and their daily lives. *Modern design is intended to implement the lives of free individuals.*

Such an ideal leaves no room for total standardization in the furnishings of a home. Fragments of the past, for instance, are often used to accent and enrich modern rooms. Modern design for the home is more appropriately used to create an atmosphere of 'the good life' than of 'a brave new world.'

## Streamlining Is Not Good Design

An exception to this may seem to be the widespread and superficial kind of design known as streamlining used to style nearly any object from automobiles to toasters. Its theme is the magic of speed, expressed in teardrop shapes, fairings and a curious ornament of parallel lines—sometimes called *speed whiskers.* The continued misuse of these devices has spoiled them for most designers, though naturally engineers use teardrop shapes and fairings where they are efficient, on high-velocity objects.

## The Future of Modern Design

Exceptions aside, there is a constantly growing public for modern design which is responsive to the world's changing requirements. The vanguard of modern design, prophetic and exploratory, will tend to shock many people and inspire a few. Daring or conservative, modern design embodies the values of our age, based on democracy and industrialization; designers seek to express these values through that direct blend of efficiency and beauty which in any age characterizes good design.

Good design in any period is simply: *the best its designers produce.* How can good design be found today among the many things available? First, it would be sensible to look for the characteristics already mentioned, a thorough merging of form and function, and an awareness of human values expressed in relation to industrial production for a democratic society. This search is not as difficult as it sounds; like any perception, it is sharpened by practice.

## Form and Function in a Dining Room Table

How does one know if form and function are merged? Try looking at a wooden dining table—how is the edge of the top treated? Is it merely a practical rounding, colored to match the top surface, or an elaborate inlay and band of veneer to hide the real edge grain? Or is the natural strength of plywood (most table tops would be too heavy and expensive in solid wood, now that our techniques give good plywood) expressed by showing its neat striping? The rounded edge is functional, but does not express the beauty of the material. The veneering needlessly hides a respectable material behind the costly skill of an old handicraft technique. *The simple declaration of the real form of the material succeeds in revealing a practical, uncomplicated, sensible beauty.* Cheaper plywoods have less regular stripings at the edge, so a good clear striping along the ends and sides of a table top would also be proof of a superior material.

How are the legs joined to the top? A good design will make a beautiful feature of the process. A poor one will depend on behind the scene strengtheners, sturdy, but ignored in the appearance of the table. How are the legs spaced? A good design will allow people to sit at the table comfortably and at the same time it will be a beautifully proportioned structure. When looking at this aspect, take into account the stretchers or other elements used to stiffen the legs and keep the table steady. How do they contribute to the whole design? Any household object, from pressure cooker to drapery fabric, can be examined in this same sense.

[ . . . ]

## The Requirements of Beauty

Besides these two stringent tests [is it sensible and attractive? Does it enhance your life?], good design may well be asked to live up to the three qualities which Thomas Aquinas listed as requisite to beauty: integrity, clarity, harmony.

*Integrity* is most surely expressed in the oneness of form and function already mentioned.

*Clarity* is forwarded by a maxim of modern design: let all functional parts be visible and all visible parts, functional (another way of stating the unity of form and function).

*Harmony* may well be thought of as inward and outward. Inward harmony will be found where there is an agreeable relationship between the components of an object. Outward harmony will be found where the object is able to take its place graciously in a larger ensemble.

These rules of thumb, or similar ones, can guide the successful hunt for good design.

NOTES

---

1. Western Pennsylvania Conservancy, "WPC-Fallingwater," <*http://www.wpconline.org/ fallingwater/family/edgar_jr.htm*>, (accessed 24 December 2002).

# 1951-1975

# 1951

## Raymond Loewy, "The MAYA Stage"

The renowned industrial designer Raymond Loewy (1893–1986) was born in France, where he studied engineering before entering the French Army during World War I. He moved to New York in 1919, where he worked in illustration, window dressing, and advertising before founding his own industrial design firm in 1929. Over the next fifty-odd years, his office designed trains, Greyhound buses, Coke bottles, International Harvester farm machines, the Skylab, and innumerable other products (including corporate identities and logos) for some of the world's largest companies. From the 1940s through the 1970s, his was a household name in the United States. In these excerpts from his immensely popular 1951 autobiography, *Never Leave Well Enough Alone*, Loewy describes his strategy for creating the "Most Advanced Yet Acceptable" design solution for any given product.

Excerpted from Raymond Loewy, *Never Leave Well Enough Alone* (New York: Simon & Schuster, 1951): 277–283. © Laurence Loewy, 1995. Reprinted by permission of Laurence Loewy of Loewy Design.

Being design consultants to one hundred and forty companies, most of them blue-ribbon corporations, and having been in very close contact with the consumer's reactions, we have been able to develop what I might call a fifth sense about public acceptance, whether it is the shape of a range, the lay-out of a store, the wrapper of a soap, the style of a car, or the color of a tugboat. This is the one phase of our profession that fascinates me no end. Our desire is naturally to give the buying public the most advanced product that research can develop and technology can produce. Unfortunately, it has been proved time and time again that such a product does not always sell well. There seems to be for each individual product (or service, or store, or package, etc.) a critical area at which the consumer's desire for novelty reaches what I might call the shock-zone. At that point the urge to buy reaches a plateau, and sometimes evolves into a resistance to buying. It is a sort of tug of war between attraction to the new and fear of the unfamiliar. The adult public's taste is not necessarily ready to accept the logical solutions to their requirements if this solution implies too vast a departure from what they have been conditioned into accepting as the norm. In other words, they will only go so far. Therefore, the smart industrial designer is the one who has a lucid understanding of where the shock-zone lies in each particular problem. At this point, a design has reached what I call the MAYA (Most Advanced Yet Acceptable) stage.

How far ahead can the designer go stylewise? This is the all-important question, the key to success or failure of a product. Its satisfactory solution calls for an understanding of the tastes of the American consumer.

We designers are realists; we like to deal in facts. Here, however, there are no yardsticks, no ways to chart a curve of public reaction to advanced design. Nevertheless, there are a few reasonably well-established facts among all these variables, and they can help us in our thinking. Being an engineer at heart, I have tried to introduce some order into this confused morass of human aesthetic behavior . . . in simple terms, design acceptance.

As a first groping effort in this direction I would like to express the Raymond Loewy Associates' ideas on the subject. One ought to bear in mind that the conclusions are necessarily empiric, and that while we speak of manufactured products in general, they apply more particularly to the automotive field.

1. Mass production of a successful given product by a powerful company over a period of time tends to establish the appearance of this particular item as the norm in its own field. (The public more or less accepts it as the standard for "looks" or styling.)
2. Any new design that departs abruptly from this norm involves a variable risk to its manufacturer. (We shall analyze the character of this risk later on; it has both positive and negative aspects.)
3. The risk increases as the square of the design gap between norm and advanced model in the case of a large manufacturer. (In plain language, for a big corporation a little style goes a long way.)
4. The risk increases as the cube of the design gap in the case of a smaller manufacturer or independent automobile manufacturer. (It is more difficult for these to establish a norm because they cannot blanket the nation with products in their design style.)
5. If the small manufacturer or the independent automobile maker succeeds in establishing a norm of his own, he may induce the large corporation to widen the design gap between their current and next models in an attempt to establish a new and different norm. Or, on the contrary, the large manufacturer may retaliate by reducing the gap in order to reaffirm forcefully the validity of his own norm and thereby discredit departing attempts of the competition. (Their salesmen will say to the prospective customer, "I wouldn't buy that stuff, it is too extreme. You won't like it.") The big company usually carries the field through sheer weight of mass manufacture.

6. The consumer is influenced in his choice of styling by two opposing factors: (a) attraction to the new and (b) resistance to the unfamiliar. As Kettering[1] said, "People are very open-minded about new things—so long as they are exactly like the old ones."

7. When resistance to the unfamiliar reaches the threshold of a shock-zone and resistance to buying sets in, the design in question has reached its MAYA stage—Most Advanced Yet Acceptable stage.

8. We might say that a product has reached the MAYA stage when 30 per cent (to pick an arbitrary figure) or more of the consumers express a negative reaction to acceptance.

9. If design seems too radical to the consumer, he resists it whether the design is a masterpiece or not. In other words, the intrinsic value of the design cannot overcome resistance to its radicality at the MAYA stage. There are some constants in the problem:

   a. The teen-age group is most receptive to advanced ideas.

   b. Two unmarried individuals each having high MAYA coefficients have a lower common coefficient as soon as they marry. (In other words, their collective taste becomes more orthodox, they fall into a bread-and-butter form of conservative buying habits.)

   c. The older age groups are influenced increasingly by the style opinion of the teen-age group. (This process is accelerating.)

   d. The wife is often the deciding factor at the time of the purchase. Her influence seems to decrease in direct proportion to the length of the marriage, reaches a plateau, and then reverses itself in later years.

   e. The MAYA stage varies according to topography, climate, season, level of income, etc. (For instance, an advanced design sells better in Texas than in North Dakota. Dark color is more popular in Pennsylvania than in Texas. A radical design will find good acceptance in larger cities, university towns, resorts; poor acceptance in mining towns, the farm belt, etc.)

In summary, let us say that any advanced design involves risk to the manufacturer. I believe there is no alternative between taking some degree of such risk or slow but certain eventual disappearance of the firm.

The smart manufacturer seems to be the one who is willing to take what General Eisenhower calls a "calculated risk." The theory expressed above, however empiric, may assist him in his calculation.

What does *risk* mean? There are as many definitions of it as there are persons. Our own thinking is somewhat as follows:

First, a large and successful corporation can get along year after year without taking more than a minimum of calculated risk. Its own norm acts as a style flywheel. This balance can be maintained until an equally heavy-weight corporation succeeds in establishing its norm along different lines.

Second, a smaller or independent manufacturer may survive for a considerable time on the basis of minimum risk so long as he follows the accepted style norm closely as it has been established by the leading manufacturer. But the company will not progress and forge ahead. A case of pernicious sales anemia sets in, resulting in eventual extermination.

Third, assuming that quality, engineering, and price are correct, calculated risk is the open gate to improved business for the smaller manufacturer. It is the key to successful operation and business expansion.

Fourth, the calculated risk should be such that it never takes the design beyond the MAYA stage, outside of some desperate business cases. These I call "Commando styling," borrowing the expression from the medical "Commando operation," where enormous sections of bone or tissue are removed from a condemned cancer patient as a last and desperate surgical gamble.

Fifth, there are reasonably accurate ways and means of pre-ascertaining the MAYA level of a given product in a given consumer's climate. This "climate" refers to: the state, location in the state, income, local characteristics, etc.

The above theory, tentative as it may be, has some value. We have made good use of it in the design of thousands of products, packages, structures, etc., for more than a hundred corporations.

Needless to say, the use of mathematical symbols—the cube, square root, etc.—does not pretend to be accurate. The terms are used figuratively to express a relationship which cannot be measured.

Guiding our clients in the virgin forest of advanced design is not our only task as trusted advisers. For instance, whenever a new product is developed and ready for the production okay, we use our imagination to the utmost in order to discover ahead of time any feature that might be distorted, misunderstood, or a subject for unpleasant jokes. To illustrate this point, we have stopped, at the last minute, a design for a household appliance that conveyed, under certain conditions of light, the semblance of a frog's head. Or a certain type of cooling unit, whose grille intake and two side knob controls mildly resembled a shark. Everyone remembers the case of a well-known automobile, an excellent car which, unfortunately, became known as the "Pregnant Six." This did not help sales. Or take the case of this particular book, which I first titled "ENTER i." One reader might say that "all I got from ENTER i was a mild case of ENTER-i-TIS"; which would do the book no good.

As far as age groups are concerned, it is definitely established that the teen-age group is far more receptive to advanced design than the next age group: say from twenty to forty. After forty, the resistance increases fast. In other words, the dream of the alert industrial designer would be to design for teen-agers. But manufacturers realize that this is a low-revenue group, which is very regrettable.

I might venture to say that if the teen-age "design receptiveness" could be extended to the twenty-five-year age level, products could, in many cases, be manufactured along more advanced lines with assurance of easy sales. The older strata would soon be sold too, by contagion selling. But regardless of all this, I would say that the teen-age segment of America is of enormous benefit to the whole economy of the country in a great variety of fields and services, as it spurs advanced thinking. Its influence is many times superior to the limited buying power of the group. It acts as a booster to the whole country.

Personally, I have a deep affection for those boys and girls and I respect their taste. Whether or not they fall periodically for some silly fad that does harm to no one, their basic taste remains fundamentally correct. So more power to you, kids, the nerve center of the nation.

## NOTES

1. Probably Charles Franklin Kettering (1876–1958), an American automotive engineer who was vice president and director of research at General Motors from 1920 to 1947. "Kettering, Charles F." *Encylcopædia Britannica*, <*http://www.britannica.com/eb/article?eu=46258*>, (accessed 27 May 2003).

# 1953

# Dwight D. Eisenhower, "Peaceful Uses of Atomic Energy"

Dwight D. Eisenhower (1890–1969) was the thirty-fourth president of the United States; he served two terms, from 1953 to 1961. In his December 1953 "Atoms for Peace" speech—given at the culmination of an eventful year that had included the death of the Soviet leader Joseph Stalin, the end of the Korean War, and an intensification in Senator Joseph McCarthy's anti-communist rhetoric—Eisenhower proposed before the General Assembly of the United Nations that the countries of the world pool atomic information and materials under the auspices of an international agency.[1] The speech led to the creation in 1957 of the International Atomic Energy Agency. Although during the Cold War most people lived in fear of the awesome destructive capacity of atomic weapons, the prospect of a future in which energy would be plentiful, cheap, and safe captivated the imagination of many designers and consumers.

Excerpted from Dwight D. Eisenhower, "Peaceful Uses of Atomic Energy," an address before the General Assembly of the United Nations, New York City, December 8, 1953, reprinted in *Public Papers of the Presidents of the United States: Dwight D. Eisenhower, 1953* (Washington, D.C.: U.S. Government Printing Office, 1960): 815–816, 820–822.

[ . . . ]

I feel impelled to speak today in a language that in a sense is new— one which I, who have spent so much of my life in the military profession, would have preferred never to use.

That new language is the language of atomic warfare.

The atomic age has moved forward at such a pace that every citizen of the world should have some comprehension, at least in comparative terms, of the extent of this development of the utmost significance to every one of us. Clearly, if the peoples of the world are to conduct an intelligent search for peace, they must be armed with the significant facts of today's existence.

My recital of atomic danger and power is necessarily stated in United States terms, for these are the only incontrovertible facts that I know. I need hardly point out to this Assembly, however, that this subject is global, not merely national in character.

On July 16, 1945, the United States set off the world's first atomic explosion. Since that date in 1945, the United States of America has conducted 42 test explosions.

Atomic bombs today are more than 25 times as powerful as the weapons with which the atomic age dawned, while hydrogen weapons are in the ranges of millions of tons of TNT equivalent.

Today, the United States' stockpile of atomic weapons, which, of course, increases daily, exceeds by many times the explosive equivalent of the total of all bombs and all shells that came from every plane and every gun in every theatre of war in all of the years of World War II.

A single air group, whether afloat or land-based, can now deliver to any reachable target a destructive cargo exceeding in power all the bombs that fell on Britain in all of World War II.

In size and variety, the development of atomic weapons has been no less remarkable. The development has been such that atomic weapons have virtually achieved conventional status within our armed services. In the United States, the Army, the Navy, the Air Force, and the Marine Corps are all capable of putting this weapon to military use.

But the dread secret, and the fearful engines of atomic might, are not ours alone.

In the first place, the secret is possessed by our friends and allies, Great Britain and Canada, whose scientific genius made a tremendous contribution to our original discoveries, and the designs of atomic bombs.

The secret is also known by the Soviet Union.

The Soviet Union has informed us that, over recent years, it has devoted extensive resources to atomic weapons. During this period, the Soviet Union has exploded a series of atomic devices, including at least one involving thermonuclear reactions.

[ . . . ]

The United States, heeding the suggestion of the General Assembly of the United Nations, is instantly prepared to meet privately with such other countries as may be "principally involved," to seek "an acceptable solution" to the atomic armaments race which overshadows not only the peace, but the very life, of the world.

We shall carry into these private or diplomatic talks a new conception.

The United States would seek more than the mere reduction or elimination of atomic materials for military purposes.

It is not enough to take this weapon out of the hands of the soldiers. It must be put into the hands of those who will know how to strip its military casing and adapt it to the arts of peace.

The United States knows that if the fearful trend of atomic military buildup can be reversed, this greatest of destructive forces can be developed into a great boon, for the benefit of all mankind.

The United States knows that peaceful power from atomic energy is no dream of the future. That capability, already proved, is here—now—today. Who can doubt, if the entire body of the world's scientists and engineers had adequate amounts of fissionable material with which to test and develop their ideas, that this capability would rapidly be transformed into universal, efficient, and economic usage.

To hasten the day when fear of the atom will begin to disappear from the minds of people, and the governments of the East and West, there are certain steps that can be taken now.

I therefore make the following proposals:

The Governments principally involved, to the extent permitted by elementary prudence, to begin now and continue to make joint contributions from their stockpiles of normal uranium and fissionable materials to an International Atomic Energy Agency. We would expect that such an agency would be set up under the aegis of the United Nations.

[ . . . ]

[An] important responsibility of this Atomic Energy Agency would be to devise methods whereby this fissionable material would be allocated to serve the peaceful pursuits of mankind. Experts would be mobilized to apply atomic energy to the needs of agriculture, medicine, and other peaceful activities. A special purpose would be to provide abundant electrical energy in the power-starved areas of the world. Thus the contributing powers would be dedicating some of their strength to serve the needs rather than the fears of mankind.

[ . . . ]

**N O T E S**

1. "Eisenhower, Dwight D." *Encyclopædia Britannica*, <*http://www.britannica.com/eb/article?eu= 32714*>, (accessed 24 December 2002).

# 1955

## Henry Dreyfuss, "Joe and Josephine"

Like Norman Bel Geddes (in whose office he briefly worked), the American industrial designer Henry Dreyfuss (1904–1972) got his start in stage and set design. However, as an industrial designer in the 1930s, he became renowned for his attention to user convenience, comfort, and preferences; his roster of clients grew to include (among many others) Bell Telephone, Hoover, Lockheed, and the U. S. military. He is widely considered the founder of the field of ergonomics and human factors research; his 1960 book, *The Measure of Man: Human Factors in Design*, is still used as a resource today. (Its title, however, has been updated to *The Measure of Man and Woman*.) The selections below are from Dreyfuss's 1955 book, *Designing for People*, in which he outlined many of his design principles and goals.

Excerpted from Henry Dreyfuss, "Joe and Josephine," chapter two of *Designing for People* (New York: Simon & Schuster, 1955): 26–28, 30–31, 36–43. Reprinted by permission of John Dreyfuss.

I f this book can have a hero and a heroine, they are a couple we call Joe and Josephine.

Joe and Josephine are austere line drawings of a man and a woman, and they occupy places of honor on the walls of our New York and California offices. They are not very romantic-looking, staring coldly at the world, with figures and measurements buzzing around them like flies, but they are very dear to us. They remind us that everything we design is used by people, and that people come in many sizes and have varying physical attributes. Joe enacts numerous roles. Within twenty-four hours he may determine the control positions on a linotype, be measured for an airplane chair, be squeezed into an armored tank, or be driving a tractor; and we may prevail upon Josephine to do a day's ironing, sit at a telephone switchboard, push a vacuum cleaner around a room, type a letter. No matter what they are doing, we observe their every position and reaction. They are a part of our staff, representing the millions of consumers for whom we are designing, and they dictate every line we draw.

Joe and Josephine did not spring lightly to our walls from the pages of a book on anatomy. They represent many years of research by our office, not merely into their physical aspects but into their psychology as well.

Merely assembling average measurements from anatomical drawings would not have been difficult. However, the concern of the industrial designer is with the mass public, and it was necessary to determine the extreme dimensions, for we must consider the variations from small to large in men and women. After all, people come in assorted rather than average sizes.

Joe and Josephine have numerous allergies, inhibitions, and obsessions. They react strongly to touch that is uncomfortable or unnatural; are disturbed by glaring or insufficient light and by offensive coloring; they are sensitive to noise, and they shrink from a disagreeable odor.

Our job is to make Joe and Josephine compatible with their environment. The process is known as human engineering. From the mountainous data we assembled, sifted, and translated, we filled the gaps between human behavior and machine design. We have collected detail[ed] measurements of heads and of all the extremities and of thighs and forearms and shoulders and every other conceivable part of the body; we are familiar with the amount of pressure the

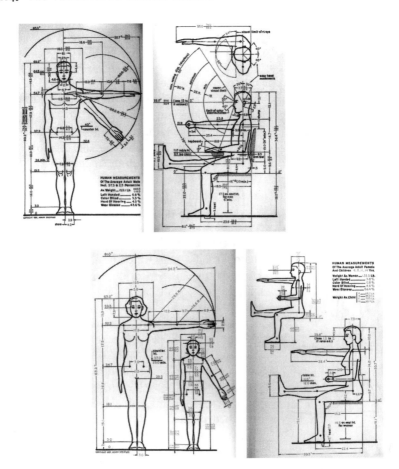

average foot can comfortably exert on a pedal; we know how hard a hand can effectively squeeze; the reach of an arm—for we must know how far buttons and levers can be placed away from the central controls of a machine; size of earphones, telephone operators' headsets, helmets for the armed services, binoculars—all are determined by our information on head sizes. From these facts we arrived at this maxim—the most efficient machine is the one that is built around a person.

[ . . . ]

Joe and Josephine have children, and we have charts for them at all ages. They were important contributors during our work on a bicycle; months of study went into the placement of the handle bars, seats, and pedals. An adjustable rig without wheels was built, and children took turns riding it while pictures recorded their posture as the handle bars, seat, and pedals were shifted in position. It was determined that the best posture for cruising was similar to

that taken in walking, the easiest posture for racing similar to that taken in running. Movies of children riding their own bicycles to school were taken in various parts of the country. As frequently happens, the films furnished unexpected information. They showed that clothes, which quite naturally varied in different climates, were a factor in bicycle design and had to be taken into account; that it was logical to make use of muscular memory rather than change the pedal motion, and that it was easier for a child to ride a bicycle that was a little too large for him than one that was too small.

Consider Josephine as a telephone operator. It wasn't too long ago that she had the mouthpiece of the phone strapped to her chest and the earphones clamped to her head. If she turned her head a half inch her voice faded. Certainly there is nothing more fatiguing than keeping one's head in a fixed position. Telephone engineers' ingenuity, plus new materials, provided the basis for the modern headset with its featherweight plastic mouthpiece attached to the earphone by an aluminum rod, which allows complete freedom of motion.

Obviously, the industrial designer has many an occasion to ponder upon the female figure. Such meditation can have humorous aspects. Our first sketch of Josephine was purposely drawn, shall we say, conservatively. The office staff immediately complained that she was the most sexless-looking woman they'd ever seen—in fact, her silhouette looked like a boy. Everyone had a suggestion, mostly along Marilyn Monroe and Jane Russell lines. Some questioned her height, arguing that she seemed too short in stature. It was decided this illusion was probably caused by the influence of dress designers, who use tall models to enhance their styles. Eventually the chart was made over with increased femininity, and Josephine is now better-looking than the average woman she portrays.

For many years we have

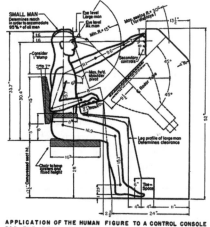

APPLICATION OF THE HUMAN FIGURE TO A CONTROL CONSOLE FOR THE BELL TELEPHONE LABORATORIES, INC.

retained an outstanding medical practitioner as a consultant on affairs of anatomy. In effect this physician is Joe's and Josephine's family doctor, and often is summoned halfway across the continent to help clients' engineers to determine the proper position and size and shape of a control board or the proper relation of the seating and controls of a tractor.

In addition, Joe and Josephine are also frequently checked by all kinds of specialists, ear doctors, neurologists, psychologists, and opticians, for ours is a preventive kind of research.

How well Joe and Josephine can see is a vital consideration in design. It is matched in importance only with how legible the industrial designer can make what they look at. As with our human engineering charts on the other four senses, we have a vision table. But sometimes mere statistics are not enough. When we designed our first typewriter years ago, our research showed that stenographers often complained of headaches at the end of the day. Irritable bosses could not possibly be entirely at fault, and further study finally proved that the shiny black lacquer used on typewriters harshly reflected the overhead lights directly into the girls' eyes, causing eyestrain and headaches. We proposed the dull, wrinkle-finish lacquer now universally used.

[ . . . ]

Color can make Joe and Josephine gay or sad; aid their digestion or make them ill; relax them or produce fatigue. It can suggest youth or age. It has therapeutic value in the neuropsychiatric ward and can influence human relations through its use as background in consulting rooms, homes, and schools. There are those who think it can stimulate conversation or create an atmosphere of belligerent silence. It can suggest intimacy or induce hostility. It can make things look larger or smaller, lower or taller, suggest heat or cool. That this recognition of the influence of color is not necessarily a twentieth-century development is indicated by the fact that bibulous English gentlemen of two or three hundred years ago are said to have preferred duck-egg green walls in their libraries, believing that somehow this color enabled them to imbibe large quantities of port without becoming noticeably intoxicated.

Our office was engaged to keep passengers from feeling pressed flat in a ship's salon measuring eighty feet long but of necessity only seven feet nine inches high, the distance between decks. Color came to our aid. By using contrasting colors on adjacent walls and on the ceilings, we were able to create the illusion of greater height in the rooms.

Color has become increasingly important to the industrial designer in recent years. For example, a dark "heavy" color in an airplane can give a sense of security, and a light color can suggest lack of weight in a vacuum cleaner and help sell it.

[ . . . ]

For the present, the greatest revolution in color has been the replacement of the utilitarian but depressing and light-consuming black in factories and on machinery by quiet grays. Not far behind is the use of pleasant greens for factory walls. Color experts have little trouble convincing plant owners of its desirability after showing that green reduces eyestrain and nerve strain, enabling machine operators to work more efficiently.

No instrument has yet been devised to measure Joe's and Josephine's color reaction, but we know that their color association falls into a familiar pattern. There is the safety-color code in which yellow or yellow-and-black bands indicate striking hazards such as low beams, stairways, and edges of platforms. Orange or Chinese red indicates dangerous hazards such as electrical fuse boxes, cutting edges, and emergency switches. Green indicates safety and first-aid equipment. Blue tags or signs denote that an object is out of order or is not to be moved. White indicates traffic control and waste receptacles. For pipeline identification, yellow or orange indicates dangerous materials such as acids, gasses, and steam, blue indicates protective materials such as fluids to combat dangerous materials, red denotes fire-protection equipment such as a sprinkling system, and purple denotes costly materials.

We introduced light gray-green in the interiors of military vehicles to replace white. The reasons were obvious—white involves the danger of glare and soils easily. In addition, the white underside of an open hatch presents a perfect target. On the contrary, white is often specified in other situations—for instance, the tops of airplane fuselages, oil storage tanks, and the roofs of buildings. Here white reflects the sun's heat and reduces interior temperatures.

Sound bombards Joe and Josephine from all directions. Fifty years ago many of the sounds they heard were pleasant—the singing of birds, the movements of horses, the hum of insects. The rise of industry has brought the thunder of rivet guns, the clanging and roar of traffic, and the scream of tires rounding a curve or stopping abruptly. Painful sound registers 130 decibels, thunder 120, the average auto 70, normal conversation 60, but even a whisper registers 25. Clearly there is no complete escape. Noise as a cause of inefficiency in factories costs American industry millions of dollars daily. Great progress has been made in silencing disruptive noises. Heavy machine tools are decibels quieter than they were a decade ago, and modern factories have become comparatively noiseless through installation of covers for noisy parts of machinery and the use of acoustic materials.

Joe and Josephine are affected also by odors, pleasant and unpleasant. Most odorous substances have large molecules, so that they diffuse very slowly. For this reason, smells may linger. For instance, cigarette odor may cling to clothes for six hours or more, musk cannot be removed even after three washings. Odors cling tenaciously to dark materials more so than to light ones, in this sequence— black, blue, green, red, yellow, white. Basic odors are flowery, putrefactive, aromatic, burnt, fruity, ethereal, pungent. The industrial designer must consider all this in his work. The pungency of leather, for instance, can become unpleasant if too much of it is used in the interior of an airplane.

In pursuit of the correct handle or lever, the average distance a person can reach without strain, the color that will produce relaxation in a waiting room, and other precise details, we have filled our files with valuable data, which we use over and over. We know that pulling force is greater than pushing, that handles under half an inch in diameter are likely to cut into the hand under heavy loading, and handles more than one and one quarter inches in diameter feel fat and give a feeling of insecurity. We know that a thirty-five-pound foot pressure is about right for normal brake-pedal design, with a sixty-pound maximum, and pressure on the accelerator should be ten to fifteen pounds, and that a resting foot exerts six to seven pounds. We know that a circular dial scale, as on a speedometer, is easier to read than a linear one, that a printed page in lower-case letters can be read more quickly than one in capitals. Our files show that from six to nine percent of American men and four to seven per cent of American women are left-handed. Fortunately, most objects, such as the electric iron, can be used ambidextrously, but sometimes left-handedness can provide a problem. We know that about 15,000,000 persons—12,000,000 adults and 3,000,000 children—have some hearing loss, which is a consideration in designing the telephone. We know that approximately 3.5 per cent of the nation's men and .2 per cent of its women are color-blind, a consideration, certainly, in designing traffic signals.

From all this, it is apparent that the industrial designer's task is twofold—to fit a client's wares to Joe's and Josephine's anatomies, and to explore their psychology and try to lessen the mental strains of this pressure age. It is not enough to seat them comfortably at their work. There is a responsibility also to remove the factors that impair digestions, cause headaches, backaches, fatigue, and give them a feeling of insecurity.

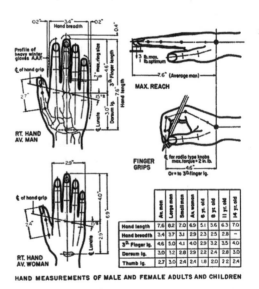

HAND MEASUREMENTS OF MALE AND FEMALE ADULTS AND CHILDREN

# 1958

# Program of the Hochschule für Gestaltung, Ulm

The Hochschule für Gestaltung (HfG) in Ulm, Germany began operation in 1953 and, in 1955, moved into buildings designed by its director, the Swiss architect/designer/artist/writer Max Bill (1908–1994). Bill, who had studied at the Bauhaus as a young man, designed the HfG's buildings and structured its curriculum to reflect and promote the goals of the Bauhaus on an international level. The "Ulm School of Design" (as it is often called in English), though in operation for only a short time—it closed in 1968 due to financial trouble—had a lasting impact on international design, particularly in the field of electronics. The spare, elegant, functionalist Ulm aesthetic was in marked contrast to the colorful exuberance of much of the popular design of the period.

Excerpted from the first issue of *Ulm: Quarterly Journal of the Hochschule für Gestaltung* (October 1958): 1–2, 4, 6, 18, 20, 22.

**T**he Hochschule für Gestaltung educates specialists for two different tasks of our technical civilization:

The design of industrial products (industrial design department and building department);

The design of visual and verbal means of communication (visual communication department and information department).

The school thus educates designers for the production and consumer goods industries as well as for present-day means of communication: press, films, broadcasting, television, and advertising. These designers must have at their disposal the technological and scientific knowledge necessary for collaboration in industry today. At the same time they must grasp and bear in mind the cultural and sociological consequences of their work.

The Hochschule für Gestaltung is conceived as a school for a maximum number of 150 students, in order to ensure a favourable proportion between the number of students and faculty. Faculty and students come from many different countries, thus giving the school an international character.

The training lasts four years, inclusive of one year's foundation course, and concludes with the diploma of the Hochschule für Gestaltung.

Wood, metal, plaster, and photography workshops are available for practical work.

The school also combines teaching and research in an institute for industrial design and in an institute for industrialized building. An institute for communication is under construction.

The school contains living quarters and social facilities for faculty and students.

The Hochschule für Gestaltung is a private institution. The Geschwister-Scholl Foundation, which has financial and legal responsibility for the school, was founded in 1950 by Inge Aicher-Scholl in memory of her brother Hans and sister Sophie, who were executed in 1943 by the Nazi regime.

The buildings were designed by Max Bill; construction began in September, 1953, and the school was officially opened on 2 October 1955. Until 1956 Max Bill was the director of the Hochschule für Gestaltung; since then the school has been directed by a Faculty Board.

[ . . . ]

## Foundation Course

All students entering in the same year follow a one year's foundation course before being accepted into one of the four departments.

The foundation course has four purposes:

1: it introduces the students to the work of the departments, above all to the methods on which this work is based;
2: it makes the students conversant with the most important questions of our technical civilization, and in this way communicates the horizons of actual design problems;
3: it trains the students to work together in various disciplines and thus prepares them for teamwork, i.e., for work in committees of specialists, each of whom understands the problems and outlook of his collaborators;
4: it adjusts levels in previous education which are due to the fact that the students not only come from varying professions but also from many countries with differing educational systems.

## Practical & Theoretical Courses

- Visual Method (Experiments and research in two and three dimensions on the basis of studies in perception, symmetry, topology)
- Workshop Practice (Wood, metal, plaster, photography)
- Means of Presentation (Technical drawing, letter forms, language, free drawing)
- Methodology (Introduction to mathematical logic, permutations and combinations, topology)
- Sociology (Changes in the social structure since the Industrial Revolution)

- Perception Theory (Introduction to the main theories and problems of visual perception)
- Cultural History of the 20th Century (Painting, sculpture, architecture, literature)
- Mathematics, Physics, Chemistry (Courses designed to adjust differences in previous education)

## Industrial Design Department

The purpose of the department is to train designers of industrial products. The development of new kinds of methods of fabrication has faced the designer with problems which can no longer be mastered from previous artistically-based standpoints. The education of the designer must give greater emphasis to the scientific and technological disciplines which now, as they will in the future, guide the operational processes in industrial production, and which ever more critically determine the end product. Today, the designer of industrial products must be capable of using the foundations of professionally-based knowledge for his work, which will be in close collaboration with constructors, production engineers, and economists. Above all, he must be in a position of awareness of the cultural and sociological context in which his activity takes place.

[ . . . ]

## Building Department

The industrialized building department has a comprehensive but limited theme: the application of modern methods of production to building techniques.

Traditional methods of building are no longer sufficient to cover the present-day need for surface buildings of all kinds, and there is clearly an urgent necessity for industrialization in this field.

The building department trains architects capable of performing this task.

[ . . . ]

## Visual Communication Department

In many phases of social life, men are nowadays addressed, linked, or put into contact with one another through visual information. The purpose of the department is to design such information in a way that corresponds to its function. Thus, typography, graphic design, photography, exhibition, film, and television techniques are handled as an homogeneous field, which is termed 'visual communication' in accord with international usage.

The research in the department aims at relating visual statements as clearly as possible to their subject. For this, methods must be developed which make use of the knowledge which has been won in recent decades in the field of perception and meaning.

[ . . . ]

### Information Department

The department educates writers for the press, broadcasting, television, and film: means of communication, which on an ever-increasing scale shape modern society and determine its way of working.

The department works in close collaboration with the visual communication department. It aims at training writers who know and master the problems, methods, and techniques of the various means of communication, rather than those who specialize from the outset in one particular field. Work in the department concentrates on experimental study.

[ . . . ]

# 1959

## Richard Nixon and Nikita Khrushchev, "The Kitchen Debate"

In the midst of the Cold War, Vice President Richard M. Nixon (1913–1994; later to become thirty-seventh president of the United States, 1969–1974) visited the Soviet Union in conjunction with the American National Exhibition in Moscow, a fair that was intended to display "the American way of life" to the Soviet people. Nixon played host to Soviet Premier Nikita S. Khrushchev (1894–1971; premier, 1958–1964) on a tour of the exhibition, during the course of which they debated the merits of capitalism and communism and sparred over matters of policy. The extent to which consumer goods were the subject of discussion may seem surprising, but to many Americans (and probably to many Soviets, judging from Khrushchev's defensive tone), the ready availability in the United States of good-quality consumer products was one of capitalism's best rejoinders to communism.

Richard Nixon and Nikita Khrushchev, "The Kitchen Debate," from "Nixon and Khrushchev Argue in Public as U.S. Exhibit Opens; Accuse Each Other of Threats," *The New York Times* (July 25, 1959): 1–3. Copyright ©1959 by The New York Times Co.; reprinted by permission.

[ . . . ]

Khrushchev: [ . . . ] **"We have existed not quite forty-two years and in** another seven years we will be on the same level as America.

"When we catch you up, in passing you by, we will wave to you. Then if you wish we can stop and say: Please follow up. Plainly speaking, if you want capitalism you can live that way. That is your own affair and doesn't concern us. We can still feel sorry for you but since you don't understand us—live as you do understand.

[ . . . ]

Nixon: [ . . . ] "I can only say that if this competition in which you plan to outstrip us is to do the best for both of our peoples and for peoples everywhere, there must be a free exchange of ideas. After all, you don't know everything—"

Khrushchev: "If I don't know everything, you don't know anything about communism except this fear of it."

Nixon: "There are some instances where you may be ahead of us, for example in the development of the thrust of your rockets for the investigation of outer space; there may be some instances in which we are ahead of you—in color television, for instance."

Khrushchev: "No, we are up with you on this, too. We have bested you in one technique and also in the other."

[ . . . ]

Nixon (halting Khrushchev at model kitchen in model house): "You had a very nice house in your exhibition in New York. My wife and I saw and enjoyed it very much. I want to show you this kitchen. It is like those of our houses in California."

Khrushchev (after Nixon called attention to a built-in panel-controlled washing machine): "We have such things."

Nixon: "This is the newest model. This is the kind which is built in thousands of units for direct installation in the houses."

He added that Americans were interested in making life easier for their women. Mr. Khrushchev remarked that in the Soviet Union they did not have "the capitalist attitude toward women."

Nixon: "I think that this attitude toward women is universal. What we want to do is make easier the life of our housewives."

He explained that the house could be built for $14,000 and that most veterans had bought houses for between $10,000 and $15,000.

Nixon: "Let me give you an example you can appreciate. Our steel workers, as you know, are on strike. But any steel worker could buy this house. They earn $3 an hour. This house costs about $100 a month to buy on a contract running twenty-five to thirty years.

Khrushchev: "We have steel workers and we have peasants who also can afford to spend $14,000 for a house." He said American houses were built to last only twenty years, so builders could sell new houses at the end of that period. "We build firmly. We build for our children and grandchildren."

Mr. Nixon said he thought American houses would last more than twenty years, but even so, after twenty years many Americans want a new home or a new kitchen, which would be obsolete then. The American system is designed to take advantage of new inventions and new techniques, he said.

Khrushchev: "This theory does not hold water."

He said some things never got out of date—furniture and furnishings, perhaps, but not houses. He said he did not think that what Americans had written about their houses was all strictly accurate.

[ . . . ]

Nixon (pointing to television screen): "We can see here what is happening in other parts of the home."[1]

Khrushchev: "This is probably always out of order."

Nixon: "Da [yes]."

Khrushchev: "Don't you have a machine that puts food into the mouth and pushes it down?[2] Many things you've shown us are interesting but they are not needed in life. They have no useful purpose. They are merely gadgets. [ . . . ]"

[ . . . ]

Nixon (indicating a floor sweeper that works by itself and other appliances): "you don't need a wife."

Khrushchev chuckled.

Nixon: "We do not claim to astonish the Russian people. We hope to show our diversity and our right to choose. We do not wish to have decisions made at the top by government officials who say that all homes should be built in the same way. Would it not be better to compete in the relative merits of washing machines than in the strength of rockets. Is this the kind of competition you want?"

Khrushchev: "Yes, that['s] the kind of competition we want. But your generals say: 'Let's compete at rockets. We are strong and we can beat you.' But in this respect we can also show you something."

[ . . . ]

NOTES

1. The television screen had a closed-circuit feature that allowed it to function like a security monitor.

2. Khrushchev may be referring to the farcical "feeding machine" featured in Charlie Chaplin's 1936 film *Modern Times.*

# 1963

## Ann Ferebee, "Is Industrial Design Color Blind?"

Ann Ferebee, an American, is the author of *A History of Design from the Victorian Era to the Present* (1970) and numerous other writings on product design, architecture, and urban design. She currently serves as director of the Institute for Urban Design in New York. Ferebee wrote the essay "Is Industrial Design Color Blind?" during the height of the Civil Rights Movement, when many whites at long last became aware of, and concerned about, the lack of racial diversity in the professional and business worlds.

---

---

On the Monday after a bomb killed four girls in Birmingham's Sixteenth Street Baptist Church, INDUSTRIAL DESIGN'S editor typed out an attack against possible racial discrimination within the design community. But was it relevant, he asked? On reflection, the staff knew nothing about discrimination in design; it didn't even know whether there were Negro designers. In order to find out, we spot checked design societies, schools, and offices.

The first call, to Ramah Larisch at the ASID,[1] began with a question. "Does the ASID have Negro members?" we asked. Mrs. Larisch explained that the ASID[2] had no Negro members because it had never had an application from a Negro. At the IDI Anne Davis was asked the same question. "We have no conscious policy of racial discrimination," said Miss Davis, answering a question which had not been asked. Two days later Miss Davis reported back with what sounded like relief that the IDI had some Negro members after all—one was an officer in the Chicago chapter. "You see," said Miss Davis, "since we make no distinction on our application forms, I've corresponded with these members for years without knowing they were Negroes."

Testing for color blind design firms we learned that both the Teague and Dreyfuss offices had had Negro designers or architects in the past but not at the moment. Then we called Betty Reese, vice president for public relations at

Loewy/Snaith. "Right now we have a Negro in product design, Joe Lawe, a Negro in store design, John Blackwell, and there's a new man on our marketing staff—but of course, he's not a designer." Pointing out that it was a social rather than a professional problem, Miss Reese said, "At Loewy/Snaith we hire talent. Period. That's why I don't think you've got a story."

Nevertheless, we walked around to the Loewy/Snaith office that afternoon for a talk with Joe Lawe. Lawe graduated from Pratt four years ago, worked on the Canadian National account at the Valkus office, and then joined the Loewy/Snaith product section one year ago. "My only brush with discrimination came while I was still at Pratt," said Lawe. Although it was commonly believed then that Detroit didn't hire Negro designers, Lawe's advisor urged him to sign up for an interview when the recruiting officer from a major manufacturer appeared at the school. With puzzling loyalty, Lawe does not name the auto manufacturer. But he says that after its interviewer promised to send him a job application form, the manufacturer wrote him that there were no openings on the design staff. The recruiting officer later explained to Lawe's advisor that he had been unaware of his company's attitude until then.

We also talked to Madeleine Ward, a Negro design student now at Parsons. "Until now, we have never thought it would be possible for us as Negroes to help mould our country. But through industrial design I am reaching other people besides Negroes for the first time in my life." Although Miss Ward attended Brooklyn's grammar and high schools, it was not until she entered the New York School of Interior Design and, later, Parsons, that she sat in a classroom in which more than 20 per cent of the students were white.

## Making the Scene

Miss Ward put us on the trail of Tom Rock and Art Dickerson, two experienced designers who are Negroes and who don't mind talking about it. Both men had impressive job records—Rock with Belle Kogan, George Nelson, Reino Aarnio, and OITF, and Dickerson with Jens Risom and L. G. Shelburne Associates—but both said they had worried, on occasions when they had *not* landed jobs, whether this was because of color. Like the Ward and Lawe families, Rock's had thought the competition in design would be hard for a Negro to buck. But Rock asked his father, "How is anything ever going to happen if you don't show up on the scene?"

Like Miss Reese, Muriel Feder, whose employment service specializes in design talent, thought a story on discrimination in design was irrelevant. But we asked her anyway whether she had trouble placing Negro designers and architects. "The question has never come up," she said. When I send a Negro designer for an interview, I don't alert the client to his color. Is the reverse true, we wondered. Do clients hire *because* the designer is a Negro? "Right now an Ohio client is begging me for a Negro architect to help design a new Negro college," said Mrs. Feder.

A bit dismayed that the design scene had not revealed more discrimination, we placed a call to Dr. John Morsell, assistant to Roy Wilkins at the NAACP. We reported to him the only case of job discrimination we had uncovered—a large Madison Avenue design office which turned down a Negro designer because its biggest client lived in Atlanta. Morsell said that this kind of thinking is disappearing and that the way to make it disappear faster is to test it. N[ei]man-Marcus, he said, had done well with a Negro architect in Dallas and Skidmore, Owings and Merrill had no trouble when they sent a Negro architect to Charleston. Dr. Morsell added that it would help if vocational counselors in high schools informed talented young Negroes about industrial design. Glancing at the pale-faced talent in ID's office, we realized later that we'd forgotten to ask Dr. Morsell a final question: why had we never met a Negro magazine writer?

**N O T E S**

1. The American Society of Industrial Designers, established 1955.
2. The Industrial Designers Institute, established 1951. ASID, IDI, and three other organizations merged in 1965 to become IDSA, the Industrial Designers Society of America.

# 1964

# Edward Carpenter, "Statement: The Designing Women"

The American Edward K. Carpenter writes extensively on urban, environmental, industrial, and exhibition design. This 1964 essay, published not long after the release of Betty Friedan's best-selling 1963 book, *The Feminine Mystique*, is a logical sequel to Ann Ferebee's essay on race that appeared in the same magazine in 1963.

Reprinted in its entirety from Edward Carpenter, "Statement: The Designing Women," *Industrial Design*, vol. 11, no. 6 (June 1964): 72–74. Used with permission from *I. D. Magazine* ©1964. Not for reprint without express written permission of the publisher, or parent company F&W Publications, Inc.

What happens to girls who graduate from industrial design courses? They marry designers and withdraw from the profession, says one designer; and although many of them do, just as airline stewardesses marry men connected with their work, many do not. What does happen to women designers, why they decide to become industrial designers in the first place, and what attributes they bring to their work are questions whose answers are as disparate as the women themselves. The story of women in design has a plot much like the story of women in any activity outside the home: since emancipation, with the right to vote in 1920, women have had a chance to prove that they can do anything a man can do and they have done so in droves. In design work, however, there is not really much for a woman to prove, except that she has talent and can exercise it. For design, with its emphasis on color, form, and texture, is closer to the traditional woman's world than are, say, parachute jumping and wrestling. And for that reason alone, women have more to contribute to design than to other professions.

To find out about women in design we talked with people who educate designers, people who find them jobs, people who hire them, and with women designers themselves. Although the survey was informal and the findings sometimes valueless because of their variety, the answers and opinions often showed striking unanimity. Most people agree that more women are finding their way into design than ever before, and many believe firmly that this trend is right and good for both design as a profession and consumers as a genre. No one, of course, denies that some women, such as Belle Kogan, Fr[e]da Diamond, and Florence Knoll (see *ID*, April, 1961), are outstanding designers. And many recognize that contributions by women in work only indirectly related to actual industrial design have helped the profession: Ada Louise Huxtable and Jane Mitarachi in writing, and Anne Louise Davis and Ramah Larisch in organization work, to name but four.

One of the reasons industrial design has more women is simply that it now has more practitioners. In the beginning formal design training was, of course, hard to get, and the composite experience needed to become a competent designer was harder for a woman to seek out than for a man. Writing in the *American Artist* in November, 1963, Alfred Werner said of the 19th century art training what by extension applied later on to design: "It all remained on an amateur level however great the talent of the individual. For, while women might get some instruction from private teachers, before the end of the 19th century only men were admitted to academies of art—and a few daring women disguised as boys were smuggled in." Clearly training in the graphic and industrial arts has become more cosmopolitan. Still, even when schools started offering industrial design courses, those doing so were often trade schools located in large cities; and if a woman was willing to brave the evils of New York or Chicago to follow her calling, her parents were perhaps less enthusiastic. Now with industrial design being taught in large universities coed design students can share both the comparative safety of university communities and the fun of university social life. Perhaps these twin advantages are luring more women to design. Some think so; at least one design educator thinks not. She speaks almost bitterly of the lack of awareness of industrial design among girl students and fears that many may be kept away because of an awe of technical things. Her fear is at least partially justified, for although just as many women as men have technical aptitudes, these aptitudes are more encouraged in men than in women. As they grow up, men play with Erector sets, tinker with cars, and build rockets in their basements. What technical gifts a woman has are more likely directed to the sewing room than the tool shop. And when she gets older she may not as readily look for the kind of outlet industrial design offers her technical gifts. At the same time many women have backgrounds like Lucia DeRespinis's. Lucia, an industrial designer who married a designer but who still works for George Nelson & Co., confounding many sages, says that her father had a home workshop and as a child she was always doing projects with her father, making small motors, working with materials.

Yet despite these aptitudes and abilities some firms hesitate to hire women designers. According to a report presented to President Kennedy last fall by the Commission on the Status of Women, "The reasons given by employers for differential treatment cover a considerable range. Frequently they say they prefer male employees because the non-wage costs of employing women are higher. They say that the employment pattern of younger women is in and out of the labor force. They say that women's rates of sickness, absenteeism, and turnover are higher than men's, that the hiring of married women introduces one more element into the turnover rate because the residence of a married couple is normally determined by the man. They say that though attendance rates of older women are often better than those of men, insurance and pensions for older workers are expensive, and that compliances with protective labor legislation applying to women is sometimes disruptive of schedules. They say that men object to working under women supervisors." Design firms experience all these problems and because of them may be reluctant to hire women. Some firms, on the defensive against today's militant liberalism, feel touchy about their reluctance. Donald Desk[e]y Associates denies that they refuse to hire women, but when asked how many they now employ, maintains a massive silence. At the other end of the scale are manufacturers like General Motors who hire all the competent women designers they can get. "We try to keep a balance between men and women," they say, and they complain that they never get enough good women to keep the balance intact. Women are more attuned to the problems other women experience in getting into, riding in, and getting out of cars, GM feels; and if a designer couples her feminine feeling for high heels and run-prone stockings with competent design ability GM is anxious to have her. At General Motors many women seem to gravitate to the interior styling studio, where they work with fabrics, textures, and colors—not because of policy at GM but because women feel most at home there. At least one independent design office shares GM's aggressive attitude toward women designers. Goertz Industrial Design, at present a womanless office, hopes a woman will bring a fresh look to the consumer products Goertz designs. Although most consumer products are bought and used by women, these products are designed by men. Goertz feels a woman designer with a distinctly feminine approach can lead items away from their entrenched, intransient mold.

But if women can bring a feminine attitude to design work, this same feminism may be a drawback in working relations with men. Politicians and voters are asking Margaret Chase Smith, the first woman to run for the Presidency, how she would stand up to Khrus[h]chev. And similarly the employer of a woman designer might wonder how she would stand up to male clients. Not all her success will depend on her ability to meet a man on his own ground, with aggressiveness and intractability. But some women, Queen Elizabeth and Joan of Arc to mention two, have been remarkably successful at even that. Others compete in subtler ways. Last summer Jane Doggett and Dorothy Jackson, whose firm Architectural Graphics did the graphics for the recently completed Memphis, Tennessee, airport, met with members of the Airlines Technical Committee to explain why individual airline counters there had to have their names printed in similar type face. Expecting violent protest, the girls—one vivacious, one quiet, both very feminine, were steeled for a protracted argument and explanation. Instead their announcement met with almost complete silence. After several moments of waiting one small man towards the end of the long, oval table raised his hand and asked if his airline, Trans Texas, could have the Texas star after its name. Misses Doggett and Jackson said it couldn't. And the meeting adjourned. "I think each representative was afraid to be the one to speak up first, so no one did," Miss Doggett said later.

That women bring qualities of personality, temper[a]ment and aptitude to design that men do not is highly questionable. Mostly these characteristics are the same in both men and women. Where the sexes differ they do so as individuals because of upbringing and training. One design spokesman complains, for example, that the work of women coming from design schools has few feminine touches. "The schools have given their design a masculine stamp," he says with obvious disappointment. And women designers agree. "It takes about five years after getting out of school to work out one's own style of design," says Lucia DeRespinis.

But in any event the important fact is that more women are entering the profession. "In my first job," says Margery Markley, who has her own New York office, "there was much reluctance to hire a woman; when I left they said they didn't want to be without one." Probably part of this corporate change of heart was because of Miss Markley's personality. But too, it illustrates the quick acceptance offered the woman who has something valuable and special to contribute.

# 1965

## Ralph Nader, *Unsafe at Any Speed*

The American lawyer, consumer advocate, environmentalist, and 2000 Green Party presidential candidate Ralph Nader (1934– ) was instrumental in the creation of the United States' 1966 National Traffic and Motor Vehicle Safety Act, which gave the government the power to set safety standards for all automobiles sold in the United States.[1] The Act was created largely in response to his 1965 best-seller, *Unsafe at Any Speed: The Designed-In Dangers of the American Automobile*, which exposed common design flaws in American cars and, in particular, condemned General Motors' Chevrolet Corvair as unsafe to drive. In the following selections, Nader castigates the automotive industry for focusing on "styling" rather than on safety.

---

Excerpted from "The Stylists: It's the Curve that Counts," chapter six of *Unsafe at Any Speed: The Designed-In Dangers of the American Automobile* by Ralph Nader (New York: Grossman, 1965; copyright ©1965, 1972 by Ralph Nader): 210–1, 226–7, 230–1. Used by permission of Viking Penguin, a division of Penguin Putnam Inc.

---

The importance of the stylist's role in automobile design is frequently obscured by critics whose principal tools are adjectives. The words are familiar: stylists build "insolent chariots," they deal with tremendous trifles to place on "Detroit Iron." Or, in the moralist's language, the work of the stylists is "decadent, wasteful, and superficial."

The stylists' work cannot be dismissed so glibly. For however transitory or trivial their visible creations may be on the scale of human values, their function has been designated by automobile company top management as *the* prerequisite for maintaining the annual high volume of automobile sales—no small assignment in an industry that has a volume of at least twenty billion dollars every year.

It is the stylists who are responsible for most of the annual model change which promises the consumer "new" automobiles. It is not surprising, therefore, to find that this "newness" is almost entirely stylistic in content and that engineering innovation is restricted to a decidedly secondary role in product development.

In the matter of vehicle safety, this restriction has two main effects. First, of the dollar amount that the manufacturer is investing in a vehicle, whatever is spent for styling cannot be spent for engineering. Thus, the costs of styling divert money that might be devoted to safety. Second, stylistic suggestions often conflict with engineering ideas, and since the industry holds the view that "seeing is selling," style gets the priority.

Styling's precedence over engineering safety is well illustrated by this statement in a General Motors engineering journal: "The choice of latching means and actuating means, or handles, is dictated by styling requirements. . . . Changes in body style will continue to force redesign of door locks and handles." Another feature of style's priority over safety shows up in the paint and chrome finishes of the vehicle, which, while they provide a shiny new automobile for the dealer's floor, also create dangerous glare. Stylists can even be credited with overall concepts that result in a whole new variety of hazard. The hard-top convertible and the pillarless models, for example, were clearly the products of General Motors styling staff.

[ . . . ]

Systematic engineering design of the vehicle could minimize or prevent many pedestrian injuries. The majority of pedestrian-vehicle collisions produce injuries, not fatalities. Most of these collisions occur at impact speed of under twenty-five miles per hour, and New York City data show that in fatality cases about twenty-five per cent of the collisions occurred when the vehicles involved were moving at speeds below fourteen miles per hour. It seems quite obvious that the external design and not just the speed of the automobile contributes greatly to the severity of the injuries inflicted on the pedestrian. Yet the external design is so totally under the unfettered control of the stylist that no engineer employed by the automobile industry has ever delivered a technical paper concerning pedestrian collision. Nor have the automobile companies made any public mention of any crash testing or engineering safety research on the problem.

But two papers do exist in the technical literature, one by Henry Wakeland and the other by a group of engineers at the University of California in Los Angeles. Wakeland destroyed the lingering myth that when a pedestrian is struck by an automobile it does not make any difference which particular design feature hits him. He showed that heavy vehicles often strike people without causing fatality, and that even in fatal cases, the difference between life and death is often the difference between safe and unsafe design features. Wakeland's study was based on accident and autopsy reports of about 230 consecutive pedestrian fatalities occurring in Manhattan during 1958 and early 1959. In this sample, case after case showed the victim's body penetrated by ornaments, sharp bumper and fender edges, headlight hoods, medallions, and fins. He found that certain bumper configurations tended to force the adult pedestrian's body down, which of course greatly increased the risk of the car's running over him. [ . . . ]

[ . . . ]

The narrowing of the difference between automobiles to minor styling distinctions is not the only unhealthy result of the stylists' dominance. Even more discouraging has been the concomitant drying-up of engineering ingenuity. As the stylists have steadily risen to pre-eminence, the technological imagination of automotive engineers has slowed to a point where automobile company executives themselves have deplored the lack of innovation. Ford vice president Donald Frey recognized the problem clearly when he said in an address delivered in January 1964, "I believe that the amount of product innovation successfully introduced into the automobile is smaller today than in previous times and is still falling. The automatic transmission [adopted in 1939 on a mass-production basis][2] was the last major innovation of the industry."

The head of Mr. Frey's company, Henry Ford II, seemed troubled by the same question in his address to the same group. He said, "When you think of the enormous progress of science over the last two generations, it's astonishing to realize that there is very little about the basic principles of today's automobile that would seem strange and unfamiliar to the pioneers of our industry. . . . What we need even more than the refinement of old ideas is the ability to develop new ideas and put them to work."

Neither of these automobile executives, of course, makes the obvious connection that if an industry devotes its best efforts and its largest investment to styling concepts, it must follow that new ideas in engineering—and safety—will be tragically slow in coming.

NOTES

1. "Nader, Ralph" *Encyclopædia Britannica*, <*http://www.britannica.com/eb/article?eu=55993*>, (accessed 26 December 2002).
2. The brackets are Nader's.

# 1966

## Robert Venturi, *Complexity and Contradiction in Architecture*

The American architect and designer Robert Venturi (1925– ), who in this 1966 essay challenged Mies van der Rohe's modernist dictum that "Less is more" by countering that "More is not less" and "Less is a bore," was one of the first and most influential theorist-practitioners of postmodern architecture. In both *Complexity and Contradiction in Architecture* (1966) and *Learning from Las Vegas* (1972; coauthored with Denise Scott Brown and Steven Izenour), Venturi argued for an architecture that privileged "messy vitality over obvious unity." Venturi's and other postmodern architects' writings had a direct impact on the field of industrial design, most noticeably in the development of increasingly colorful and playful consumer goods in the 1980s.

Excerpted and reprinted by permission from Robert Venturi, *Complexity and Contradiction in Architecture* (© 1966 The Museum of Modern Art, New York): 16–17 (references omitted).

I like complexity and contradiction in architecture. I do not like the incoherence or arbitrariness of incompetent architecture nor the precious intricacies of picturesqueness or expressionism. Instead, I speak of a complex and contradictory architecture based on the richness and ambiguity of modern experience, including that experience which is inherent in art. Everywhere, except in architecture, complexity and contradiction have been acknowledged, from Gödel's proof of ultimate inconsistency in mathematics to T. S. Eliot's analysis of "difficult" poetry and Joseph Albers' definition of the paradoxical quality of painting.

But architecture is necessarily complex and contradictory in its very inclusion of the traditional Vitruvian elements of commodity, firmness, and delight. And today the wants of program, structure, mechanical equipment, and expression, even in single buildings in simple contexts, are diverse and conflicting in ways previously unimaginable. The increasing dimension and scale of architecture in urban and regional planning add to the difficulties. I welcome the problems and exploit the uncertainties. By embracing contradiction as well as complexity, I aim for vitality as well as validity.

Architects can no longer afford to be intimidated by the puritanically moral language of orthodox Modern architecture. I like elements which are hybrid rather than "pure," compromising rather than "clean," distorted rather than "straightforward," ambiguous rather than "articulated," perverse as well as impersonal, boring as well as "interesting," conventional rather than "designed," accommodating rather than excluding, redundant rather than simple, vestigial as well as innovating, inconsistent and equivocal rather than direct and clear. I am for messy vitality over obvious unity. I include the non sequitur and proclaim the duality.

I am for richness of meaning rather than clarity of meaning; for the implicit function as well as the explicit function. I prefer "both-and" to "either-or," black and white, and sometimes gray, to black or white. A valid architecture evokes many levels of meaning and combinations of focus: its space and its elements become readable and workable in several ways at once.

But an architecture of complexity and contradiction has a special obligation toward the whole: its truth must be in its totality or its implications of totality. It must embody the difficult unity of inclusion rather than the easy unity of exclusion. More is not less.

[ . . . ]

Rationalizations for simplification are still current, however, though subtler than the early arguments. They are expansions of Mies van der Rohe's magnificent paradox, "less is more." Paul Rudolph has clearly stated the implications of Mies' point of view: "All problems can never be solved. . . . Indeed it is a characteristic of the twentieth century that architects are highly selective in determining which problems they want to solve. Mies, for instance, makes wonderful buildings only because he ignores many aspects of a building. If he solved more problems, his buildings would be far less potent."

[ . . . ]

[ . . . ] Forced simplicity results in oversimplification. [ . . . ] Blatant simplification means bland architecture. Less is a bore.

[ . . . ]

# 1969

## R. Buckminster Fuller, *Operating Manual for Spaceship Earth*

The visionary American architect, designer, and social critic Richard Buckminster ("Bucky") Fuller (1895–1983) was an early proponent of high-efficiency, environmentally responsible design. His streamlined Dymaxion cars and houses of the late 1920s and 1930s (whose names derived from a combination of the words "dynamic," "maximum," and "tension") were radical reinterpretations of traditional transportation and housing forms. The highly efficient 4D-Timelock and Dymaxion house designs, which Fuller intended to be low-cost, mass-produced, easily transportable solutions to the global housing problem, met with little commercial success. However, the geodesic dome that he patented in 1954—which enclosed a maximum amount of space with a minimum amount of building material—became a popular form of architecture in the 1960s and 1970s. In these excerpts from his book, *Operating Manual for Spaceship Earth*, written while he was a professor at Southern Illinois University, Carbondale, Fuller emphasizes the need to conserve the earth's resources—a message that was forcefully driven home to many Americans during the energy crisis of the 1970s.

Excerpted from R. Buckminster Fuller, *Operating Manual for Spaceship Earth* (Carbondale, Ill.: Southern Illinois University Press, 1969): 123–5, 128. Courtesy, The Estate of R. Buckminster Fuller.

[ . . . ]

The fossil fuel deposits of our Spaceship Earth correspond to our automobile's storage battery which must be conserved to turn over our main engine's self-starter. Thereafter, our "main engine," the life regenerating processes, must operate exclusively on our vast daily energy income from the powers of wind, tide, water, and the direct Sun radiation energy. The fossil-fuel savings account has been put aboard Spaceship Earth for the exclusive function of getting the new machinery built with which to support life and humanity at ever more effective standards of vital physical energy and reinspiring metaphysical sustenance to be sustained exclusively on our Sun radiation's and Moon pull gravity's tidal, wind, and rainfall generated pulsating and therefore harnessable energies. The daily income energies are excessively adequate for the operation of our main industrial engines and their automated productions. The energy expended in one minute of a tropical hurricane equals the combined energy of all the U.S.A. and U.S.S.R. nuclear weapons. Only by understanding this scheme may we continue for all time ahead to enjoy and explore universe as we progressively harness evermore of the celestially generated tidal and storm generated wind, water, and electrical power concentrations. We cannot afford to expend our fossil fuels faster than we are "recharging our battery," which means precisely the rate at which the fossil fuels are being continually deposited within Earth's spherical crust.

We have discovered that it is highly feasible for all the human passengers aboard Spaceship Earth to enjoy the whole ship without any individual interfering with another and without any individual being advantaged at the expense of another, provided that we are not so foolish as to burn up our ship and its operating equipment by powering our prime operations exclusively on atomic reactor generated energy. The too-shortsighted and debilitating exploitation of fossil fuels and atomic energy are similar to running our automobiles only on the self-starters and batteries and as the latter become exhausted replenishing the batteries only by starting the chain reaction consumption of the atoms with which the automobiles are constituted.

[ . . . ]

This all brings us to a realization of the enormous educational task which must be successfully accomplished right now in a hurry in order to convert man's spin-dive toward oblivion into an intellectually mastered power pull-out into safe and level flight of physical and metaphysical success, whereafter he may turn his Spaceship Earth's occupancy into a universe exploring advantage. If it comprehends and reacts effectively, humanity will open an entirely new chapter of the experiences and the thoughts and drives thereby stimulated.

[ . . . ]

Returning you again to our omni-befuddled present, we realize that reorganization of humanity's economic accounting system and its implementation of the total commonwealth capability by total world society, aided by the computer's vast memory and high speed recall comes first of all of the first-things-first that we must attend to to make our space vehicle Earth a successful man operation. We may now raise our sights, in fact must raise our sights, to take the initiative in planning the world-around industrial retooling revolution. We must undertake to increase the performance per pound of the world's resources until they provide all of humanity a high standard of living. We can no longer wait to see whose biased political system should prevail over the world.

[ . . . ]

# 1971

## Victor Papanek, *Design for the Real World*

Designer and citizen of the world Victor Papanek (1927–1998) was born in Austria, grew up in England, studied design and architecture in the United States, taught at universities in the United States, Canada, Denmark, Sweden, and the United Kingdom, and practiced design around the globe for such organizations as the United Nations Educational, Scientific and Cultural Organization (UNESCO) and the World Health Organization (WHO). He published his book, *Design for the Real World*, in 1971; it has since been translated into over twenty languages. In it, building on the work of Buckminster Fuller (who wrote its introduction), Ralph Nader (see *Unsafe at Any Speed*), and environmentalists such as Rachel Carson (author of *Silent Spring*, 1962), Papanek castigated practitioners of industrial design for wasting both natural and human resources on the design of unnecessary, dangerous, and environmentally harmful products. In a direct challenge to the doctrine of artificial obsolescence (see Earnest Elmo Calkins, "Consumer Engineering"), Papanek claimed that designers needed to work for positive social good, and, failing that, to "stop working entirely."

Excerpted from Victor Papanek, *Design for the Real World: Human Ecology and Social Change* (New York: Bantam Books, 1971): 14–16, 18–19, 23, 25–26. Copyright 1984 by Victor Papanek. Published by arrangement with Academy Chicago Publishers.

There are professions more harmful than industrial design, but only a very few of them. And possibly only one profession is phonier. Advertising design, in persuading people to buy things they don't need, with money they don't have, in order to impress others who don't care, is probably the phoniest field in existence today. Industrial design, by concocting the tawdry idiocies hawked by advertisers, comes a close second. Never before in history have grown men sat down and seriously designed electric hairbrushes, rhinestone-covered file boxes, and mink carpeting for bathrooms, and then drawn up elaborate plans to make and sell these gadgets to millions of people. Before (in the "good old days"), if a person liked killing people, he had to become a general, purchase a coal mine, or else study nuclear physics. Today, industrial design has put murder on a mass production basis. By designing criminally unsafe automobiles that kill or maim nearly one million people around the world each year, by creating whole new species of permanent garbage to clutter up the landscape, and by choosing materials and processes that pollute the air we breathe, designers have become a dangerous breed. And the skills needed in these activities are taught carefully to young people.

In an age of mass production when everything must be planned and designed, design has become the most powerful tool with which man shapes his tools and environments (and, by extension, society and himself). This demands high social and moral responsibility from the designer. It also demands greater understanding of the people by those who practice design and more insight into the design process by the public. Not a single volume on the responsibility of the designer, no book on design that considers the public in this way, has ever been published anywhere.

In February of 1968, *Fortune* magazine published an article that foretold the end of the industrial design profession. Predictably, designers reacted with scorn and alarm. But I feel that the main arguments of the *Fortune* article are valid. It is about time that industrial design, *as we have come to know it,* should cease to exist. As long as design concerns itself with confecting trivial "toys for adults," killing machines with gleaming tailfins, and "sexed-up" shrouds for typewriters, toasters, telephones, and computers, it has lost all reason to exist.

Design must be an innovative, highly creative, cross-disciplinary tool responsive to the true needs of men. It must be more research-oriented, and we must stop defiling the earth itself with poorly-designed objects and structures. [ . . . ]

Looking at the books on design in seven languages, covering the walls of my home, I realized that the one book I wanted to read, the one book I most wanted to hand to my fellow students and designers, was missing. Because our society makes it crucial for designers to understand clearly the social, economic, and political background of what they do, my problem was not just one of personal frustration. So I decided to write the kind of book that I'd like to read.

This book is written from the viewpoint that there is something basically wrong with the whole concept of patents and copyrights. If I design a toy that provides therapeutic exercise for handicapped children, then I think it is unjust to delay the release of the design by a year and a half, going through a patent application. I feel that ideas are plentiful and cheap, and it is wrong to make money off the needs of others. I have been very lucky in persuading many of my students to accept this view. Much of what you will find as design examples throughout this book has never been patented. In fact, quite the opposite strategy prevails: in many cases students and I have made measured drawings of, say, a play environment for blind children, written a description of how to build it simply, and then mimeographed drawings and all. If any agency, anywhere, will write in, my students will send them all the instructions free of charge. I try to do the same myself. [ . . . ]

[ . . . ]

In an environment that is screwed up visually, physically, and chemically, the best and simplest thing that architects, industrial designers, planners, etc., could do for humanity would be *to stop working entirely*. In all pollution, designers are implicated at least partially. But in this book I take a more affirmative view: It seems to me that we can go beyond not working at all, and work positively. Design can and must become a way in which young people can participate in changing society.

Ever since the German Bauhaus first published its fourteen slender volumes around 1924, most books have merely repeated the methods evolved there or added frills to them. A philosophy more than half a century old is out of place in a field that must be as forward-looking as this.

As socially and morally involved designers, we must address ourselves to the needs of a world with its back to the wall while the hands on the clock point perpetually to one minute before twelve.[1]

[ . . . ]

All men are designers. All that we do, almost all the time, is design, for design is basic to all human activity. The planning and patterning of any act towards a desired, foreseeable end constitutes the design process. Any attempt to separate design, to make it a thing-by-itself, works counter to the inherent value of design as the primary underlying matrix of life. Design is composing an epic poem, executing a mural, painting a masterpiece, writing a concerto. But design is also cleaning and reorganizing a desk drawer, pulling an impacted tooth, baking an apple pie, choosing sides for a back-lot baseball game, and educating a child.

Design is the conscious effort to impose meaningful order.

[ . . . ]

The mode of action by which a design fulfills its purpose is its function.

"Form follows function," Louis Sullivan's battle cry of the 1880's and 1890's, was followed by Frank Lloyd Wright's "Form and function are one." But semantically, all the statements from Horatio Greenough to the German Bauhaus are meaningless. The concept that what *works* well will of necessity *look* well, has been the lame excuse for all the sterile, operating-room-like furniture and implements of the twenties and thirties. A dining table of the period might have a top, well proportioned in glistening white marble, the legs carefully nurtured for maximum strength with minimum materials in gleaming stainless steel. And the first reaction on encountering such a table is to lie down on it and have your appendix extracted. Nothing about the table says: "Dine off me." *Le style international* and *die neue Sachlichkeit*[2] have let us down rather badly in terms of human value. Le Corbusier's house as *la machine à habiter*[3] and the packing-crate houses evolved in the Dutch *De Stijl* movement reflect a perversion of aesthetics and utility.

[ . . . ]

**N O T E S**

1. This may be a reference to the "Doomsday Clock" maintained by the *Bulletin of the Atomic Scientists*.
2. The International Style and the New Objectivity (forms of early twentieth-century architectural modernism).
3. The machine for living in.

# 1973

# Richard Nixon, "Address to the Nation About Policies To Deal With the Energy Shortages"

The "Energy Crisis" of the 1970s was the result of a September/October 1973 decision by members of the Organization of Petroleum Exporting Countries (OPEC) to raise world oil prices by 70 percent. The situation became even more desperate when, in retaliation for the United States support of Israel in the Yom Kippur War, OPEC raised prices another 130 percent and put into effect an embargo on oil shipments to the United States and the Netherlands. On November 7 of that year, President Richard Nixon addressed the American public, urging them to take measures at home and at work to conserve energy and to reduce their dependence on foreign oil. Although the embargo was only temporary, additional price increases were levied over the next few years; a barrel of crude oil that cost $3.00 in the United States in 1973 cost ten times that amount in 1980.[1] The Energy Crisis had a lasting effect on the design of houses, automobiles, and consumer goods; fuel efficiency, which had never been a priority for most American designers and consumers, suddenly became a necessity.

Richard Nixon, "Address to the Nation About Policies To Deal With the Energy Shortages," 7 November 1973, from *Public Papers of the Presidents of the United States: Richard Nixon, 1973* (Washington, D.C.: U.S. Government Printing Office, 1975): 916–920.

# G *ood evening:*

I want to talk to you tonight about a serious national problem, a problem we must all face together in the months and years ahead.

As America has grown and prospered in recent years, our energy demands have begun to exceed available supplies. In recent months, we have taken many actions to increase supplies and to reduce consumption. But even with our best efforts, we knew that a period of temporary shortages was inevitable.

Unfortunately, our expectations for this winter have now been sharply altered by the recent conflict in the Middle East. Because of that war, most of the Middle Eastern oil producers have reduced overall production and cut off their shipments of oil to the United States. By the end of this month, more than 2 million barrels a day of oil we expected to import into the United States will no longer be available.

We must, therefore, face up to a very stark fact: We are heading toward the most acute shortages of energy since World War II. Our supply of petroleum this winter will be at least 10 percent short of our anticipated demands, and it could fall short by as much as 17 percent.

Now, even before war broke out in the Middle East, these prospective shortages were the subject of intensive discussions among members of my Administration, leaders of the Congress, Governors, mayors, and other groups. From these discussions has emerged a broad agreement that we, as a nation, must now set upon a new course.

In the short run, this course means that we must use less energy—that means less heat, less electricity, less gasoline. In the long run, it means that we must develop new sources of energy which will give us the capacity to meet our needs without relying on any foreign nation.

The immediate shortage will affect the lives of each and every one of us. In our factories, our cars, our homes, our offices, we will have to use less fuel than we are accustomed to using. Some school and factory schedules may be realigned, and some jet airplane flights will be canceled.

This does not mean that we are going to run out of gasoline or that air travel will stop or that we will freeze in our homes or offices anyplace in America. The fuel crisis need not mean genuine suffering for any American. But it will require some sacrifice by all Americans.

We must be sure that our most vital needs are met first—and that our least important activities are the first to be cut back. And we must be sure that while the fat from our economy is being trimmed, the muscle is not seriously damaged.

To help us carry out that responsibility, I am tonight announcing the following steps:

First, I am directing that industries and utilities which use coal—which is our most abundant resource—be prevented from converting from coal to oil. Efforts will also be made to convert powerplants from the use of oil to the use of coal.

Second, we are allocating reduced quantities of fuel for aircraft. Now, this is going to lead to a cutback of more than 10 percent of the number of flights and some rescheduling of arrival and departure times.

Third, there will be reductions of approximately 15 percent in the supply of heating oil for homes and offices and other establishments. To be sure that there is enough oil to go around for the entire winter, all over the country, it will be essential for all of us to live and work in lower temperatures. We must ask everyone to lower the thermostat in your home by at least 6 degrees so that we can achieve a national daytime average of 68 degrees. Incidentally, my doctor tells me that in a temperature of 66 to 68 degrees, you are really more healthy than when it is 75 to 78, if that is any comfort. In offices, factories, and commercial establishments, we must ask that you achieve the equivalent of a 10-degree reduction by either lowering the thermostat or curtailing working hours.

Fourth, I am ordering additional reductions in the consumption of energy by the Federal Government. We have already taken steps to reduce the government's consumption by 7 percent. The cuts must now go deeper and must be made by every agency and every department in the Government. I am directing that daytime temperatures in Federal offices be reduced immediately to a level of between 65 and 68 degrees, and that means in this room, too, as well as in every other room in the White House. In addition, I am ordering that all vehicles owned by the Federal Government—and there are over a half-million of them—travel no faster than 50 miles per hour except in emergencies. This is a step which I have also asked Governors, mayors, and local officials to take immediately with regard to vehicles under their authority.

Fifth, I am asking the Atomic Energy Commission to speed up the licensing and construction of nuclear plants. We must seek to reduce the time required to bring nuclear plants on line—nuclear plants that can produce power—to bring them on line from 10 years to 6 years, reduce that time lag.

Sixth, I am asking that Governors and mayors reinforce these actions by taking appropriate steps at the State and local level. We have already learned, for example, from the State of Oregon, that considerable amounts of energy can be saved simply by curbing unnecessary lighting and slightly altering the school year. I am recommending that other communities follow this example and also seek ways to stagger working hours, to encourage greater use of mass transit and carpooling.

How many times have you gone along the highway or the freeway, wherever the case may be, and see hundreds and hundreds of cars with only one individual in that car? This we must all cooperate to change. Consistent with safety and economic considerations, I am also asking Governors to take steps to reduce highway speed limits to 50 miles per hour. This action alone, if it is adopted on a nationwide basis, could save over 200,000 barrels of oil a day—just reducing the speed limit to 50 miles per hour.

Now, all of these actions will result in substantial savings of energy. More than that, most of these are actions that we can take right now—without further delay.

The key to their success lies, however, not just here in Washington but in every home, in every community across this country. If each of us joins in this effort, joins with the spirit and the determination that have always graced the American character, then half the battle will already be won.

But we should recognize that even these steps, as essential as they are, may not be enough. We must be prepared to take additional steps, and for that purpose, additional authorities must be provided by the Congress.

I have therefore directed my chief adviser for energy policy, Governor Love, and other Administration officials, to work closely with the Congress in developing an emergency energy act.

I met with the leaders of the Congress this morning, and I asked that they act on this legislation on a priority, urgent basis. It is imperative that this legislation be on my desk for signature before the Congress recesses this December.

Because of the hard work that has already been done on this bill by Senators Jackson and Fannin and others, I am confident that we can meet that goal and that I will have the bill on this desk and will be able to sign it.

This proposed legislation would enable the executive branch to meet the energy emergency in several important ways:

First, it would authorize an immediate return to daylight saving time on a year-round basis.

Second, it would provide the necessary authority to relax environmental regulations on a temporary, case-by-case basis, thus permitting an appropriate balancing of our environmental interests, which all of us share, with our energy requirements, which, of course, are indispensable.

Third, it would grant authority to impose special energy conservation measures, such as restrictions on the working hours for shopping centers and other commercial establishments.

And fourth, it would approve and fund increased exploration, development and production from our naval petroleum reserves. Now, these reserves are rich sources of oil. From one of them alone—Elk Hills in California—we could produce more than 160,000 barrels of oil a day within 2 months.

Fifth, it would provide the Federal Government with the authority to reduce highway speed limits throughout the Nation.

And finally, it would expand the power of the Government's regulatory agencies to adjust the schedules of planes, ships, and other carriers.

If shortages persist despite all of these actions and despite inevitable increases in the price of energy products, it may then become necessary—may become necessary—to take even stronger measures.

It is only prudent that we be ready to cut the consumption of oil products, such as gasoline, by rationing or by a fair system of taxation, and consequently, I have directed that contingency plans, if this becomes necessary, be prepared for that purpose.

Now, some of you may wonder whether we are turning back the clock to another age. Gas rationing, oil shortages, reduced speed limits—they all sound like a way of life we left behind with Glenn Miller and the war of the forties. Well, in fact, part of our current problem also stems from war—the war in the Middle East. But our deeper energy problems come not from war, but from peace and from abundance. We are running out of energy today because our economy has grown enormously and because in prosperity what were once considered luxuries are now considered necessities.

How many of you can remember when it was very unusual to have a home air-conditioned? And yet, this is very common in almost all parts of the nation.

As a result, the average American will consume as much energy in the next 7 days as most other people in the world will consume in an entire year. We have only 6 percent of the world's people in America, but we consume over 30 percent of all the energy in the world.

Now, our growing demands have bumped up against the limits of available supply, and until we provide new sources of energy for tomorrow, we must be prepared to tighten our belts today.

[ . . . ]

**N O T E S**

1. "Petroleum Exporting Countries, Organization of," *Encyclopædia Britannica,* <*http://www.britannica.com/eb/article?eu=61005*>, (accessed 24 December 2002).

# 1976-2000

# 1976

# Alexander Kira, "Historical Aspects of Personal Hygiene Facilities"

Alexander Kira, an American architect and ergonomics specialist, is a professor emeritus of architecture at Cornell University and a former director of its Center for Housing and Environmental Studies. His 1966 book *The Bathroom*, which was significantly expanded in 1976, offered a groundbreaking approach to the design of bathroom spaces and fixtures: matter-of-fact analysis of the mechanics of male and female urination, defecation, hand-washing, bathing, etc., combined with analysis of the social and cultural factors that shape the way those activities are performed.

Excerpted from *The Bathroom*, 2nd ed., by Alexander Kira, copyright ©1966 by Alexander Kira (New York: Viking Press, 1976): pp. 5–6, 8–9 (references omitted). Used by permission of Bantam Books, a division of Random House, Inc.

**M**an has always and everywhere been faced with the same fundamental problems of personal hygiene that concern us today. The ways in which he has coped with them have, however, varied enormously, not only from one culture to another but also from one era to another. While available technology has certainly played a role in this, by far the most important determinants have been our various philosophical, psychological, and religious attitudes regarding the human body and its processes and products. These attitudes are not only central to our conceptions of ourselves as human beings but are also held strongly and are often embodied in religious laws and enforced by legal sanctions. All the world's religions, in all their branchings and shadings, have had viewpoints and teachings on the body, sex, birth, death, illness, menstruation, elimination, and cleansing. As we shall see later, these have often been contradictory and have obviously been strongly influenced by the social climate of the period as well as by the then current medical knowledge and opinion. Virtually the only absolutes in this entire area of human existence have been those natural and involuntary bodily processes over which we have no control whether we like the facts or not.

The availability of technology, as we are constantly being reminded, is essentially a question of sociopolitical demand. Technology per se has had relatively little life of its own. As our recent experiences with the space program, with pollution controls, and with consumer-product safety have amply demonstrated once again, technology is to a very large degree a variable that can be speeded or slowed according to the social and cultural demands of an era. While we can create new technologies to satisfy our demands, we can also ignore particular technologies and allow them to lie idle for years. Thus, on the one hand, we have the legacy of civilizations such as the Minoan and the Roman, which created stupendous feats of engineering and produced hygiene facilities with piped hot and cold running water, water-flushed sewage systems, and steam rooms, and, on the other hand, a notable lack of such facilities centuries later, when basic technology was considerably more advanced.

[ . . . ]

During the thirties, and particularly during and immediately after World War II, a number of ingenious improvements were proposed and even tried, mostly in terms of prefabrication. None, however, were successful, and few of the ideas ever found their way into practice. The actual significant progress that has been made in this period is quite small, so much so that the average bathroom today is barely distinguishable from one built forty years ago. To a large extent, the forces responsible for this are to be found, both in the United States and abroad, within the structuring of the plumbing industry, which has followed the pattern peculiar to the home-building industry: field erection and assembly of thousands of independently produced and often unrelated items. With few exceptions, the bathroom has rarely been conceived of as an entity, certainly not by the plumbing industry. But our attitudes toward personal hygiene have also kept us from giving the problem the attention it deserves, as we will examine in detail later. In a great many ways, the average bathroom supplied by the average builder and architect is still minimal in every respect—in terms not only of contemporary needs but also of contemporary technology, values, and attitudes.

# 1984

## Klaus Krippendorff and Reinhart Butter, "Product Semantics: Exploring the Symbolic Qualities of Form"

The German-American Klaus Krippendorff is a professor of communication at the Annenberg School for Communication at the University of Pennsylvania; Reinhart Butter, also a German-American, is a professor of industrial design at The Ohio State University. Both men received diplomas in design from the Hochschule für Gestaltung, Ulm (see introduction to "Program of the HfG, Ulm), and they have since collaborated on many projects, including this influential 1984 article, which appeared in the special "product semantics" issue of *Innovation* that they coedited.

Excerpted from Klaus Krippendorff and Reinhart Butter, "Product Semantics: Exploring the Symbolic Qualities of Form," *Innovation,* vol. 3, no. 2 (spring 1984): 4, 6, 8–9. Reprinted with permission from *Innovation* (spring 1984), the Quarterly of the Industrial Designers Society of America; p: 703.707.6000; f: 703.787.8501; e: *idsa@idsa.org*; w: *www.idsa.org.*

I n its broadest sense, design is the conscious creation of forms to serve human needs. It sharply contrasts with the habitual reproduction of forms. While the history of design is not free of faddish and sometimes unconscious shifts in focus (witness the merging of craftsmanship with mass production by the Bauhaus, of technology with ergonomics at the Ulm School and of styling with market considerations on Madison Avenue), design has also broadened its scope of consciousness.

Probably the most noteworthy development in design today, giving evidence of this greater scope, is its concern for the cognitive meanings, symbolic functions and cultural histories of form. We can trace this concern to developments in Ulm some 25 years ago which are now coming to fruition by the name of "product semantics." *Product semantics is the study of the symbolic qualities of man-made forms in the context of their use and the application of this knowledge to*

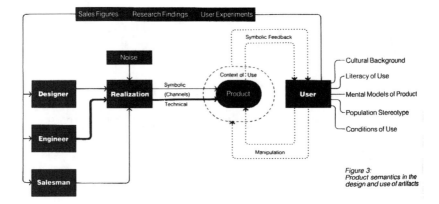

Figure 3:
Product semantics in the
design and use of artifacts

*industrial design.* It takes into account not only the physical and physiological functions, but the psychological, social and cultural context, which we call the symbolic environment. Product semantics is an effort to understand and to take full responsibility for the symbolic environment into which industrial products are placed and where they should function by virtue of their own communicative qualities. Through product semantics, designers can demystify complex technology, improve the interaction between artifacts and their users and enhance opportunities for self-expression.

[ . . . ]

The knowledge product semantics provides about how objects work within the context of their use cannot entirely be expressed in terms of linear communication between a designer and a user. The crucial difference lies in the individuality of the users' interpretations which evolve in the circular process of their involvement with the designers' products. [ . . . ] Figure 3 depicts a designer whose circumstances realistically restrict him to be a mere contributing communicator, albeit a very important one.

[ . . . ]

## Channels Influencing Product Use

The meanings relevant to product design may be communicated through four symbolic channels.

- Information displays, [ . . . ]
- Graphic elements or two-dimensional markers, [ . . . ]
- A product's form, shape and texture [ . . . and]
- Indications of a product's internal states. [ . . . ]

These four channels of communication may be redundant in that the information they provide to the user overlaps. Redundancy often aids understanding. But these channels may also produce conflicts by giving contradictory messages to a user, or they may fail to provide enough information, causing misapplications or operational errors to occur. Product semantics heavily relies on the principles of communication characteristic of these channels, and we will point to some typical mistakes designers may make in using them here.

[ . . . ]

## Four Semantic Infelicities in Design

[ . . . ]

The first and most elementary kind of infelicity has the effect of rendering different products indistinguishable or unidentifiable by a user. [ . . . ]

A second kind of infelicity results in the users' inability to manipulate a product in desired ways. [ . . . ]

The third kind of infelicity prevents a user from exploring the nature of a product either to improve its operation or to find new applications without outside help. [ . . . ]

A fourth kind of infelicity results from a product's inability to fit the symbolic environments in which users must operate them. [ . . . ]

The four kinds of infelicities discussed here are neither exhaustive nor exclusive. Rather, they illustrate where designers can make mistakes in the symbolic domain and where product semantics can provide insight into why they come about. They designate different failures in the circular dependency depicted in Figure 3 and pertain to different levels in that dependency. The first level—product identification—requires the user to merely look at an object from different perspectives and interpret relevant clues to judge what kind of object it is. The second level—self-evident operation—additionally requires the user to handle an object, to move it about or alter its controls and obtain feedback from those actions. It also requires that the user experience operational success or failure. The third level—explorability of forms—invites the user to play with the object, acquire a working knowledge of it and perhaps invent novel applications. And the fourth level—coherence with the symbolic context—concerns a user who interprets an object in conjunction with others and who may describe the whole arrangement in terms of personal style, individual expression, social attributes and aesthetic value. Product semantics deals with all these levels, promising to make designers aware of the symbolic processes underlying them.

[ . . . ]

## The State of the Art

Product semantics is still in its infancy. Many designers are dissatisfied with previous approaches and have become aware of the importance of the symbolic role of products. But enhanced awareness is only the first stage of and a prerequisite for the emergence of product semantics. A second stage is the development of concepts and a suitable language in which to talk about the symbolic qualities of products, the user-product interfaces, the construction of cognitive models, the transmission of meanings through the channels at a designer's disposal, the infelicities that may occur and so on. The papers in this issue [of *Innovation*] give evidence of movement in this direction. While work is progressing, results are admittedly rudimentary, scar[c]e in number and isolated from other approaches. Many new ideas will have to be generated, tested and weeded out before we can speak of having a suitable language. In a third stage, empirical investigations are particularly essential to validate the propositions in this language. Those few research efforts that have demonstrably yielded fruits are rarely unquestionably valid and generalizable to support teaching and communication among designers at this time. What we need is a collection of generally applicable research methods that will not restrict us by saying what is right and what is wrong, but that will show us where the range of practical options is.

Product semantics is not a new style. It is not a ticket to intrude into the privacy of the individual users. Nor is it a new functionalism turned psychological. It is a serious study of the meanings that emerge in human interactions with objects. Its application enriches our imagination and aims to prevent the range of failures we have become aware of only recently. This issue of *Innovation* demonstrates our state of knowledge and points out the direction we wish to move toward.

# 1984

## Barbara Radice, "Memphis and Fashion"

The international design group Memphis was founded in Milan, Italy, in 1981 by the Austro-Italian architect and designer Ettore Sottsass (1917– ). The group challenged modernist dogmas about functionalism and rationalism by creating boldly colored and patterned decorative arts and furniture that were intended to be both flashy and faddish. The Italian critic Barbara Radice (1943– ), who, in these selections describes the group's aims and outlook, was simultaneously a member of Memphis's inner circle and a chronicler and critic of its works.

Excerpted from Barbara Radice, *Memphis: Research, Experiences, Results, Failures, and Successes of New Design* (New York: Rizzoli, 1984): 185–187 (references omitted). Reprinted by permission of the author.

**M**emphis was started with the idea of changing the face of international design, and it chose the most effective, direct, and hazardous way to do so. It showed that the change not only was possible, but had already taken place, that it involved worldwide aspirations and personalities and that it was a radical one. Born in an anomalous way, outside of academic culture, Memphis also made its début in a flashy way. It came up with a large number of products presented to the beat of good rock music and with a way-out type of display and allure. The idea was to attract attention, and the response was immediate. The opening was followed by a tidal wave of interest among the public and the press. The resulting gossip and arguments, the passionate or amused support, the harsh, drastic criticism, the interviews, the publicity—all this very quickly made Memphis not only a successful cultural movement, but a myth, a sort of liberating symbol with which many people wished to identify. To put it in the words of a twelve-year-old American girl who wrote to ask for a piece of furniture for her bedroom, Memphis was already "like a rock star." This overnight stardom momentarily embittered those who, in spite of themselves, had been caught up in the whys and wherefores of that success. Nevertheless it ended up representing, for those same people, the response to many embarrassing doubts and questions. It showed, in other words, that Memphis was "a fad," "just" a fad. With a little bitterness, then, one could catch one's breath.

Quite differently, with a mixture of joy and anxious astonishment, the people on the other side of the moon caught their breath too. Memphis architects and designers and their friends and supporters saw the fact of being a fad, of moving "à la mode" and "comme la mode,"[1] as a sign of great vitality.

Arata Isozaki pointed out: "The important thing about Memphis is also the way it appeared to the world. Normally a furniture manufacturer announces a product, prints a catalogue, and so on and so forth. Memphis appeared suddenly, as fashion does, and it had a very strong impact all over the world...things always change rapidly anyhow. At the Bauhaus, the tubular chairs were designed between 1920 and 1925, no earlier and no later. The designers of those chairs changed style later, but the objects lived on. They are still produced even today."

Memphis never feared fashion, being a fashion, or going out of fashion. On the contrary it foresaw and adjusted from the outset to this fluid state of variability. I quote from my introduction to the catalogue, the statement that perhaps caused the greatest uproar at the time of the presentation in 1981: "We are all sure that Memphis furniture will soon go out of style."

The whole Memphis idea is oriented toward a sensory concentration based on instability, on provisional representation of provisional states and of events and signs that fade, blur, fog up and are consumed. "It is no coincidence," says Sottsass, "that the people who work for Memphis don't pursue a metaphysical aesthetic idea or an absolute of any kind, much less eternity. Today everything one does is consumed. It is dedicated to life, not to eternity." Memphis works for contemporary culture, it designs for consumption. When Memphis designers say they design "for communication" they cast off the alibis of useful, "clean," lasting design, design that solves functional (or social . . . ?) problems. Their brand of communication consists in presenting an object that is attractive by virtue of its elusive, evanescent, consumable, perversely "useless" and consequently infinitely desirable qualities. Communication—true communication—is not simply the transmission of information (which in the case of a "product" is always unilateral, from the product to the consumer). Communication always calls for an exchange of fluids and tensions, for a provocation, and a challenge. Memphis does not claim to know what people "need," but it runs the risk of guessing what people "want." With the same words Ruthie (in the song, "Stuck Inside of Mobile with the Memphis Blues Again," which gave Memphis its name) answers Bob Dylan, who discourages her advances under the Panama moon, protesting his fidelity to a debutante. Ruthie says: "Oh but your debutante just knows what you need, but I know what you want." The two things often don't coincide at all.

Memphis doesn't give away or solve anything. Memphis, as I said before, seduces. It seduces by virtue of its enigmatic and contradictory qualities. It seduces because the void of values that it has created by refusing to solve problems, to be logical, definitive, positive, stable, or lasting represents a challenge to common sense-good taste-respectability. It seduces because it is impassive in happily declaring that it is meant to be consumed.

Naturally there's a trick, and the trick is part of the challenge. Memphis has unabashedly, almost obscenely stripped-off the aura of usefulness and the more arcane aura of art (which many of its enemies shrewdly continued to attribute to it). It has gambled all its charm on this emptying of meaning, and with this turn of the screw has won the "fatal" powers of the absolute object, of which Baudrillard speaks: "An absolute object is an object whose value is null and whose quality is indifferent but which escapes objective alienation because it becomes more an object than the object, and this gives it a fatal quality."

The fatal quality mentioned by Baudrillard is the quality an object acquires when it becomes a fetish, and it ceases to show its use-value, when it relinquishes the "risible claim of assigning to every event a cause and a cause to every event," and declares that only "effects" are absolutely necessary.

This is also the secret quality of fashion. A quality transgressive of all value judgements and codes, for it is tied to the arbitrary charm of the ephemeral. A quality that eludes, *because* it is ephemeral, the solidity and viscosity of feeling and of history, that is, it eludes duration (eternity) and pledges itself to extinction (to life).

Memphis objects, like fashion, are purely tautological, they are "immoral." As I attended Memphis openings in London, Los Angeles, Milan, Tokyo,

San Francisco, and New York, I often wondered about the strange power of these objects—a power extending over an extremely heterogeneous public, a power capable of transforming a furniture show into an ecstatic event, a momentary collective trance, a sort of esoteric initiation that marks the passage into a special cultural caste.

Memphis, I told myself, is not just a cultural event, it is an erotic event, an erotic-consumer rite that absorbs anxieties and recycles energies; it is a lubricating essence, a fine tuning of metabolism, a focusing of perspectives. At least this is the kind of effect it has—even on nonspecialists, even on the skeptics who reject it but feel it, and above all on young people.

Memphis, like the fruit of the tree of knowledge, contains a promise and a challenge inextricably bound up with, and metamorphosed into one another. The trick I mentioned earlier is that Memphis objects, by emptying themselves of meaning and charging themselves with enigma, go back to being ritual objects, propitiatory diagrams, ceremonial formulas. They offer life, not an explanation but a sense, arbitrary as it may be; the sense of life in self-contemplation.

Memphis, like fashion, works on the fabric of contemporaneity, and contemporaneity means computers, electronics, videogames, science-fiction comics, Blade Runner, Space Shuttle, biogenetics, laser bombs, a new awareness of the body, exotic diets and banquets, mass exercise and tourism. Mobility is perhaps the most macroscopic novelty of this culture. Not only physical mobility but also and above all mobility of hierarchies and values; and mobility of interpretations which has liquefied the contours and solidity of things, shrinking the long, lazy waves of our "Weltanschauung"[2] to increasingly high frequencies until they burst and evaporate in a dust of hypotheses, in a whirl of events. What matters to us is not their substance but their appearance, their virtual image. It is the world of TV screens, the world of shadow, where, as in Zen stories, it is never clear whether you dream you are a butterfly or the butterfly dreams it is you.

Memphis has plunged into the flow of this mobility and acts as a reflector, as a radar, as a talisman capable of harmonizing with the subtle ripples of this perennial, accelerated metamorphosis. At least it tries to.

At Memphis they say that even a design must "happen" in real time. It must move, in other words, in the fluid logic of variability and produce objects destined for total and immediate consumption, objects as intense as apparitions, as magic as curses, concentrates of existential lust. Objects whose charisma, whose "secret name," should be outlined by the concentration, compactness and speed of the energies they are able to contain and unleash rather than diluted in the boredom of an aphonic, and equally arbitrary design, of stability, solidity, and duration. Memphis quality is of no interest, nor can it be known how long it will "last." One might say that it is a quality concerned with the exact opposite of "duration," with self-destruction, annihilation, disappearance, which is also the magic formula of our destiny, of life which in order to glitter must fade and liberate, as radioactive fall out, the shivers and omens of the end.

NOTES

1. "in fashion" and "like (or as) fashion"
2. "world view" or philosophy of life

# 1984

## Dieter Rams, "Omit the Unimportant"

The German architect and industrial designer Dieter Rams (1932– ) began working for the German consumer appliance company Braun in 1955, shortly after Otl Aicher and Hans Gugelot of the Ulm Hochschule für Gestaltung (see introduction to "Program of the HfG, Ulm") had created a new, more modern corporate identity for the company. As head of product design at Braun for many decades, Rams established his "less, but better" design ethic as Braun's house style.

Reprinted in its entirety from Dieter Rams, "Omit the Unimportant," *Design Issues* 1:1 (Spring 1984): 24–26. ©1984 by the Massachusetts Institute of Technology. Reprinted by permission of MIT Press.

Every industrial product serves a specific purpose. People do not buy a specific product just to look at it, rather because it performs certain functions. Its design must conform in the best possible way to the expectations that result from the function the product fulfills. The more intensive and explicit the product's use, the clearer the demands on design. That all sounds very obvious, but anyone who looks at our environment will discover a host of products whose design is not substantiated by any functional necessities. Often you can count yourself lucky if the design is not disturbing during use. Rigid functionalism of the past has been somewhat discredited in recent years. Perhaps justly so because the functions a product had to fulfill were often seen too narrowly and with too much puritanism. The spectrum of people's needs is often greater than designers are willing, or sometimes able, to admit. Functionalism may well be a term with a multitude of definitions; however, there is no alternative.

One of the most significant design principles is to omit the unimportant in order to emphasize the important. The time has come for us to discover our environment anew and return to the simple basic aspects, for example, to items that have unconstricted obvious-seeming functionalism in both the physical and the psychological sense. Therefore, products should be well designed and as neutral and open as possible, leaving room for the self-expression of those using them.

Good design means as little design as possible. Not for reasons of economy or convenience. Arriving at a really convincing, harmonious form by employing simple means is surely a difficult task. The other way is easier and, as paradoxical as it may seem, often cheaper, but also more thoughtless with respect to production. Complicated, unnecessary forms are nothing more than designers' escapades that function as self-expression instead of expressing the product's functions. The reason is often that design is used to gain a superficial redundance.

The economy of Braun design is a rejection of this type of approach. Braun products eliminate the superfluous to emphasize that which is more important. For example, the contours of the object become more placid, soothing, perceptible, and long-living. Much design today is modish sensation and the rapid change of fashion outdates products quickly. The choices are sensible: disciplined simplicity or forced, oppressive, stultifying expression. For me there is only one way: discipline.

Every manufactured item sends out signals to the mind or emotions. These signals—strong or weak, wanted or unwanted, clear or hidden—create feelings. But the most important factor is whether the item can communicate its use. Of course, a product's effect is also important. What sentiments does it evoke? People are very much directly influenced and emotionally moved by the design of items surrounding them, often without realizing this immediately.

My own experience can be summarized in two theses. First, items should be designed in such a way that their function and attributes are directly understood. For design, this is an opportunity and a challenge. Until recently, this task hasn't been taken very seriously and the opportunity hasn't been used enough. The self-explanatory quality of most products is low, especially in innovative fields where it is very important that a product's utility is understood without the frustrating continuous studies of user's instructions. Design riddles are impudent and products that are informative, understandable, and clear are pleasant and agreeable. Of course, getting products to "talk" by means of design is a demanding task. Creativity, experience, tenacity, ability, and diligence are necessary.

Second, the fewer the opportunities used to create informative design, the more design serves to evoke emotional responses. This is not always conscious but more or less instinctive, created by fireworks of signals that the products send out. Often these responses are so intense that they are confusing. I try to fight against them. I don't want to be dominated, nor do I want to be excited, stup[e]fied, or amazed. I refuse to be surprised by the steadily increasing dynamic of taste. I refuse, as well, to submit to widespread demands or structures of the market without asking for the product's use.

The latest design trends are intended to evoke emotions by trivial, superficial means. It is not a question of information for use, nor a problem of insight and perception in a broader sense. The issue is stimuli: new, strong, exciting, and therefore aggressive signals. The primary aim is to be recognized as intensely as possible. The aggressiveness of design is expressed in the harshness of combat to attain first place in people's perception and awareness and to win the fight for a front place in store display windows.

I don't support dull or boring design but I do take a stand against the ruthless exploitation of people's weaknesses for visual and haptic signals, which many designers are engaged in. The festival of colors and forms and the entertainment of form sensations enlarges the world's chaos. To out-do each other with new design sensations leads nowhere. The alternative is to return to simplicity. And that requires working hard and seriously.

This task is not only for designers. Participation is required by all those involved in developing new products, and by the public as well. Aggressive individuality must be abandoned. We should not forego innovation, but reject novelty as the sole aim. Our culture is our home, especially the everyday culture expressed in items for whose forms I am responsible. It would be a great help if we could feel more at home in this everyday culture, if alienation, confusion and sensory overload would lessen.

Instead of trying to outdo our rivals, we designers should work together more seriously and thoughtfully. Designers are critics of civilization, technology, and society. But contrary to the many qualified and unqualified critical minds of our time, designers cannot stop there. They must continue to look for something new, something that ensues from the criticism and that can stand up against it. In addition, they cannot remain at the level of words, reflections, considerations, warnings, accusations, or slogans. They must transpose their insights into concrete, three-dimensional objects.

Of the many issues that confront designers, the increase of violence seems to be the most threatening. Destructive, aggressive tendencies are gaining momentum and counteract the idea on which design was founded. It is a frontal attack. I work in the hope of designing objects that are useful and convincing enough to be accepted and lived with for a long time in a very obvious, natural way. But such objects do not fit into a world of vandalism, aggression, and cynicism. In this kind of world, there is not room for design or culture of any type.

Design is the effort to make products in such a way that they are useful to people. It is more rational than irrational, optimistic and projected toward the future rather than resigned, cynical, and indifferent. Design means being steadfast and progressive rather than escaping and giving up. In a historical phase in which the outer world has become less natural and increasingly artificial and commercial, the value of design increases. The work of designers can contribute more concretely and effectively toward a more humane existence in the future.

# 1985

## The Japan Management Association, "Just-In-Time at Toyota"

The Japan Management Association (JMA) is a nonprofit organization that was established in 1942 under the auspices of Japan's Ministry of International Trade and Industry; its goal is to "pursue innovation in management that will result in improved quality and productivity" in Japanese business enterprises.[1] *Kanban: Just-In-Time at Toyota,* published by the JMA in Japanese in 1985 and in English in 1986, outlines a set of management strategies developed by executive vice president Taiichi Ohno (1912–1990) of Toyota Motor Co. that constituted perhaps the greatest revolution in management theory since Frederick Winslow Taylor's "scientific management" of the early 1900s.

The Japan Management Association, *Kanban: Just-In-Time at Toyota: Management Begins at the Workplace,* edited by the Japan Management Association and translated by David J. Lu (1985; English translation, Stamford, Conn. and Cambridge, Mass.: Productivity Press, 1986): 24, 66, 68–69, 72–73. Reprinted from *Kanban: Just-In-Time at Toyota,* edited by the Japan Management Institute. English translation copyright ©1986 Productivity Inc.; 800-394-6868; *www.productivityinc.com.*

**A**n ideal condition for manufacturing is where there is no waste in machines, equipment and personnel, and where they can work together to raise the added value to produce profit. The most important concern for us is how closely we can approach this ideal.

To make the flow of things as close as possible to this ideal condition— whether they be between operations, between lines, between processes or between factories—we have devised a system in which the materials needed are obtained *just-in-time*—that is, exactly when needed and in the quantity needed.

On the other hand, for this ideal condition to occur in the line operations, including machines and equipment, if there is abnormality, everything must be stopped immediately at the discretion of the worker or workers involved. (Machines must be endowed with the same faculty.) The reasons for the occurrence of abnormality must be investigated from the ground up. This is what we call *automation with a human touch*.

We believe it is best to manufacture everything in a balanced manner. This *load-smoothing production* serves as the base for the two pillars of the Toyota system, namely the just-in-time and automation-with-a-human-touch approaches.

[ . . . ]

The term *just-in-time* was invented by Mr. Kiichiro Toyoda, the first president of Toyota. But it was Mr. Ohno who took up the challenge. Indeed, Mr. Ohno is responsible for the creation of the Toyota system as we know it today.

[ . . . ]

[ . . . ]

[ . . . I]f a process can supply items that are needed at the time needed and in the quantity needed by other processes, the waste as discussed above can be eliminated from the workplace and improvement can move one step forward. To accomplish this, management must abandon the practice of giving production plans to each and every one of the processes, or of making the preceding process transport its products to the subsequent process. This system does not make it clear how much the subsequent process really needs, and the preceding process is liable to overproduce. Productivity suffers when a process produces an unnecessary amount or transports to the next process materials not needed by the latter.

A new idea is born to reverse this process. It is done with the subsequent process withdrawing from the preceding process what it needs. Instead of the preceding process sending to the next process what it has produced, the flow is changed in such a way that *the subsequent process withdraws from the preceding process what it needs when it needs it. The preceding process produces exactly the same quantity as is withdrawn.* In this way, all of those variegated problems mentioned earlier can be solved.

The final point of manufacturing processes is the final assembly line. This is made into a point of departure, and a production plan is shown only to the final assembly line. In it is shown what types of cars, and in what quantity, are needed, and when they are needed. The assembly line goes to the preceding process to withdraw parts it needs. In this way, steps are taken to retrace the entire manufacturing process backward, and even the division of rough raw materials can become simultaneously connected with the rest of the manufacturing process in a chain-like fashion. Conditions to fulfill the requirements of the just-in-time system are satisfied, and the management man-hours can be significantly reduced.

[ . . . ]

It is not easy to stop the line when work is in progress. When the line is stopped even momentarily, the amount of production will fall, and no supervisor cherishes the thought. At Toyota, lines are stopped—but this does not mean we like doing it.

In any event, Toyota's lines stop now and then. When they stop, they stop only for a few seconds. This is done in order to make the entire line function smoothly. We stop the lines with the ultimate goal of never stopping those lines again.

This is a true story:

There was a supervisor at Toyota, whom we shall call Mr. A, who steadfastly refused to stop his line. Then there was another supervisor, whom we shall call Mr. B, who would do as suggested in stopping the line.

Mr. B did not hesitate stopping his line, so initially it stopped too frequently. The number of cars assembled on this line was drastically cut and no production plan could be maintained. The line stopped, however, because of the many problems which, while known to the workers, had never been brought to Mr. B's attention.

By stopping the line, the problems were made obvious. They were solved one after another. After three weeks, the situation reversed. Mr. B's line outperformed that of Mr. A. The latter kept on thinking that to stop the line meant lowering efficiency and bringing a loss to the company.

It may sound paradoxical, but for us to stop the line means to ensure that it will become a stronger line which will not have to be stopped for the same reason again. The goal is to create an ideal line, and the company is willing to bear the loss in stopping the line. Thus, when the line is stopped, supervisors scramble to solve the problems.

Supervisors who can never say "Stop the line" are failures. Equally at fault are those supervisors who stop the same line two or three times for the same reason.

[ . . . ]

**NOTES**

1. Japan Management Association, "Welcome to JMA," *<http://www.jma.or.jp/service/prof.html>*, (accessed 23 December 2002)

# 1988

## C. Thomas Mitchell, "The Product As Illusion"

Tom Mitchell is the founder and director of the Center for Design Process, a research lab devoted to exploring methods of user responsive designing. He teaches at Indiana University and is the author of four books on design. The following excerpts are from Mitchell's essay in the 1988 anthology, *Design After Modernism*, in which he argues for the creation of "new, post-industrial design methods" that focus on user experiences rather than on the physicality of products themselves.

Excerpted from *Design After Modernism: Beyond the Object*, edited by John Thackera (New York: Thames and Hudson, 1988): 208, 214. © C. Thomas Mitchell, 1988. Reprinted by permission of the author.

Traditional methods of product design have proved unsuitable in application to new information technology design tasks such as the making of computer software. A number of high technology industries in Japan and the United States have been compelled to abandon traditional design methods, which were developed for the mechanistic design of the industrial era, and develop new, post-mechanical design methods.

The transition from mechanistic to post-mechanical design methods closely parallels the changes which have taken place in science itself. The mechanistic science which provided the impetus for the industrial revolution has been seriously challenged throughout this century by new scientific concepts such as quantum mechanics, relativity and, most recently, non-equilibrium thermodynamics. Each of these theoretical developments abandons the static, objective world view of classical science and stresses instead the importance of dynamic processes in which the observer's presence is an inseparable element of the scientific effect itself.

[ . . . ]

By creating systems which focus upon people's experience of using their product, rather than upon the physicality of the product itself, software makers have created new roles for themselves. Like the avant-garde artists, software makers assume the passive role of providing systems in which everyone may participate. Unlike traditional product design, which is intended solely as a means of producing physical objects, post-industrial designing, as typified by software making, is a continuous and non-instrumental thought process participated in equally by software makers and users.

For new, post-mechanical design tasks, such as the making of computer software, current product design methods are completely inapplicable. 'The Product' as a solely physical entity is an illusion of the mechanistic era which can no longer be sustained in an age preoccupied with information. In place of the concept of design as simply a means of producing objects, develops an understanding of designing as a continuous and non-instrumental thought process, a creative act in which everyone, designers and non-designers alike, may participate equally. The designer's role in the post-mechanical era is to make the design process equally accessible to everyone. In order to realize this programme, design, like the avant garde of art before it, must abandon aesthetics and become instead a socially oriented process in which, like the new scientists, we are all both spectators and actors.

# 1990

## Americans With Disabilities Act
## (U.S. Public Law 101-336)

The United States' "Americans With Disabilities Act" of 1990 had a number of immediate and obvious effects on design and the built environment. It mandated that public facilities and services of all sorts, including transportation and communication, be made accessible to persons with disabilities. Although its impact was most evident in architecture and transportation design, the passing of the ADA signaled an awareness on the part of legislators—and fostered an increased awareness among architects and designers—that large numbers of people were not well served by traditional forms of architecture and design. Although many designers' interest in "universal design," "barrier-free design," or "design for disability" predated the 1990 act (as early as the 1940s, Henry Dreyfuss and others had been working on designs for those with disabilities, and much of the work of the well-known Swedish Ergonomi Design Gruppen occurred in the 1970s and 1980s), it was not until the 1990s that household products designed for use by persons with limited strength and/or mobility—such as OXO's "Good Grips" line—became common on store shelves.

Excerpted from Public Law 101–336 (Americans With Disabilities Act of 1990), from *The ADA Handbook* (Washington, D.C.: U.S. Government Printing Office, 1991): 1, 3–4.

**A**n Act: To establish a clear and comprehensive prohibition of discrim nation on the basis of disability.
[ . . . ]

(a) Findings. The Congress finds that

(1) some 43,000,000 Americans have one or more physical or mental disabilities, and this number is increasing as the population as a whole is growing older;

(2) historically, society has tended to isolate and segregate individuals with disabilities, and, despite some improvements, such forms of discrimination against individuals with disabilities continue to be a serious and pervasive social problem;

(3) discrimination against individuals with disabilities persists in such critical areas as employment, housing, public accommodations, education, transportation, communication, recreation, institutionalization, health services, voting, and access to public services;

(4) unlike individuals who have experienced discrimination on the basis of race, color, sex, national origin, religion, or age, individuals who have experienced discrimination on the basis of disability have often had no legal recourse to redress such discrimination;

(5) individuals with disabilities continually encounter various forms of discrimination, including outright intentional exclusion, the discriminatory effects of architectural, transportation, and communication barriers, overprotective rules and policies, failure to make modifications to existing facilities and practices, exclusionary qualification standards and criteria, segregation, and relegation to lesser services, programs, activities, benefits, jobs, or other opportunities;

(6) census data, national polls, and other studies have documented that people with disabilities, as a group, occupy an inferior status in our society, and are severely disadvantaged socially, vocationally, economically, and educationally;

(7) individuals with disabilities are a discrete and insular minority who have been faced with restrictions and limitations, subjected to a history of purposeful unequal treatment, and relegated to a position of political powerlessness in our society, based on characteristics that are beyond the control of such individuals and resulting from stereotypic assumptions not truly indicative of the individual ability of such individuals to participate in, and contribute to, society;

(8) the Nation's proper goals regarding individuals with disabilities are to assure equality of opportunity, full participation, independent living, and economic self-sufficiency for such individuals; and

(9) the continuing existence of unfair and unnecessary discrimination and prejudice denies people with disabilities the opportunity to compete on an equal basis and to pursue those opportunities for which our free society is justifiably famous, and costs the United States billions of dollars in unnecessary expenses resulting from dependency and nonproductivity.

(b) Purpose. It is the purpose of this Act

(1) to provide a clear and comprehensive national mandate for the elimination of discrimination against individuals with disabilities;

(2) to provide clear, strong, consistent, enforceable standards addressing discrimination against individuals with disabilities;

(3) to ensure that the Federal Government plays a central role in enforcing the standards established in this Act on behalf of individuals with disabilities; and

(4) to invoke the sweep of congressional authority, including the power to enforce the fourteenth amendment and to regulate commerce, in order to address the major areas of discrimination faced day-to-day by people with disabilities.

# 1991

## Kenichi Ohmae, "Global Products"

The Japanese Kenichi Ohmae (1943– ) is known worldwide as a "management guru"; he has written dozens of books and was a longtime partner in the international management consulting firm McKinsey & Co.[1] These excerpts from the 1999 revised edition of Ohmae's influential book, *The Borderless World*, which addresses the issue of globalization, are virtually unchanged from the original 1991 edition (with the exception that the list of brand names that fulfill Ohmae's criteria for global products has expanded).

Excerpted from Kenichi Ohmae, *The Borderless World: Power and Strategy in the Interlinked Economy,* revised edition (New York: HarperCollins, 1999): 24–27. Copyright © 1991 by McKinsey & Co., Inc. Reprinted by permission of HarperCollins Publishers Inc.

I n high-school physics I learned about a phenomenon called diminishing primaries. If you mix together the primary colors of red, blue, and yellow, what you get is black. If Europe says its consumers want a product in green, let them have it. If Japan says red, let them have red. No one wants the average. No one wants the colors all mixed together. It makes sense to take advantage of, say, any technological commonalities in creating the paint. But local managers close to local customers have to be able to pick the color.

When it comes to product strategy, managing in a borderless world doesn't mean managing by averages. It doesn't mean that all tastes run together into one amorphous mass of universal appeal. And it doesn't mean that the appeal of operating globally removes the obligation to localize products. The lure of a universal product is a false allure.

[ . . . ]

[ . . . ] Remember the way tabloids used to cover major beauty contests? They would create a composite picture using the best features from all of the most beautiful entrants—this one's nose, that one's mouth, the other one's forehead. The portrait that emerged was never very appealing. It always seemed odd, lacking in distinctive character. But there will always be beauty judges—and car buyers—in, say, Europe, who, though more used to continental standards, find a special attractiveness in the features of a Japanese or a Latin American. So much the better.

For some kinds of products, however, the kind of globalization that Harvard's Ted Levitt writes about makes excellent sense. One of the most obvious is battery-powered products, such as cameras, watches, and pocket calculators. These are all part of the "Japan game"—that is, they come from industries dominated by Japanese electronics companies. What makes these products successful across the Triad?[2] Popular prices, for one thing, based on aggressive cost reduction and global economies of scale. Also important, however, is the fact that many general design choices reflect an in-depth understanding of the preferences of leading consumer segments in key markets throughout the Triad. Rapid model changes during the past decade have helped educate consumers about the "fashion" aspects of these products and have led them to base their buying decisions in large measure on such criteria.

With other products, these same electronics companies use quite different approaches. Those that make stereophonic equipment, for example, offer products based on aesthetics and product concepts that vary by region. Europeans tend to want physically small, high-performance equipment that can be hidden in a closet; Americans prefer large speakers (and televisions, for that matter) that rise from the floor of living rooms and dens like the structural columns of ancient temples. Of course, the high end of American consumers prefer the European approach. But it is a relatively small segment. [ . . . ] To repeat: Approaches to global products vary.

Fashion-oriented, premium-priced branded goods make up another important cluster of these global products. Gucci, Louis Vuitton, and Prada bags are sold around the world, unchanged from one place to another. They are marketed in virtually the same way. They appeal to an upper-bracket market segment that shares a consistent set of tastes and preferences. Not everyone in the United States or Europe or Japan belongs to that segment. But for those who do, the growing commonality of tastes qualifies them as members of a genuinely cross-Triad, global segment. This global fashion segment has grown enormously over the last decade, as the information is shared widely throughout the developed and developing world. Of particular importance are sporting goods and casual wear. Nike, Reebok, and Adidas compete for global athletes to wear their products, and the major global events are filled with the swoosh and other insignia. American casual wear, carrying names such as The Gap, Eddie Bauer, Land[s'] End, and L. L. Bean, have become global brands. If not, they can be ordered via fax or off the Internet; customers pay handsomely for the feeling of wearing the shoes and shirts in which Michael Jordan and Tiger Woods are outfitted when they compete. There is even a global segment for top-of-the-line automobiles, such as Rolls-Royce and Mercedes-Benz. You can—in fact, should—design such cars for select buyers around the globe. But you cannot do that with Nissans or Toyotas or Hondas. These companies had to create a completely separate image and distribution channels to compete effectively with the "German segment" in the United States—for example, Infiniti, Lexus (called "Celsior" in Japan), and Acura, respectively. Truly universal products are few and far between.

## Insiderization

Some may argue that this definition of universal products is unnecessarily narrow, that many such products exist that do not fit neatly into top-bracket segments: Coca-Cola, Heinz, Del Monte, things like that. On closer examination, however, these turn out to be very different sorts of things. Think about Coca-Cola for a moment. Before it got established in each of its markets, the company had to build up a fairly complete local infrastructure and do the groundwork to establish local demand.

Access to markets was by no means assured from day one; consumer preference was not assured from day one. In Japan, the long-established preference was for carbonated lemon drinks known as *saida*. Unlike Gucci bags, consumer demand did not "pull" Coke into these markets; the company had to establish the infrastructure to "push" it. Today, because the company has done its homework and done it well, Coke is a universally desired brand. But it got there by a different route: local replication of an entire business system in every important market over a long period of time.

For Gucci-like products, the ready flow of information around the world stimulates consistent primary demand in top-bracket segments. For relatively undifferentiated, commodity-like products, demand expands only when corporate muscle pushes hard. If Coke is to establish a preference, it has to build it, piece by piece.

## NOTES

1. "Biography of Kenichi Ohmae," <*http://www.ohmae-report.com/pro/bioe.html*>, (accessed 23 December 2002).
2. Ohmae's term for the United States, Europe, and Japan—the three markets he deems most important to the success of global companies.

# 1992

## David H. Rice, "What Color Is Design?"

The American industrial designer David H. Rice is president of the Washington, D.C.–based firm DesignCom, and founded and serves as chair of the Organization of Black Designers (OBD), a 7,700-member national nonprofit professional association dedicated to promoting "the visibility, education, empowerment and interaction of its membership and the understanding and value that diverse design perspectives contribute to world culture and commerce."[1] In this 1992 essay from *Interior Design* magazine, Rice addresses racial and cultural diversity (or the lack thereof) in American industrial design.

Reprinted in its entirety from *Interior Design*, vol. 63, no. 1 (January 1992): 34–35. © Reed Business Information. Reprinted by permission of *Interior Design* magazine.

I have attended many design shows and exhibits in the past several years, shows sponsored by industry leaders in design and manufacturing. I have attended with great anticipation, but my enthusiasm was consistently turned into dismay, and not a little indignation. Why was there not one black designer represented in any of these shows?

As the recent AIGA (American Institute of Graphic Arts) conference and workshop in New York ("Why is Graphic Design 93% White?") indicated, the number of people of color in the various design professions is woefully small, particularly in regard to African Americans. According to a recent article in *Architecture* (April 1991, p. 52), out of 44,470 regular members of the American Institute of Architects, only 380 are black. There are roughly 30 million black people in America, so why is this number so ridiculously low? There are no figures for other design professions, including interior design, because none of their professional design organizations has done a study.

This is a truly sad and shocking state of affairs. In a globally competitive world, America cannot afford to lose the wonderful contributions that can be made by a creative and vital segment of its population. African Americans have, against great odds, made tremendous contributions to the fine and performing arts, and we can and are doing the same in the applied arts fields of design. But there still needs to be greater opportunity. The number of blacks in the design disciplines is min[u]scule, and the design professions in America are missing the richness that cultural diversity and unique ethnic perspective brings to our greater society.

There is a tremendously rich heritage of design that flows from African roots. The greatest architectural wonders of the world—the Great Pyramids—still rest there. Africans were casting bronze and smelting iron thousands of years before Europeans. African fabric design is some of the most creative and vibrant in the world. The first furniture ever created came from Africa. Then why this great lack of representation of black designers in the design professions?

In many ways, design in America is sterile and dead, lacking in valid context and cultural relevance. Frankly, it is too inbred with the ideas and values of primarily white American males. The country and the world are more diverse than that. America has the richest musical heritage of any nation on earth, due primarily to the magnificent diversity our music industry encompasses. Through it, we influence almost every other culture in the world. What if our design industry reflected the same kind of creative fervor and diversity as our music industry? Instead, we have the very narrow productions of a monolithic cognoscenti, a group that engages in regular sessions of self-congratulations and self-aggrandizement—i.e., the same designers on the same design juries, winning the same awards year after year.

The majority culture in America is, in fact, an amalgam of cultures. We need to express minority values and experiences so that the whole can function more harmoniously. It is crucial to provide unlimited outlets of expression and participation for all of our ethnic populations because their experiences inform and enrich the lives of our whole society.

There are, of course, black interior designers and black architects and black industrial designers, but where are the lamps, chairs, seating systems and fabrics they have designed? When did Herman Miller or Artemide or any other major manufacturer last contract with a black designer to design a product?

The design industry is missing out on a reservoir of ideas, concepts, perhaps whole new design realities that black designers can bring to the design disciplines. There are also glaring oversights by the design industries of product markets that are unexploited due to lack of capital investment and lack of interest. The U. S. Federal Government Bureau of Labor Statistics Consumer Expenditures Section reports that black American consumer spending power is $186 billion per year. Total GNP for black Americans is $300 billion per year. How many products are designed to appeal to this market? Are Nike and McDonald[']s the only possibilities? In these tough economic times, we talk about global marketing, but there is a huge market right here in the U. S. that, due to cultural myopia, has never been adequately tapped. The lack of access to traditional capital sources for black design entrepreneurs prevents the development of this huge market.

Without employment, there can be no mentors. This can be a devastating obstacle to young black students entering the design arena. Feelings of isolation and rejection can lead to a sense of inadequacy. The scarcity of established black design professionals, and the virtual invisibility in schools and design publications of those that do exist, has not only meant few role models for young black designers, but fewer job opportunities. It's a vicious circle.

In answer to the mounting frustrations shared by many talented black designers, the Organization of Black Designers (OBD) was formed to create a greater awareness of the presence and lack of presence of African Americans in design. OBD encompasses the fields of interior, industrial, fashion and graphics/packaging design. The organization has three specific goals. Education: OBD is currently establishing a national mentor program and a scholarship fund for high school students. Visibility: OBD is promoting greater networking by black designers and the design establishment. An archival program is also in the works. Empowerment: OBD is encouraging black designers to start their own firms and to become design entrepreneurs by developing new products and systems.

Currently OBD is compiling a national data base of black designers. Already the organization is raising the awareness of the design community as evidenced by the large number of phone calls and letters requesting membership information or names of designers as candidates for employment. The OBD data base currently lists roughly 1,300 designers, mostly black, working in areas ranging from textile design to automotive design. Membership in OBD is open not only to African American designers, but also to any designer interested in being part of the issues and activities the organization endorses.

Initiatives to address the great racial disparity in the design industry are currently being undertaken by the Industrial Designers Society of America (IDSA), the American Institute of Graphic Arts (AIGA), the American Design Council (ADC), and the Society of Environmental Graphic Designers (SEGD). Obviously, this is an admirable and desirable goal, but first there should be recognition and economic opportunity for those of us who are already here, those of us who have struggled long and hard for far too little opportunity, acknowledgement and engagement by the established design community. That recognition should come in the form of exhibitions, publications, awards, fellowships and, most importantly, work—not token work, but serious work in the form of commissions, retainers and contracts.

Good design has no racial bounds, but the industry does not fully reflect that truth. Talented and capable black designers and architects exist. We are here, we are competent, and we welcome the support and assistance of the members of the entire design community.

## NOTES

1. "Organization of Black Designers," <*http://www.core77.com/OBD/welcome.html*>, (accessed 26 December 2002).

# 1996

# Charles Jencks, "The Post-Modern Information World and the Rise of the Cognitariat"

With his 1977 book, *The Language of Post-Modern Architecture*, the American/ English critic, theorist, and architect Charles Jencks (1939– ) helped popularize the term "postmodernism" in the design fields. A prolific author, he has written dozens of books and innumerable essays on twentieth-century architecture and cultural theory. The selections below are from the fourth edition of Jencks's repeatedly rewritten "transitext" or "evolvotome," *What Is Post-Modernism?*, in which he writes of postmodernism not as an artistic or architectural style but, rather, as a set of socioeconomic conditions.

Excerpted from Charles Jencks, *What is Post-Modernism?*, 4th. ed. (London: Academy Editions, 1996): 50–54 (references omitted). Copyright © 1996 by Charles Jencks. Reproduced by permission of John Wiley & Sons Limited.

**I**n the late nineteenth century, the French poet Comte de Lautréamont defined beauty as 'the fortuitous encounter of a sewing machine and an umbrella on a dissection table'. Bizarre, convulsive juxtaposition—sometimes beautiful and very unusual. In the late twentieth century a traditionally-garbed Bedouin can be found riding a camel across the desert while having, beneath his robes, a business suit, mobile phone and laptop computer. I have been on the tenth floor of a High-Tech tower in Tokyo and watched seven traditional Japanese weddings going on at once. Today incongruity is usual.

The most visible shift in the post-modern world is towards pluralism and cultural eclecticism; an heterogeneity which was never intentional. Pluralism is mostly a by-product of communication and global capitalism, and many nations would wish it away. But the globe has been irreversibly united by current technologies into an instantaneous, twenty-four-hour information world, the post-industrial successor to a modern world based on relatively, by today's standards, snail-paced industry.

Some nations are dissolving, and all national identities are hybridising. Cultural boundaries are now crossed easily because of increasing trade, ease of travel and immediate world communication. This has led to 'space-time compression', the 'global village', which miniaturises the earth spatially and temporally to the equivalent of a small town—perhaps even a computer console. The space and time necessary for a transaction, meeting or media event has imploded drastically while the speed with which capitalism forces styles to change and products to innovate has also modified our taste for change in schizophrenic ways. Media cultures are at once more stereotyping—and in that sense conservative—and hooked on constant marginal variation.

Such combustible changes have created 'the post-modern condition', bringing unique opportunities and problems. This duality is why the condition cannot be entirely supported or condemned; the only intelligent attitude is critical selection, to choose or 'eclect' the positive elements and try to suppress the negative (not that this is always possible). For instance, the much proclaimed 'end of work', which the post-industrial society is bringing, shows a Janus face; there is both more leisure time and job insecurity, work variety and exploitation. But no country has yet been able to have the former goals without the latter by-products.

To understand the post-modern condition is to grasp such contrasts. This mental act is hard because there is no one principle. How does one decode a kaleidoscope, or comprehend city traffic? Not by focusing down, but by panning up to see the general pattern. The post-modern condition shows a series of simultaneous slides from one situation to another; none of them are complete, all of them are hybrid.

There is the partial shift from mass-production to segmented production (from Fordism to Post-Fordism); the slide from a relatively integrated mass-culture to many fragmented taste cultures (minoritisation); from centralised control in government and business to peripheral decision-making; from repetitive manufacture of identical objects to the fast-changing manufacture of varying objects; from few styles to many genres; from national identification to both local and global consciousness.

There are many more related changes than this short list implies, but one of the deep causes of change is what Daniel Bell fully analysed in 1973 as the Post-Industrial Society (sixty years after it had been predicted); others call it the 'Third Wave', or 'information society'. Several related events brought it into existence.

Contemplate this kaleidoscope of change. In 1956, in the USA, for the first time the number of white collar workers outnumbered blue collar workers, and by the late 1970s America had made the shift to an information society, with relatively few people—13 per cent—involved in the manufacture of goods. Most workers—60 per cent—were engaged in the manufacture of signs and symbols, information and knowledge. Whereas a modernised society depended on most people mass-producing objects in a factory (30 per cent), the post-modernised one depends on the segmented production of ideas and images in an office (by about the same percentage). Very few of the population today are farmers—in the modern world of 1900 they constituted 30 per cent of the labour force; in the post-modern world they make up from 3 to 10 per cent (USA and Japan). The service sector has fluctuated over the last ten years at around 11 to 12 per cent of the workforce, about the same percentage as unemployment.

In the post-modern world, a fundamental social fact is the revolutionary growth of those who create and pass on information. Put another way, it is the sudden emergence of a new class; the numerical domination of the proletariat by the cognitariat. These new workers are neither working class nor really middle class, but rather paraclass. They cut across customary boundaries and make for volatile political allegiances. Who can predict how the electorate will feel next week? Statistically, most of the paraclass are clerks, secretaries, insurance people, stockbrokers, teachers, managers, governmental bureaucrats, lawyers, writers, bankers, technicians, programmers, accountants, and ad-men. Indeed, in the First World there is a plague of public relations agents and those manipulating the 'consciousness industry'. Why has this happened? Because prime time television and prime space in the quality media are both in very short supply (given the near infinite demand). You can mine gold in many countries, but there is only one *New York Times,* BBC, and *Le Monde.* In the post-modern world the fierce competition is for media validation and this multiplies another part of the cognitariat—the chattering classes, the opinion-formers and the opinionated.

Salaries of the cognitariat differ as much as their way of life and status and are finely graded, from cognicrats at the top to cogniproles at the bottom. The fundamental fact of the post-industrial society is that, as Daniel Bell made clear in the 1970s, knowledge, not ownership, is power. To navigate through the burgeoning information world takes social skills, a certain intelligence and applied knowledge. This is why, in spite of all the new labour-saving devices, the work done by the cognicrats at the top has not diminished. As John Kenneth Galbraith has shown, with his concept of the 'technostructure', it now takes a small army of experts to launch any advanced industrial product such as a new car; teams of accountants, lawyers, advertisers, not to say designers, technicians and inventors. If there is any final control in this situation it is not just owner-ship, but the ability to manipulate knowledge. This is where the ultimate power rests—with the cognicrats and their teams of market analysts and experts.

Class-analysis of the old type does not work in this new situation; the pro-letariat versus the capitalist. The cognitariat paraclass is too big and amorphous to find the old, sharp divisions. Perhaps a new polarisation is emerging, as Will Hutton argues of Britain: 'the 30/30/40 society'. The bottom 30 per cent are the unemployed or economically inactive, the top 40 per cent are the full-time employed and self-employed, and the middle 30 per cent are the part-timers and casual workers—the relatively insecure. While these structural facts exist throughout the post-modern world, they do not relate closely to individual iden-tity as, for instance, did working class culture. Furthermore, there is some mobil-ity within the cognitariat and certainly lots of job changing. Thus, social distinctions dissolve and cultural identifiers—accent, dress, social attitudes and values—become fuzzy. Lastly, the new productive mode called flexible speciali-sation, 'flexitime', leads to a constant rotation of jobs. This is a defining aspect of the emergent Post-Fordism.

Post-Fordism is just as essential to the post-modern condition as post-indus-trialisation. It gathers momentum after the oil shock of 1973 and the economic stagnation of large Fordist enterprises that had been the cornerstone of moder-nity ever since Henry Ford defined the modern corporation in the 1920s. By the early 1980s the strongest growth was Post-Fordist; that is, in small, fast-chang-ing companies of less than fifty people who are networked by computer and other media. Flexible specialisation, just-in-time production, allowing small stockpiles and a quick response to changing fashions, characterise the system. A company such as Benetton manages many such dispersed networks and engages in little if any actual production.

Post-Fordist and Fordist enterprises are necessarily tightly interwoven. All advanced economies are radically hybrid, and no single sector leads them. In the typical case they are interrelated wholes, with one-third of the economy being Fordist, one-third Post-Fordist, and the remaining third state supported. Such purified types as 'socialism' or 'capitalism' do not capture this mixture. Perhaps the compound 'socitalism'—socialised capitalism—gets closer to the truth; that advanced economies depend on dynamic mixtures between the large, the small, the state and the hybrid whole. As the Post-Communist world shows, it is much easier to socialise capitalism than capitalise socialism. The economies which are most resilient recognise the marketplace, but do not fetishise competition and privatisation. That is why the 'social market' became the catchphrase by the late eighties, and many European countries tried to get the exact mixture of socital-ism right. The problem is that this balance changes dynamically in the global market.

So much for basic abstractions. It may sound rather benevolent; in the First World it has meant the end of the working class and the decline of class antagonisms. The 60 to 80 per cent of the population in the paraclass is, in some material ways, better off than was its modern predecessor. But the obvious downside is present in virtually all post-modern societies; a widening gap between rich and poor, those who command an information-society and those who are left behind; the loss of working class culture and the despair of those now trapped in a new underclass.

Another negative consequence of these fast-moving trends is the confusion of identities and beliefs so that cults and sects and trivial private affairs dominate the news. Is it a surprise that the private lives of Prince Charles and Princess Diana monopolised the British media for three years? Or that the OJ Simpson Trial and 'the Sarin Gas Sect' (as it is quaintly known) were top of the consciousness industry in America and Japan for a year? Reformed actors such as Ronald Reagan dominate vast numbers of the population—in spite of the fact that very few may believe in these media-masks very deeply. After Reagan vacated the presidency, his followers dropped him with a shrug when he took up advertising in Japan. Easy belief equals easy disillusion; not even anger sticks to the Teflon President.

The way once effective media-bytes are soon forgotten can be brought out by a series of questions. Can you remember who called Reagan's deficit spending 'voodoo economics'? George Bush, the man who would continue the voodoo. And who beat him with the one-liner, 'It's the economy, stupid'? Yes, Clinton, the president whose popularity went *down* when the economy went *up*. Moral? Politicians cannot remember their own slogans, which have little bearing on the truth, anyway. It is no surprise they are believed in only weakly. Weak thought, weak belief and social insecurities are some of the endemic problems of the post-modern condition.

# 1998

## Kenji Ekuan, "Japanese Aesthetics"

Kenji Ekuan (1929– ), widely considered Japan's foremost industrial designer, is the founder and president of the GK Design Group (established 1957), the first group design practice in postwar Japan.[1] In *The Aesthetics of the Japanese Lunchbox*, Ekuan argues that it is Japanese designers' adherence to the country's traditional values and aesthetics that has made its products so successful in the global marketplace.

Excerpted from Kenji Ekuan, *The Aesthetics of the Japanese Lunchbox* (Cambridge, Mass.: MIT Press, 1998): 79, 81, 177–8, 180. Reprinted by permission of MIT Press.

The movement to produce a thinner electronic calculator beginning in the latter half of the 1960s adumbrated a new notion of quality. It was sought to render the calculator both almighty in a multi-functional sense and as small as possible, that is, to establish multi-functionality and miniaturization as equal values. Packing numerous functions into something and making it smaller and thinner are contradictory aims, but one had to pursue contradiction to its limit to find a solution. Here we note the emphasis on "almighty but small," with small size implying strength, or the concept of "small but powerful." It was this sense of values—itself indicative of the basic configuration of the Japanese mind—that drove the development of such contemporary products as mini-calculators, cameras, and cars.

Smallness and thinness—these qualities may themselves be guiding principles of civilization. Lightness betokens an aesthetic of conservation. The innate disposition that detects beauty in avoiding waste has vast potential.

A sense of beauty that lauds lightness and simplicity—desire that precipitates functionality, comfort, luxury, and diversity. Fulfillment of beauty and its concomitant desire will be the aim of design in the future. It is only when such things are achieved—small but powerful, thin but almighty, and simple yet diverse—that we attain a conservation aesthetic grounded in desire.

When modern man first entertained such desires, a tendency arose to manufacture large, thick, heavy, complex objects, with an inevitable loss of efficiency and refinement. Instead, today's shift from big-is-better to small-is-beautiful heralds a lifestyle driven by an aesthetic of conservation. Smallness, thinness, lightness, and simplicity applied to tools and equipment have yielded very superior items. This suggests an index for rating the maturity of our late twentieth-century civilization.

[ . . . ]

We Japanese are said to possess the sharpest artistic predisposition of any people, and this has also born[e] magnificent fruit in applied engineering and technology. For Japan has exerted great efforts toward mastering and using the *technē* of the West.

[ . . . ]

Tradition has it that we Japanese lack originality and are adept only at imitating foreign behavior and products. It is certain that we are gifted imitators. But whether or not Japan has its own originality is a different problem altogether.

Japan imports its raw materials from abroad. This has been the custom since the prehistoric Jomon age. We begin by replicating an imported object—and later make out of it something quite superior to the original. During the formative Nara and Heian periods (645–1185), the government set up a special workshop for precise imitation of foreign things. Materials were provided to craftsmen of all sorts to copy whatever was brought from China. Even the Meiji government of the last century did the same thing at first, but later discontinued such facilities. We Japanese believe we cannot understand the soul of foreign things, so we attempt to grasp this by making an imitation. Japan was once thought of as a net borrower in terms of culture, but today we have succeeded in refashioning civilization and sending it out again as Japanese. The reason Japanese products sell abroad is the drawing power and flavor of this unique distillation.

**N O T E S**

1. GK Design Group, "GKDI_SITE," <*http://www.gkdi.com/#*>, (accessed 23 December 2002).

# 1999

## Hartmut Esslinger, "Frog Stands For . . ."

Hartmut Esslinger (1944– ), a German product designer, founded Esslinger Design in 1969; the company morphed into the international design firm frog (or frogdesign), which became famous in the early 1980s for its design of Apple's now-iconic Macintosh computer. Frog's/Esslinger's well-known slogan that "form follows emotion" is a clear challenge to the modernist adage that "form follows function."

Excerpted from *Frog: Form Follows Emotion*, edited by Fay Sweet (New York: Watson-Guptill, 1999): 7. Reprinted by permission of Ivy Press.

F rog stands for the best in creative design services. We are a new kind of world-class business: a global creative network that generates substantial return on investment for our clients in every sense of the term. Our charter is to evolve with courage, grace, and a pure heart, to always focus on being the leader, and to embrace new forms of creative collaboration. We achieve this by embodying a magic mixture of characteristics that include being radical, inspirational, and optimistic; fun, flexible, and young of mind. But most important we are ethical, tolerant, caring, and hardworking. Then, 'form follows emotion.'

# 1999

## Donald Norman, "Time for a Change: Design in the Post-Disciplinary Era"

American Donald Norman is a cofounder of the Nielsen Norman Group, an executive consulting firm that promotes human-centered development processes for products and services. Formerly a vice president of advanced technology at Apple and Hewlett Packard, he is now a professor of computer science at Northwestern University. In this 1999 essay, he reiterates some of the ideas he laid out in his influential 1988 book, *The Design of Everyday Things*, arguing that designers' focus on aesthetics often comes at the expense of usability.

Reproduced in its entirety from Donald Norman, "Time for a Change: Design in the Post-Disciplinary Era," *Innovation*, vol. 18, no. 2 (summer 1999): 16–17. Reprinted with permission from *Innovation* (summer 1999), the Quarterly of the Industrial Designers Society of America; p: 703.707.6000; f: 703.787.8501; e: *idsa@idsa.org*; w: *www.idsa.org*.

**W**hat do I look for in a product or service? Sensible things. I want products that are attractive and that look and feel good. I want them to fit nicely in my home, office or wherever else I might use them. I want to be able to understand how to use them without reading a manual. They should be safe, endangering neither me nor anyone else. All of these aspects matter to me as a user. They make up the user experience.

I'm not happy with what I see. Products are difficult to use. They are unsafe. Or they flout style for the sake of style, without regard for the consequences upon use. Bad design, all of it.

In part, bad design results from producing design for the interest of design. This is exacerbated by design prizes that focus only on a product's appearance. Bad design results from a process that ignores the whole product.

Good design, on the other hand, results from interdisciplinary, human-centered product development. This approach addresses the whole product, fulfilling the needs of the user and the business that manufactures the product. It takes into account the total user experience.

Defining the user experience requires at least five different activities:

- field observation, which is best done by applied anthropologists;
- product design, best done by a team of industrial designers, human factors experts and engineers;
- rapid prototyping, by industrial designers, model makers, artists and programmers;
- user testing, usually done by psychologists;
- user manual writing, best done by technical writers.

All five of these activities play an essential role in creating the total user experience. All of these user experience experts must work together as a team from conception through shipping to the start of the next design cycle. In addition, these people must work harmoniously with others who are involved in the product development process, particularly manufacturing and marketing.

In the current product development process, each discipline makes its contribution to product design in isolation and then complains bitterly that other people ruined the outcome. I have heard designers grumble that their clients undo their work. They develop a great design, but by the time the product is shipped it has been completely distorted. "Can you help us stop companies from ruining the design?" designers ask.

This question points out the fundamental flaw in understanding the role of design. Design cannot be separated from the other considerations of a product. The person who 'ruined' the design probably was trying to improve some other dimension of the product. The design must have been unsatisfactory in some way. This happens when the industrial design team's work is completed without consideration of all the relevant variables and then the team is frozen out of the final decision process.

Industrial designers and human-factor engineers often are kept out of the loop because they argue for superior aesthetics or usability at the expense of everything else. This attitude may win design prizes, but it bankrupts companies. All design is a series of tradeoffs. Cost, time to market, compatibility with previous products, making a brand statement—these are important factors.

It's time for a change. It is time to break out of the segregation that keeps the various disciplines tightly locked in their own boxes. It is time for a post-disciplinary revolution.

Each of the legs of product development—industrial design, engineering, user experience, marketing and manufacturing—is essential to good design. The disciplines have to work as a team throughout the *entire* development process, together making the necessary tradeoffs to better satisfy the needs of the customer and the company.

This is not always easy. People from other disciplines have different educational backgrounds, different sensibilities and work styles. The same words may have entirely different meanings when used in other disciplines. It can take weeks, months or even years before working as a team goes smoothly. But time allows each discipline to gain an appreciation of the contributions that others can make.

Real collaboration results in superior design. This means that industrial designers, as well as everyone else involved in the product development process, must learn to be team players, doing what is best for the company and the product rather than focusing on any single aspect or feature of the product. They must recognize that the best design does not always lead to the best product.

At the end of the day, what makes something beautiful is whether or not it works.

# Index

This index is alphabetized word-by-word and uses American rather than British spellings.
Page references in bold indicate selections in this book that were written by that author. Page references in *italics* indicate illustrations.
Proper names of persons, places, publications, businesses, and other organizations that are mentioned only in passing, or only in the notes, are generally not indexed.
A distinction is maintained in the index between *manufacture* (hand production) and *machinofacture* (machine production).

 **Books from Allworth Press**

Allworth Press is an imprint of Allworth Communications, Inc. Selected titles are listed below.

**Designing for People**
by Henry S. Dreyfuss (paperback, 6¾ × 9⅞, 256 pages, $21.95)

**Citizen Designer: Perspectives on Design Responsibility**
edited by Steven Heller and Véronique Vienne (paperback, 6 × 9, 272 pages, $19.95)

**Teaching Graphic Design: Course Offerings and Class Projects from the Leading Undergraduate and Graduate Programs**
edited by Steven Heller (6 × 9, paperback, 272 pages, $19.95)

**Looking Closer 4: Critical Writings on Graphic Design**
edited by Michael Bierut, William Drenttel, and Steven Heller (paperback, 6¾ × 9⅞, 304 pages, $21.95)

**Looking Closer 3: Classic Writings on Graphic Design**
edited by Michael Bierut, Jessica Helfand, Steven Heller, and Rick Poynor (paperback, 6¾ × 9⅞, 304 pages, $18.95)

**Graphic Design Time Line: A Century of Design Milestones**
edited by Steven Heller and Elinor Pettit (paperback, 6¾ × 9⅞, 272 pages, $19.95)

**Graphic Design History**
edited by Steven Heller and Georgette Balance (6¾ × 9⅞, 352 pages, $21.95)

**Design Issues: How Graphic Design Informs Society**
edited by DK Holland (paperback, 6¾ × 9⅞, 288 pages, $21.95)

**Design Humor: The Art of Graphic Wit**
by Steven Heller (paperback, 6¾ × 9⅞, 288 pages, $21.95)

**Design Culture: An Anthology of Writing from the AIGA Journal of Graphic Design**
edited by Steven Heller and Marie Finamore (paperback, 6¾ × 10, 320 pages, $19.95)

Please write to request our free catalog. To order by credit card, call 1-800-491-2808 or send a check or money order to Allworth Press, 10 East 23rd Street, Suite 510, New York, NY 10010. Include $5 for shipping and handling for the first book ordered and $1 for each additional book. Ten dollars plus $1 for each additional book if ordering from Canada. New York State residents must add sales tax.

To see our complete catalog on the World Wide Web, or to order online, you can find us at *www.allworth.com*.